The Bible Speaks Today

Series editors: Alec Motyer (OT)
John Stott (NT)
Derek Tidball (Bible Themes)

The Message of
Zechariah

D1027937

Kevin Kay

The Bible Speaks Today: Old Testament series

The Bible Speaks Today New Testament *and* **Bible Themes**
series are listed at the back of this book

The Message of Zechariah

Your Kingdom Come

Barry Webb

InterVarsity Press

InterVarsity Press
P.O. Box 1400, Downers Grove, IL 60515-1426
World Wide Web: www.ivpress.com
E-mail: mail@ivpress.com

Inter-Varsity Press
38 De Montfort Street, Leicester LE1 7GP, England
World Wide Web: www.ivpbooks.com
E-mail: ivp@uccf.org.uk

InterVarsity Press® *is the book-publishing division of InterVarsity Christian Fellowship/USA*®*, a student movement active on campus at hundreds of universities, colleges and schools of nursing in the United States of America, and a member movement of the International Fellowship of Evangelical Students. For information about local and regional activities, write Public Relations Dept., InterVarsity Christian Fellowship/USA, 6400 Schroeder Rd., P.O. Box 7895, Madison, WI 53707-7895.*

Inter-Varsity Press is the book-publishing division of the Universities and Colleges Christian Fellowship (formerly the Inter-Varsity Fellowship), a student movement linking Christian Unions in universities and colleges throughout the United Kingdom and the Republic of Ireland, and a member movement of the International Fellowship of Evangelical Students. For information about local and national activities write to UCCF, 38 De Montfort Street, Leicester LE1 7GP, England.

USA ISBN 0-8308-2430-8

UK ISBN 0-85111-294-3

Printed in the United States of America ∞

British Library Cataloguing in Publication Data

A catalogue record for this book is available from the British Library.

Library of Congress Cataloging-in-Publication Data

Webb, Barry G.
  The message of Zechariah: your kingdom come/Barry Webb.
    p. cm.—(The Bible speaks today)
Includes bibliographical references (p.   ).
  ISBN 0-8308-2430-8
  1. Kingdom of God—Biblical teaching. 2. Bible. O.T.
Zechariah—Commentaries. 3. Messiah—Prophecies. I. Title. II.
Series.
  BS1665.6.K48W43 2004
  224'.9807—dc22

2003020598

P	18	17	16	15	14	13	12	11	10	9	8	7	6	5	4	3	2	1
Y	18	17	16	15	14	13	12	11	10	09	08	07	06	05	04			

To Duncan and Miriam,
just married

Contents

Part 2. Kingdom consummation

General preface

THE BIBLE SPEAKS TODAY describes three series of expositions, based on the books of the Old and New Testaments, and on Bible themes that run through the whole of Scripture. Each series is characterized by a threefold ideal:

- to expound the biblical text with accuracy
- to relate it to contemporary life, and
- to be readable.

These books are, therefore, not 'commentaries', for the commentary seeks rather to elucidate the text than to apply it, and tends to be a work rather of reference than of literature. Nor, on the other hand, do they contain the kinds of 'sermons' that attempt to be contemporary and readable without taking Scripture seriously enough.

The contributors to The Bible Speaks Today series are all united in their convictions that God still speaks through what he has spoken, and that nothing is more necessary for the life, health and growth of Christians than that they should hear what the Spirit is saying to them through his ancient – yet ever modern – Word.

ALEC MOTYER
JOHN STOTT
DEREK TIDBALL
Series editors

Preface

He appeared to them over a period of forty days and spoke about the kingdom of God.[1]

To have someone teach you the Bible is a great privilege. But some Bible studies (and teachers) are better than others. I can never remember thinking that the Bible itself was dull; it has always seemed quite wonderful to me, and moved me deeply. But some people, even with the best will in the world, have an annoying way of trivializing it, or getting between the Bible and me, causing static as I try to listen to hear its message. The problem is usually that they talk too much about themselves. That is why I have always been fascinated by the Bible studies Jesus led with his disciples – on the road to Emmaus, and in Jerusalem, during those precious forty days before his ascension.[2] No static there! There was absolutely no chance that Jesus could get in the way by talking too much about himself, because he himself *was* the message. The Bible was all about *him*; that is what he opened their eyes to see.[3] It not only transformed their understanding of the Scriptures; it also changed the disciples themselves – from people who were walking away, heads down, to people who were back where they should have been, with their heads up again, praising God with great joy.[4] That is the sort of thing that Bible study *does* to people, when Jesus does the teaching. 'Were not our hearts burning within us', they said afterwards, 'while he talked with us on the road and opened the Scriptures to us?'[5]

But wait a minute – what exactly did Jesus talk about when he took those Bible studies? Was it the Scriptures, or the Kingdom of God, or himself? It is a silly question, for he spoke of all of them at

[1] Acts 1:3.
[2] Luke 24:25–27; Acts 1:3.
[3] Luke 24:45.
[4] Luke 24:13, 17, 52.
[5] Luke 24:32.

once: 'he explained to them what was said in all the Scriptures concerning himself';[6] that is, 'He ... spoke about the kingdom of God.'[7] The Bible is about the kingdom of God, and the kingdom of God is about Jesus: that is biblical theology in a nutshell, and no-one (of course) understood and taught it better than Jesus himself.

How I wish I could have been at those Jesus-led Bible studies! Even to eavesdrop would have been awesome, like an under-graduate, mouth open, at a masterclass. But why even think about it? Those Bible studies surely belong to a vanished world. Or do they? Is it altogether beyond possibility that Jesus might draw alongside me too, and teach me? Hasn't the ascended Lord Jesus come to us in the person of the Holy Spirit to fulfil his promise to be with us *always*, and to lead us into all truth? He 'will take from what is mine', Jesus said, 'and make it known to you'.[8] Or, more pointedly still, 'I will not leave you as orphans; *I will come to you*.'[9] To be taught by the Holy Spirit as we read the Scriptures is not a second best, the scraps we might gather up like beggars after the children have eaten.[10] It is to be taught by Jesus himself – directly and personally; and that is the birthright of all God's children.[11]

Jesus has walked with me as I have written this book; I have no doubt about that. I have had the same burning heart, the same breathless wonder as those first disciples as he has opened my eyes to understand God's kingdom purposes and (dare I say it?) my place in them. It never makes you proud to be taught by Jesus. Only awestruck. It is a privilege beyond price; and to be able to pass on the riches of that experience to others is a blessing multiplied many times over.

Others have walked with me too, of course – God's 'angels' to succour me on the journey, whether they realized that is what they were or not. My wife, Alison, and daughter, Tabitha, who came with me to England so that I could give myself to the task away from the distractions of my normal hectic life. For me it was a sheer luxury, while they had to face the daunting prospect of employment and schooling in a foreign land. They did so, not grudgingly, but with joy, and for that – as well as much else – I thank them.

Thanks are due too to my colleagues and many students at Moore College in Sydney, Australia, who listened to sermon after sermon

6 Luke 24:27.
7 Acts 1:3.
8 John 16:15.
9 John 14:18; my italics.
10 Cf. Matt. 15:21–28; Mark 7:24–30.
11 1 John 2:26–27.

on Zechariah in the college chapel in the year or two before. They must have known I was up to something, and they were not wrong! I hope, though, that I was not just warming up, but also serving them then and there, and that they were blessed by it. They got some advance instalments, so to speak. So did seven postgraduate students who attended a seminar on Zechariah that I taught at Moore College in the second half of 2001. It was a treat to be able to spend quality time each week for a whole semester poring over Zechariah in their company before putting pen to paper (or fingers to keyboard). Talking through things with them helped me a lot; I hope they were helped too. Special thanks are due to Michael Stead and Geoff Ziegler, who served as my research assistants in the early stages of the project. They must have found me rather distracted at the time and wondered whether I even read, let alone appreciated, a lot of what they produced for me. Let me assure them that I appreciated it then, and much more so now that I have had the opportunity to go back over it and follow up the leads they gave me. A piece Michael wrote on Zechariah's messianism has been especially helpful. Michael also proofread the manuscript, as did Marko Jauhiainen (working on his PhD in Cambridge) and Jessica Demeny (on missionary service in India).

Finally, thanks to the Moore College Council for granting me study leave, once again. Since I've never mastered the art of writing books in harness, so to speak, I owe them a great debt for loosening the straps every now and then and letting me run free. Tyndale House, Cambridge, is a wonderful place to do research and writing of this kind, and I'm grateful to the warden Bruce Winter, his staff, and all who support their work by their giving and prayers. I count it a special privilege, once more, to be associated with Inter-Varsity Press, whose many fine publications did so much to nourish me as a young Christian – and still do.

So with gratitude to all these, and many more, I launch this new book on its journey. May what truly honours God in it flourish and bear good fruit. I hope that all else may go unnoticed, or (mercifully) be forgiven. May his kingdom come, and his will be done.

BARRY WEBB
Moore Theological College
2003

Chief abbreviations

ABD	Freedman, D. N. (ed.), *The Anchor Bible Dictionary*, 6 vols. (Doubleday, 1992)
AV	The Authorized (King James) Version of the Bible, 1611
BHS	*Biblia Hebraica Stuttgartensia*, ed. K. Elliger and W. Rudolph (Deutsche Bibelgesellschaft, 1984)
JB	The Jerusalem Bible (1966)
LXX	The Old Testament in Greek according to the Septuagint (third to first centuries BC)
Macc.	The (first or second) book of Maccabees
MT	The Hebrew (Masoretic) text of the Old Testament
NBD	J. D. Douglas (ed.), *New Bible Dictionary*, 2nd ed. (IVP, 1982)
NIV	The New International Version of the Bible (1973, 1978, 1984)
NT	New Testament
OT	Old Testament
RSV	The Revised Standard Version of the Bible (OT 1952; NT 2nd ed. 1971)
RV	The Holy Bible. Revised Version (1948)

Bibliography

Works referred to in the footnotes are cited there by surname, or surname and date or volume number.

Ackroyd, P. R., *Exile and Restoration: A Study of Hebrew Thought of the Sixth Century BC* (SCM, 1968).

Adler, M. J., *How to Read a Book: A Guide to Self-Education* (London, 1940).

Aland, K., Black, B., Martini, C. M., Metzger, B., and Wikgren, A. (eds.), *The Greek New Testament*, 4th ed. (United Bible Societies, 1983).

Andersen, F. I., 'Who built the Second Temple?' *Australian Biblical Review* 6 (1958), pp. 3–35.

Baldwin, J. G., *Haggai, Zechariah, Malachi: An Introduction and Commentary*, Tyndale Old Testament Commentaries (Tyndale, 1972).

———— 'Iddo', in *NBD*, p. 503.

Beckwith, R. T., *The Old Testament Canon of the New Testament Church and its Background in Early Judaism* (SPCK, 1985).

Bedford, Peter Ross, *Temple Restoration in Early Achaemenid Judah*, Journal for the Study of Judaism, Supplement 65 (E. J. Brill, 2001).

Belben, H. A. G., 'Fasting', in *NBD*, p. 373.

Berquist, Jon L., *Judaism in Persia's Shadow: A Social and Historical Approach* (Fortress, 1995).

Bright, J., *A History of Israel*, 3rd ed. (SCM, 1980).

Brotzman, E. R., *Old Testament Textual Criticism: A Practical Introduction* (Baker, 1994).

Cheyne, T. K., and Black, J. S. (eds.), *Encyclopaedia Biblica*, vol. 4 (Macmillan, 1903).

Childs, Brevard S., *Introduction to the Old Testament as Scripture* (SCM, 1979).

———— 'Zechariah', in Childs, *Introduction to the Old Testament as Scripture*, pp. 472–487.

Coggins, R., Phillips, A., and Knib, M. (eds.), *Israel's Prophetic Tradition: Essays in Honour of Peter R. Ackroyd* (Cambridge University Press, 1982).

Conrad, Edgar W., *Zechariah*, Readings: A New Biblical Commentary (Sheffield Academic Press, 1999).

Cook, Stephen L., *Prophecy and Apocalypticism: The Post-Exilic Social Setting* (Fortress, 1995).

Darr, K. P., 'The wall around Paradise: Ezekielian ideas about the future', *Vetus Testamentum* 37.3 (1987), pp. 271–279.

Duhm, B., *Das Buch Jesaja*, Handkommentar zum Alten Testament (Vandenhoeck & Ruprecht, 1892).

Dumbrell, W. J., *The End of the Beginning: Revelation 21–22 and the Old Testament*, Moore Theological College Lectures 1983 (Lancer, 1985), esp. pp. 61–63.

Floyd, Michael H., 'Zechariah and changing views of Second Temple Judaism in recent commentaries', *Religious Studies Review* 25 (July 1999), pp. 257–263.

Grollenberg, L. H., *Atlas of the Bible* (Nelson, 1956).

Hanson, P. D., *The Dawn of Apocalyptic* (Fortress, 1975).

Jeremias, J., *Jerusalem in the Time of Jesus* (SCM, 1969).

Jones, Douglas R., 'A Fresh interpretation of Zechariah IX–XI', *Vetus Testamentum* 12 (1962), pp. 241–259.

Kidner, F. D., *Ezra and Nehemiah: An Introduction and Commentary*, Tyndale Old Testament Commentaries (IVP, 1979).

Kitchen, K. A., and Mitchell, T. C., 'Chronology of the Old Testament', in *NBD*, pp. 188–200.

Kline, Meredith G., 'The rider of the red horse', *Kerux* 5.2 (1990), pp. 2–20.

—— 'How long?' *Kerux* 6.1 (1991), pp. 16–31.

—— 'The structure of the book of Zechariah', *Journal of the Evangelical Theological Society* 34 (1991), pp. 179–193.

—— 'Messianic avenger', *Kerux* 7.1 (1992), pp. 20–36.

—— 'The Servant and the serpent', part 2, *Kerux* 8.2 (1993), pp. 10–34.

—— 'Anathema', *Kerux* 10.3 (1995), pp. 3–30.

—— 'Marana tha', *Kerux* 11.3 (1996), pp. 10–28.

—— 'The exaltation of Christ', *Kerux* 12.3 (1997), pp. 3–29.

Lamarche, P., *Zacharie IX–XIV: Structure littéraire et messianisme* (Gabalda, 1961).

Love, Mark Cameron, *The Evasive Text: Zechariah 1–8 and the Frustrated Reader* (Sheffield Academic Press, 1999).

Mason, R., 'The prophets of the restoration', in Coggins, Phillips and Knib, *Israel's Prophetic Tradition*, pp. 137–154.

Meyers, C. L., and Meyers, E. M., *Haggai, Zechariah 1–8: A New*

Translation with Introduction and Commentary, Anchor Bible (Doubleday, 1987).

—— *Zechariah 9–14: A New Translation with Introduction and Commentary*, Anchor Bible (Doubleday, 1993).

Meyers, C. L., Meyers, E. M., and Petersen, D. L., 'Zechariah, book of', in *ABD*, vol. 6, pp. 1061–1068.

Morris, L., *The Gospel According to Matthew* (IVP, 1992).

Newman, Carey C. (ed.), *Jesus and the Restoration of Israel: A Critical Assessment of N. T. Wright's 'Jesus and the Victory of God'* (IVP, 1999).

Oesterley, W. O. E., and Robinson, T. H., *A History of Israel*, 2 vols. (Clarendon, 1932).

Patterson, R., 'Old Testament Prophecy', in Ryken and Longman, *Complete Literary Guide to the Bible*, pp. 296–310.

Petersen, David L., *Haggai and Zechariah 1–8: A Commentary*, Old Testament Library (Westminster, 1984).

—— *Zechariah 9–14 and Malachi: A Commentary*, Old Testament Library (Westminster/John Knox, 1995).

Redditt, Paul L., *Haggai, Zechariah and Malachi*, New Century Bible Commentary (Eerdmans, 1995).

Rose, W. H., *Zemah and Zerubbabel: Messianic Expectations in the Early Postexilic Period*, JSOT supplements 304 (JSOT Press, 2000).

Ryken, L., *How to Read the Bible as Literature* (Zondervan, 1985).

Ryken, L., and Longman III, T. (eds.), *A Complete Literary Guide to the Bible* (Zondervan, 1993).

Sweeney, Marvin A., *The Twelve Prophets*, vol. 2: *Micah, Nahum, Habakkuk, Zephaniah, Haggai, Zechariah, Malachi*, Berit Olam: Studies in Hebrew Narrative and Poetry (Liturgical Press, 2000).

Webb, B. G., *The Message of Isaiah: On Eagles' Wings*, Bible Speaks Today (IVP, 1996).

—— *Five Festal Garments: Christian Reflections on The Song of Songs, Ruth, Lamentations, Ecclesiastes and Esther*, New Studies in Biblical Theology 10 (IVP, 2000).

Wellhausen, J., 'Zechariah, book of', in T. K. Cheyne and J. S. Black (eds.), *Encyclopaedia Biblica* (Macmillan, 1903), vol. 4, pp. 5391–5395.

Williamson, H. G. M., *Ezra, Nehemiah*, Word Biblical Commentary (Word, 1985).

Wiseman, D. J., 'Tyre, Tyrus', in *NBD*, pp. 1227–1229.

Wright, J. S., 'Zechariah, book of', in *NBD*, pp. 1275–1276.

—— 'Zerubbabel', in *NBD*, p. 1280.

Yancey, Philip, *The Bible Jesus Read* (Zondervan, 1999).

Introduction

When Jesus taught his disciples to pray that God's kingdom would come,[1] he taught them more than how to pray: he opened his heart to them and challenged them to be inspired by the same vision he had, and for which he would go to the cross. For Jesus' whole life and ministry was about the kingdom of God. The message he preached was the good news that the time had come for the kingdom of God to be manifested on earth. In other words, that the hope of the Old Testament prophets was about to become a reality in his own living, dying and rising again, and that this would be God's doing from beginning to end. Indeed, the strong apocalyptic language in which Jesus spoke about the coming of the kingdom shows quite clearly that for him it meant nothing less than the beginning of the end of the world.[2] It was time to get ready to meet God, because the last judgment was beginning to happen.[3]

Such a view of things may seem very strange to us who live two thousand years later. But that feeling of strangeness should not make us dismiss Jesus' words out of hand, as though they stand discredited by the mere passage of time. For the same Jesus who spoke of crisis also spoke of process: of yeast hidden in a large amount of dough, and of seed slowly growing until harvest time.[4] Indeed, the prayer 'your kingdom *come*' would make no sense at all if there were no interval between the 'now' and the 'then', between inauguration and consummation. That interval is precisely the time that Jesus was preparing his disciples to live in, and he spoke of a

[1] Matt. 6:9–10.
[2] 'Apocalyptic' is from the Greek *apokalypsis* (revelation). 'Apocalyptic' language is language that conveys a revelation, especially about the end of the world. The book of Revelation in the NT, sometimes called the Apocalypse of John, is full of such language.
[3] See, e.g., Matt. 24; Mark 13.
[4] Matt. 13:33, 24–30.

great task that would have to be completed before it would come to an end: 'this gospel of the kingdom will be preached in the whole world as a testimony to all nations, *and then the end will come*'.[5] So to be a disciple of Jesus Christ is (among other things) to be fired by a great vision, and to live in the interval between its initial and final realization.

The incarnation of the Son of God, and what followed over the next three years, was a turning point in world history and in the purposes of God. It introduced a radically new situation in which everything had changed. But it was not a negation of the past, as though all that had gone before was now cancelled out as irrelevant. On the contrary, according to Jesus himself, the new thing that had happened in him was the *fulfilment* of the past, a past in which, under God's sovereign guidance and control, the kingdom of God had been slowly but certainly moving towards Bethlehem to be born.[6] The prospect of its coming had captivated the prophets and other inspired writers of the Old Testament for hundreds of years before its realization in Jesus. Like Jesus' disciples of later times, they too had lived in the tension of the now and the not yet, for they already had the vision of it (at least in outline), but not yet its realization in the Messiah, who was yet to come. For the Christian, then, a journey into the world of Zechariah and his contemporaries is not a journey into alien territory, but a pilgrimage to the land of his spiritual ancestors. It is to meet people fired by the same vision as himself, and living with many of the same tensions and challenges. That is why the study of the book of Zechariah is bound to be so enriching; it is imbued, from beginning to end, with the same heart-cry that Jesus turned into a prayer for all of us: 'Your kingdom come'.

1. Zechariah's world

The book that bears his name locates the beginning of Zechariah's ministry in *the second year of Darius* (Zech. 1:1, 7; cf. 7:1); that is, early in the reign of the Persian emperor Darius I.

The Persian Empire was created by Cyrus the Great (549–530 BC).[7] He was succeeded, first by his son Cambyses (530–522 BC), and then

[5] Matt. 24:14; my italics.
[6] I allude, of course, to the famous words of W. B. Yeats (in his poem 'The Second Coming') in which he speaks of a similar (more ominous) inevitability about the way things are presently building towards another great turning point, a (metaphorical) *second* coming.
[7] He first came into contact with the Judean exiles in 539, when he conquered Babylon.

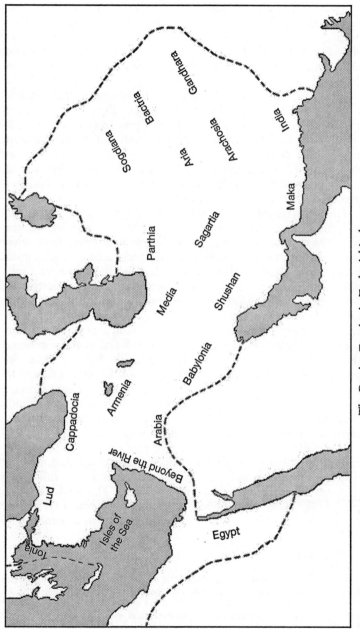

The Persian Empire in Zechariah's day

THE MESSAGE OF ZECHARIAH

by Darius (522–486 BC).[8] Darius was the son of Hystaspes, who was a prince from a different branch the same family.[9] Darius himself had been an officer in Cambyses' army. The succession was disputed after Cambyses' death, and so in the first two years of his reign Darius had to dispose of two rival claimants to the throne and put down rebellions in various places. By the end of his third year, however, he was in secure possession of an empire that extended from India to Greece, and from Armenia to Egypt.[10] For administrative purposes he divided it into twenty provinces, or satrapies, the whole of Syria-Palestine west of the Euphrates River and south to the Sinai desert being the province of Eber Nahara ('Beyond the River'). The area immediately surrounding Jerusalem was the subprovince of Yehud.[11] It was here in Yehud, and in Jerusalem in particular, that Zechariah lived and preached his message.

The name Yehud is a variant of Yehudah (Judah), the name of one of Israel's greatest ancestors, and of the tribe that was derived from him. The tribe of Judah was the leading tribe of Israel, from which the royal line of David came. In short, it was a name with a proud history. In the tenth century BC Jerusalem had been the royal capital of an Israelite empire that spanned nearly all of Syria-Palestine and the lands east of the Jordan River, and commanded respect from Egypt, Arabia and Phoenicia. It had been built by conquest under David, and prospered through trade and judicious alliances during the time of Solomon. It was almost, quite literally, at the centre of the known world – at the eastern edge of the Mediterranean Sea, astride the main trade routes linking Africa, Central Asia and the Far East. Its strategic position is reflected in the incessant struggles over control of land in the same area today. In the time of Solomon, Israel had been able to exploit its situation to the full, and became extremely wealthy. It was Israel's golden age.

More difficult times followed Solomon's death. Through mismanagement and an inability to resolve internal conflicts, much of the empire was lost, and David's descendants ended up ruling only the southern part of what had once been Israel. The north (the larger part) broke away, and formed a separate kingdom, with Samaria eventually becoming its capital. Judah became the name of the

---

[8] Kitchen and Mitchell, p. 198.

[9] The Achaemenid family.

[10] He had put down rebellions in Babylonia, Media and Armenia well before this. Egypt, however, put up stiffer resistance. It rebelled as soon as Cambyses died, and Darius did not reconquer it until the middle of 519 BC. See Berquist, pp. 51–53. India and Greece bordered Darius's empire on the east and west respectively. See Bright, Plate X (in the historical maps section at the end of Bright's book).

[11] See the map in Meyers and Meyers 1987, p. xxxvi.

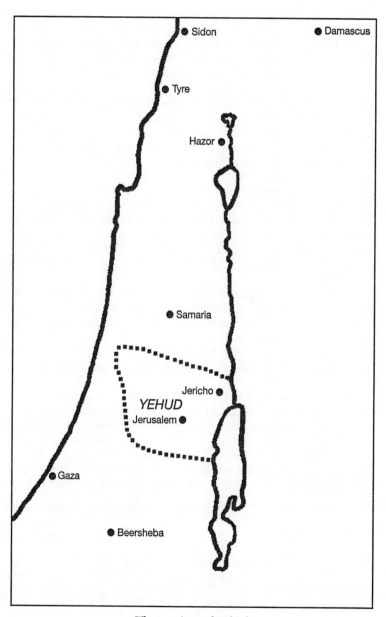

The province of Yehud

southern kingdom, since most of its citizens were of that tribe.[12] Over the following three and a half centuries, the two Israelite kingdoms came under increasing pressure from the aggressive, expansionist policies of the rising imperial powers to the east, Assyria in the eighth and seventh centuries, and Babylon in the sixth. There were times of recovery and relative prosperity, especially in the first half of the eighth century, but the general tendency, especially from then onwards, was towards decline and collapse. Weakened by conflict with one another, and harassed by neighbouring states, the two small Israelite kingdoms had no real chance, humanly speaking, of avoiding being absorbed, sooner or later, by one of the new superpowers. The northern kingdom was the first to go, succumbing finally to Assyria in 722 BC.[13] Amazingly, Judah survived for another 135 years, before falling to Babylon (Assyria's successor) in 587 BC. Judah and the surrounding area was devastated, and much of its population deported.[14] It was not until Babylon itself succumbed to Persia, some fifty years later, that those who wanted to were able to return and begin to re-establish their lives there.[15]

The Yehud that Zechariah knew was a far cry indeed from the Judah of the past. It was a small province, roughly 55 kilometres from north to south, and 65 east to west,[16] with a population of (at most) about 50,000 – less than half that of Judah before the disaster of 587 BC.[17] Jerusalem itself, where the destruction had been worst, was still sparsely inhabited.[18] It was a relatively small community, with a lot of problems.

The first area of difficulty was financial. Yehud was scarcely viable economically. It lacked the resources to engage in wealth-producing activities that required capital investment, such as mining and manufacturing, and did not have the size and influence necessary to command significant trading revenue. So it depended critically on agricultural production, which made it vulnerable to the vagaries of the weather – which was often unkind.[19] Many

---

[12] The other southern tribes, Benjamin and Simeon, were much smaller.

[13] 2 Kgs. 17:1–6.

[14] 2 Kgs. 25:1–21.

[15] See Ezra 1.

[16] I.e. 34.5 by 40.5 miles. Again, see the map in Meyers and Meyers 1987, p. xxxvi.

[17] See Ezra 2:64–65; and Bright, p. 365, note 57. Bright (p. 365), following Albright, suggests the population could 'scarcely have been much above 20,000'. But as Andersen (p. 34) has noted, 'such a low figure requires that the data in Ezra-Nehemiah about the numbers of returning exiles be taken as an exaggeration, or as covering a very extended period of migration'.

[18] See Neh. 7:4, which refers to the situation seventy-five years on.

[19] Hag. 1:5–11.

experienced severe financial hardship and struggled to survive. Zechariah's colleague Haggai captured this aspect of life in Yehud in words that will surely bring a wry smile to the faces of many of us: 'You have planted much, but have harvested little. You eat, but never have enough. You drink, but never have your fill. You put on clothes, but are not warm. *You earn wages, only to put them in a purse with holes in it.'*[20] The leaking purse (or wallet) syndrome is an affliction known in the modern world too!

The second set of problems were social. There was tension between those who had returned and those who had never gone into exile. Each side had reasons, in their own minds, to think that they were superior: the 'true' remnant through whom God's continuing commitment to Israel would be worked out.[21] There were also tensions between those whose families had belonged to the former northern and southern kingdoms respectively. The southerners (the people of Judah and Jerusalem) considered themselves more pure, racially and religiously, than their northern brethren, and were reluctant to accept them as full members of the community.[22] Finally, there was tension with people who were not of Israelite origin at all, who had taken advantage of the fall of Jerusalem to move in and settle in areas that had formerly been part of Judah.[23] So it was a very mixed, and potentially unstable, community.

The third major area of difficulty was political. Yehud had previously been part of a larger province with its administrative headquarters in Samaria, to the north. But with the repatriation of the Judean exiles, it had become a semi-independent subprovince, with its own governor. The authorities in Samaria naturally resented this reduction of their own influence in the area, and took every opportunity to block progress on the reconstruction of Jerusalem, and to represent its inhabitants in the worst possible light to the Persian authorities. According to Ezra 4 this policy of obstruction had been pursued relentlessly for almost two decades (538–520 BC), and had succeeded in bringing work on the Jerusalem temple to a complete standstill for the two years before Haggai and Zechariah began their ministries.[24]

[20] Hag. 1:6; my italics.
[21] This tension is difficult to document, and some scholars (e.g. Bedford 2001) have questioned its existence. However, that some such tension was present is prima facie likely, especially given the clear evidence of a background to it in the immediately preceding period. See Ezek. 11:14–15.
[22] See Ezra 4:1–3. The somewhat confused situation in the north had resulted from the partial resettlement of the area with non-Israelites after the northern kingdom fell to Assyria (2 Kgs. 17:24–41).
[23] This infiltration had happened mainly from Edom, to the south-east (Ezek. 35).
[24] Ezra 4:1 – 5:2.

All indications are, therefore, that life in Yehud was difficult. Its people lived daily with the painful contrast between the glories of the past and the humiliations of the present. Very little of what the returnees had eagerly expected had been realized.

2. Zechariah himself

The question 'Who am I?' is a vital one for all of us, and we try to answer it in various ways: by identifying ourselves by our occupation, for example (farmer, business person, teacher, doctor), or by our association with a particular group (a sporting fraternity, a political party or a religious denomination). In some cultures, knowing one's 'people' (race, tribe or clan) is the key. In Western societies, where such roots may be less clear, it has become common for people to expend a great deal of effort trying to trace their family history through archival research. Genealogies are one manifestation of the universal interest in our connectedness to other human beings. They are one important way of establishing our identity and our place in the world.

Zechariah has a whole book of the Bible named after him, which at once associates him with a select, famous few. However, as so often with the biblical prophets, the messenger is largely hidden behind his message. Our certain knowledge about the man behind the book is in fact fairly slight. The way he is introduced in Zechariah 1:1 seems straightforward enough: 'the prophet Zechariah son of Berekiah, the son of Iddo'. But things are not quite as simple as they appear. Literally this reads, 'Zechariah son of Berekiah son of Iddo the prophet', which could be taken in at least two ways. Conrad takes it to mean that Iddo was the prophet, and that Zechariah was only the grandson of a prophet.[25] This *could* be the meaning, but it is far more likely in my judgment that we are intended to understand that Zechariah himself was the prophet. This is an equally possible meaning, for Zechariah's short genealogy here has the same basic pattern as Jeremiah's and Ezekiel's, whose status as prophets no-one would question for a moment.[26] Furthermore,

[25] Conrad, p. 46. Conrad argues that in the book of the Twelve (Hosea–Malachi) we have a transition away from the old-style 'prophets' to new intermediaries called 'messengers', culminating in Malachi. The word Malachi means 'my messenger', and may be a title rather than a personal name.

[26] The pattern is 'X son of Y, title'. Jeremiah is literally 'son of Hilkiah from the priests in Anathoth' (Jer. 1:1), and Ezekiel is 'son of Buzi the priest' (Ezek. 1:3). Here the title is 'priest', but both genealogies entail the same kind of ambiguity as Zechariah's. What follows shows that, priests themselves or not, Jeremiah and Ezekiel were certainly prophets. Compare, however, Num. 7:18, where the ambiguity inherent in such a genealogy is explicitly resolved. Nethanel is literally 'son of Zuar leader of Issachar', but from Num. 2:5 it is clear that Nethanel is the leader, not Zuar.

Zechariah's contemporary and close associate Haggai is simply and directly called a prophet (Hag. 1:1). We may reasonably assume, then, that Zechariah too was a prophet in his own right, and not merely the grandson of one.

In fact, it is more than likely that Zechariah's grandfather was a priest rather than a prophet.[27] 'Iddo' appears to have been a fairly common name among Israelites.[28] A certain 'Iddo', however, is named in Nehemiah 12:4 as the head of one of the priestly families that had returned to Jerusalem with Zerubbabel, who later became the governor (Hag. 2:21). This places him fairly well to have been Zechariah's grandfather, and the prophet's priestly connections are further suggested by the strong interest in the temple evident in his preaching.[29]

But what of Berekiah, the prophet's father according to Zechariah 1:1? The truth is that we know almost nothing at all about him, and the mystery surrounding him is increased by the fact that he is missing in Ezra 5:1 and 6:14, where Zechariah is simply 'the son of Iddo'.[30] This has led to a flurry of speculation about whose son Zechariah actually was.[31] Some early Christian commentators said that he was the natural son of Berekiah, but the spiritual son of Iddo; that is, he was brought up by Iddo the priest in much the same way that Samuel was brought up by Eli.[32] Two recent commentators have suggested that Zechariah's father may have died young, leaving him to be raised as the de facto 'son' of his grandfather.[33] Others have argued that there were two Zechariahs with two different fathers, whose names have become conflated in the title of the book. One was responsible for Zechariah 1 – 8, and the other for Zechariah 9 – 14.[34] A far simpler and more likely explanation is the one Joyce Baldwin gives in her commentary, namely that in Ezra 5:1 and 6:14 'son' is used in the more general sense of 'descendant'.[35]

[27] Though of course 'priest' and 'prophet' are not mutually exclusive; Ezekiel was both (Ezek. 1:3; 2:5).

[28] See Baldwin, 'Iddo', p. 503, for a good summary of the occurrences of the name in various parts of the Old Testament.

[29] Cf. Ezekiel's similar interest in the temple (Ezek. 1:3; 8 – 11; 40 – 48).

[30] The NIV eases the difficulty of the missing father by (legitimately) translating 'son' as 'descendant'.

[31] See Baldwin 1972, pp. 88–89. What immediately follows is heavily indebted to her.

[32] 1 Sam. 1:1 – 2:11.

[33] Meyers and Meyers 1987, p. 92. The authors themselves do not think there is sufficient evidence to resolve the issue, but list the early death of Berekiah as one of four possibilities.

[34] See the references in Baldwin 1972, p. 88, n. 5.

[35] As reflected in the NIV translation of these verses. This extended use of 'son' is quite common in OT genealogies, and is familiar to us from the well-known designation of Jesus as 'son of David'.

Zechariah 1:1 and 1:7 give both the father and grandfather, whereas Ezra mentions only the better-known grandfather. A parallel occurs in the case of Jehu, who is called 'son of Nimshi' in 1 Kings 19:16 and 2 Kings 9:20, but 'son of Jehoshaphat son of Nimshi' in 2 Kings 9:2, 14. Zechariah 1:1 gives the fuller version of Zechariah's genealogy, as would be expected in a book that bears his name.[36]

Beyond this, we can only speculate. If Iddo was indeed his grandfather, Zechariah was probably quite young when he began his ministry.[37] As a member of one of the leading priestly families, however, he would have belonged to the upper echelons of society. He appears to have had access to the high priest Joshua (Zech. 6:9–12), and probably to the governor as well (Zech. 4:6). Consequently, he would have been a person of influence. The content of his preaching makes it clear that he was not a recluse, but a public figure who addressed a wide range of issues relating to politics, religion, and social justice. He did not hesitate to denounce sin and call for repentance (Zech. 1:2–6; 5:1–11), but the general tenor of his preaching, like that of Haggai, was positive and empowering. The book of Ezra gives brief but telling testimony to the impact that the preaching of Haggai and Zechariah had:

> Now Haggai the prophet and Zechariah the prophet, a descend-ant of Iddo, prophesied to the Jews in Judah and Jerusalem in the name of the God of Israel, who was over them. Then Zerubbabel son of Shealtiel and Jeshua son of Jozadak set to work to rebuild the house of God in Jerusalem. And the prophets of God were with them, helping them.[38]

The significant words at the end of verse 1 ('in the name of the God of Israel, who was over them') alert us to the secret of this impact. It was not due to their eloquence, nor their charismatic personalities, but to the God in whose name and by whose authority they spoke.[39] That is what it meant to be a prophet, to be the channel through which the word of the sovereign God enters history and shapes it. Not all prophets saw such a positive response to their preaching. Jeremiah, for example, had to stand at his post through almost half a century, preaching a message that went largely unheeded by his contemporaries. Zechariah's lot was a happier one. 'Success', though,

---

[36] See note 31. My previous three sentences are a near quotation of Baldwin on this point, modified slightly for stylistic reasons.

[37] Cf. Jeremiah (Jer. 1:4–8).

[38] Ezra 5:1–2.

[39] Kidner (p. 53), in a characteristically beautiful turn of phrase, speaks of 'the gentle reminder [in this verse] of man's accountability and heaven's help'.

was never the measure of a true prophet, but faithfulness to God, and to the message that had been given him to speak.

By this standard, Zechariah was a prophet indeed. His preaching from beginning to end shows him to be a man fired by the conviction that the God of Israel was the LORD of the whole earth, and that his kingdom would come and his will would be done, whatever obstacles human beings might put in its way. More than that, he believed that he and his fellows were called and privileged, then and there, to play their part in the coming of that kingdom. He was thoroughly engaged with the realities of his present situation, but never closed in by them, as though they alone set the horizons of his life. He knew that life was to be lived in the light of that day (which he believed would surely come) when there would be 'one LORD, and his name the only name', and when God – this God – would be 'king over the whole earth' (Zech. 14:9). It was Zechariah's unswerving commitment to this conviction that gave his preaching, and the book, its special character, and drew its diverse elements together into a remarkable unity.

3. The book of Zechariah

The Bible is no 'ordinary' book, and its special character can be a stumbling block to many 'ordinary' readers. A book of such extraordinary antiquity and reputed authority must be beyond them, they feel. Perhaps it is even dangerous to dabble with it; best leave it to the experts – especially the Old Testament, which (supposedly) is especially primitive and violent. For the Christian, however, such negativity is not only unwarranted, but entirely inexcusable. The reason is simple: the Old Testament was Jesus' own Bible,[40] the book (for that is what the word 'bible' means) to which he turned in his own spiritual struggles,[41] and referred to constantly in his teaching.[42] Someone who is committed to Jesus as their Lord cannot but be also a dedicated and appreciative reader of the Old Testament. Our commitment to Jesus commits us to the task (or rather adventure) of reading the same book he did, and the word 'book' itself gives us a reassuring point from which to begin. For we all know what a book is, and how, in general terms, we should approach one.[43]

[40] 'The Bible Jesus Read', as Philip Yancey put it in the title of one of his recent books (1999).
[41] I have in mind particularly his quoting of Deuteronomy and Psalms in his temptation in the wilderness (Matt. 4:1–11).
[42] Note, e.g., his appeal to Genesis in his teaching on divorce: Matt. 19:4; Mark 10:6.
[43] See Adler.

The book of Zechariah, with which we are particularly concerned here, is a book within a book. It is part of the Bible, which has two main parts: the Old Testament and the New. So we must read Zechariah more as we might read a volume in a trilogy (for example) or as a chapter in a large volume, rather than as a completely 'stand alone' work.[44] It does, nevertheless, have a sufficiently distinct character and completeness to it to be properly called a book in its own right.

We shall begin by considering its structure, which is just another way of asking the question 'What are its main parts and how are they related to one another?' The details will have to wait until we read it more closely, but it will help us to tackle this basic question in a preliminary way here. A 'bird's eye' view, or a map, can be a helpful way of becoming familiar with new territory!

a. Its structure

Some basic elements of structure strike us at once as we begin to read. Like all other books of the Bible, Zechariah is divided into chapters and verses. These divisions were not an original part of the text, but at least show us how someone else has broken it up.[45] They also give us a convenient, shorthand way of identifying where we are in the book, and of referring to its smaller parts (e.g. verses or paragraphs) that we may want to examine more closely.

More significant, however, are indications of structure that are an integral part of the text itself. The first verse of the book is clearly a heading that introduces what follows. A second, similar, heading occurs in 1:7, and a third, slightly shorter one, in 7:1. A different kind of heading occurs at the beginning of chapters 9 and 12. It is a single word in Hebrew, translated correctly in the NIV as 'An Oracle' (a prophetic message).

So far so good. Now let us turn our attention to what stands under these headings – the contents, or 'stuff', of the book. Two major blocks of material stand out clearly. There is a series of eight visions in 1:7 – 6:8, and two major oracles in chapters 9 – 14 introduced by the two headings we have already noted (the first covers chapters 9 – 11, and the second chapters 12 – 14). Moreover, both the visions and the oracles are preceded by an introduction:

---

[44] In fact, it is the eleventh of the twelve Minor Prophets, traditionally known in Judaism as 'The Book of the Twelve', or just 'The Twelve'.

[45] The division into verses is Jewish, and probably occurred during the Talmudic period (AD 135–500). The division into chapters was of later, Christian, origin and was introduced into Hebrew manuscripts in the time of Salmaon ben Ishmael (c. 1330). See Brotzman, p. 47.

the visions by 1:1–6, and the oracles by 7:1 – 8:23.[46] Finally, we observe that the series of eight visions is followed by a symbolic action, the crowning of Joshua the high priest, at the end of chapter 6 (vv. 9–15).

Putting all this together, we arrive at the following basic structure:[47]

PART 1. CHAPTERS 1 – 6

Introduction (1:1–6)

Eight visions (1:7 – 6:8; plus 6:9–15)

PART 2. CHAPTERS 7 – 14

Introduction (7:1 – 8:23)

Two oracles (chs. 9 – 11, and 12 – 14)

As we shall see, the two main parts of the book are deeply connected. The introduction to part 1 doubles up as an introduction to the whole book,[48] something underlined by the fact that the introduction to part 2 seems deliberately to echo it.[49] And, more fundamentally for how the book as a whole works, the oracles of part 2 build upon the visions of part 1.[50]

---

[46] I take the three chronological markers at 1:1, 7 and 7:1 as major (first order) markers, and the two occurrences of the single word *maśśā'* (an oracle) at 9:1 and 12:1 as minor (second order) markers. This means that chs. 7 – 8 go with what follows them rather than what precedes them. Cf. Kline, 'Structure of Zechariah' (1991), pp. 184–185.

[47] In arriving at this analysis I have been significantly helped by the work of Marvin Sweeney (see esp. pp. 573–574). Taking his cue mainly from the chronological markers in 1:1, 7 and 7:1, he breaks with the traditional (critical) division of the book into chs. 1 – 8 and 9 – 14, and sees it as having two main parts: 1:1–6 and 1:7 – 14:21), with the second part subdivided at 7:1 into 1:7 – 6:15 and 7:1 – 14:21. My own analysis differs from his in some significant ways (see previous note). Other points of difference will be noted (with explanation where appropriate) in the following exposition.

[48] Which is why it is capitalized above, in contrast to the second (minor) introduction in chs. 7 – 8. The introduction of 1:1–6 has a major heading after it as well as before it, in contrast to the introduction in chs. 7 – 8.

[49] Zech. 1:1–6 and ch. 7 both refer to the word of the LORD coming to Zechariah in a particular year of Darius, the LORD's anger with the forefathers, the words proclaimed by the earlier prophets, and the refusal of the forefathers to pay attention. Ch. 8, however, is not related to 1:1–6 in the same way. For this and other reasons already given above, I take chs. 7 – 8 as introducing chs. 7 – 14 rather than closing chs. 1 – 8.

[50] Cf. Dumbrell, pp. 193–194.

b. Its message

We have already summarized the message of Zechariah in the words 'Your kingdom come!' It is a book about the future coming of the kingdom of God, and the need to live now in the light of it.[51] We're now ready to examine that message in a little more detail. If we think of it as a rope, what are its strands, and how are they woven together? We shall look at a number of them in turn, but always with an eye to how each strand, or theme, connects with the others.

i. Repentance

This note is struck at once, in the introduction of 1:1–6: ' "Return to me," declares the LORD Almighty, "and I will return to you." ' It comes first because it is fundamental to everything that follows. Those who are expecting the kingdom of God to come must prepare themselves for it by renouncing all forms of rebellion and submitting themselves wholly to God's rightful rule over them. To use Zechariah's own powerful language, those who want to claim God's promise to 'return' to *them*, must first 'return' to *him* (1:3).

As an uncompromising preacher of repentance, Zechariah stood foursquare with the great prophets such as Isaiah, Jeremiah and Ezekiel, who had gone before him.[52] They were part of a prophetic line that ran from Moses, through men like Zechariah, to John the Baptist, and finally to Jesus, who began his public ministry with the clarion call 'The kingdom of God is near. Repent...' (Mark 1:15). For all these prophets repentance was more than a mere formality, done routinely as part of their traditional way of praying. The announcement that the kingdom of God was coming was a declaration that God was very much in charge of his world, and determined to call all of us to account for how we have lived in it.[53] It was a demand to take *God* seriously because he takes *us* seriously, and that is a very serious matter indeed. Such preaching turns people's whole lives upside down, for the values of the kingdom of God stand in sharp contrast to the values of the kingdoms we have fashioned for ourselves. Repentance, as the prophets understood it, could not simply be done in our heads, or in 'church'; if it was to be done at all it had to be done in the home, the marketplace, the courts, and the king's council. To repent meant to recognize the kingship of God.

---

[51] Cf. Kline 1990, p. 2: '[Zechariah's] overall theme, developed in visions, oracles, symbolic actions, "sermons", and "burdens", is the restoration and consummation of God's kingdom'.

[52] E.g. Is. 1:18–20; 59:20; Jer. 18:11; Ezek. 14:6; 18:30, 32.

[53] Note Amos 4:12: 'Prepare to meet your God'!

In Zechariah repentance is mentioned explicitly only in the opening few verses (1:1–6),[54] but in reality it is a theme that permeates the whole book. It surfaces in Zechariah's ominous words about a curse that has gone out over the whole land because of theft and lying (5:1–4), and about the iniquity associated with the 'basket' (representing sharp business practices; 5:5–11).[55] It shows itself in his denunciation of predatory conquerors (9:8), oppressive, exploitative rulers (10:3; 11:4–5), idolatry, false prophecy, and impurity (13:1–3), and in his reminder of the righteous anger of God that overtook the forefathers (1:2). Positively it finds expression in calls for justice, mercy and compassion, especially towards the widow, the fatherless and the alien (7:8–10; 8:16–17).

To what extent Zechariah's contemporaries heeded his preaching on this subject is difficult to know with certainty.[56] He certainly had an impact on their commitment to rebuilding the temple, as we have seen, but his sustained preaching on repentance indicates that sin persisted in many areas of their personal and community life. It is clear, though, that Zechariah believed that one day true repentance would happen: God would pour out on his people 'a spirit of grace and supplication'. They would recognize that their sin had been – at its deepest level – an attack on God himself, and turn to him in deep contrition (12:10–14). Then at last his kingdom would come and his will would be done on earth as it is in heaven (Zech. 14).

For Zechariah, then, repentance was both a requirement and a gift, a human responsibility and a sovereign work of God. It was Zechariah's responsibility to preach it, and his hearers' responsibility to do it. But deep and true repentance, the kind that ushers in his kingdom, is ultimately a miracle that only God himself can bring about. Only he can turn hearts of stone to hearts of flesh.[57] Repentance and the coming of God's kingdom are inextricably linked together; they are both ways of talking about the rule of God.

ii. The city of God
The book of Zechariah is about Jerusalem from beginning to end. It opens with a reminder of God's anger with an earlier generation – a white-hot, righteous anger that had had its outworking in the fall of Jerusalem to the Babylonians in 587 BC (1:2). The eight visions of chapters 1 – 6, however, convey good news for Zechariah's

[54] The Hebrew verb *šûḇ*, variously translated 'return', 'turn' and 'repent[ed]' in Zech. 1:2, 4, 6, is the standard word for repentance in the OT prophets.
[55] See my comments on this passage in the exposition that follows.
[56] On who are said to have repented in Zech. 1:6 (Zechariah's contemporaries, or their forefathers), see my comments in the following exposition.
[57] Ezek. 36:26–27.

contemporaries of God's intention to restore Jerusalem, and call to account the nations that have abused its people (1:14–17). Chapters 7 and 8, which introduce the second half of the book, speak of God's plan to bless Jerusalem so much in the future that people from all over the world will want to go there (8:20–23). The two oracles that follow develop this at length, culminating at the end of the book with the great, final day when the LORD will come to Jerusalem in power and glory to be acknowledged as king of the whole earth and to be worshipped by people of all nations (14:1–9, 16–21). For Zechariah, then, Jerusalem is the city of God par excellence, and its future glorification is a key aspect of the coming of God's kingdom.

For Zechariah, Jerusalem's chief glory was the presence of God in it, powerfully symbolized by the temple. For it was here in particular, as in the tabernacle of earlier times, that God had chosen to dwell among his people. We are told in Exodus that the tabernacle in the wilderness had been built at the Lord's express command, and that when it was finished he filled it with his glory – his manifest presence.[58] The same things are said about the Jerusalem temple, which was eventually built to replace the tabernacle in the time of Solomon.[59] Of course, the temple could not 'contain' God; even the highest heaven could not do that, since he is the creator and ruler of the whole universe.[60] Heaven is his throne, and the whole earth merely his footstool.[61] But – wonder of wonders – he chose to reveal himself to human beings, and to take them into a covenant relationship with himself. And the temple was the place he chose to meet with them to receive their worship, answer their prayers, and give them his blessing.[62] So Jerusalem was nothing without the temple, and the temple was nothing without God's presence. It was God's presence that made both the temple and the city glorious. With the LORD present in his temple, Jerusalem was the city of God. It was the centre of his kingdom on earth, and the place where that kingship would finally be manifested.

In this too Zechariah was in complete agreement with the earlier prophets. Isaiah and Micah had spoken of a day when 'the mountain of the LORD's temple' would be raised up as chief among the mountains, and all nations would flow to it.[63] Ezekiel, speaking to a small community of Jerusalemites in exile, had described God's

[58] Exod. 25:8; 40:34.
[59] 1 Kgs. 8, especially v. 11. In the interim a more modest temple had existed, for a time, at Shiloh (1 Sam. 1:3–9; Jer. 7:12–15).
[60] 1 Kgs. 8:27.
[61] Is. 66:1.
[62] 1 Kgs. 8:29–53.
[63] Is. 2:1–4; Mic. 4:1–4.

reluctant withdrawal from Jerusalem and the temple because of the abominations that had been practised there, and of his promise to return one day.[64] The book of Ezekiel ends with the prophet transported in a vision to a very high mountain where he sees laid out before him the city of God, the new Jerusalem, and within it a glorious new temple from which a river flows out to bring renewal to the whole earth.[65] Ezekiel's vision concludes with the words 'THE LORD IS THERE', the name by which the new Jerusalem of the future will be known.[66]

These, then, were the dreams and visions that circulated in the minds of Zechariah's contemporaries and, in their best moments, roused them to action. Zechariah became a mighty catalyst for this arousal by giving the same ideas fresh currency, and preaching them with prophetic power. The dream of a new Jerusalem was God's dream, and Zechariah, as his prophet, challenged his fellows to make it theirs as well.

iii. The 'now' and the 'not yet' of the kingdom
Of course, the problem for Zechariah's hearers was that the temple and city they were struggling to rebuild in their day wasn't even remotely like what Ezekiel had seen in his magnificent vision. The walls of Jerusalem were still in ruins, and the temple itself was small and unimpressive. It didn't even measure up to what had been there in the past, let alone what had been envisioned for the future. According to Ezra 3:12, when the foundation of this second temple was being laid some of the very old people who could remember the first one (which Solomon had built) wept when they realized how small this one was going to be in comparison to it. As Zechariah himself put it, it was a 'day of small things' (Zech. 4:10). The historical realities Haggai and Zechariah were confronted with makes their rhetoric seem almost embarrassingly extravagant. Could such things be regarded by any level-headed person as fulfilments of what God had promised, or a manifestation of his supreme kingship? Did Haggai and Zechariah perhaps get carried away and, like many false prophets and preachers before and since, lead their hearers on by filling them with false hopes, blowing bubbles that were sure to burst, sooner or later?

It would be possible to view them that way – indeed, in scholarly

[64] Ezek. 8 – 11; 43:1–9.
[65] Some (e.g. Darr, pp. 271–279) argue that only the land of Israel is on view, but the transparent allusion to the rivers flowing out of Eden in Gen. 2, and the constant reference to Ezekiel as 'son of man' (or 'son of Adam'), suggests to me that something more inclusive is in mind, even if it is implied rather than spoken about directly.
[66] Ezek. 48:35.

circles these prophets have been poorly regarded until relatively recent times.[67] But those who preserved and transmitted their words to us as Scripture apparently had a different view. They did not reject their words as the rantings of false prophets, or even relegate them to a secondary status, as they did with most of the literature that came later, in the period between the Old and New Testaments.[68] On the contrary, they included the books of Haggai and Zechariah in the second major section of the Hebrew Bible (our Old Testament),[69] along with Isaiah, Jeremiah, Ezekiel; and Amos, Hosea, Micah and the rest of the Twelve.[70] And this very high view of Zechariah, in particular, is confirmed, as we shall see, by the way it is quoted as Scripture in the New Testament.

How, then, are we to understand the strong 'kingdom of God' language Zechariah applied to the apparently insignificant events taking place in the small province of Yehud in his own day? Three things need to be borne in mind, as they are quite fundamental to Zechariah's message. First, the earlier prophets, as we have seen, had declared that Jerusalem was destined to play a key role in the future manifestation of God's kingdom on earth. By rising up and rebuilding in their own day, Zechariah and the people of Yehud showed that *they believed the promises of God and intended to live*

[67] The post-exilic prophets for a long time suffered from the negative impact of the work of Julius Wellhausen and others in the late nineteenth and early twentieth centuries. Wellhausen considered that the prophetic movement reached its peak in the preaching of the eighth-century prophets, and thereafter went into decline. The eighth-century prophets had been champions of social justice and critics of the establishment. In contrast, the post-exilic prophets were supporters of the priestly (temple) establishment, and were not as focused on justice as the primary requirement of the covenant. They were associated with the early development of Judaism, which Wellhausen saw as a religion of ceremony and law, in contrast to Christianity, which was a religion of grace, and love to one's fellow man. However, in the post-Holocaust era, the post-exilic prophets have benefited from an increasingly strong trend among biblical scholars to endeavour to understand Judaism better, to appreciate its positive features, and to repudiate anything that smacks of anti-Semitism. For a good summary of Wellhausen's views, their impact on the study of the post-exilic prophets, and developments that have taken place more recently, see Floyd, especially pp. 260–262. The work of Peter Ackroyd (e.g. *Exile and Restoration*) provided a welcome stimulus to the study of these prophets in the 1960s. Rex Mason's work (e.g. 'The prophets of the restoration') is typical of the good work being done in this area more recently.

[68] I have in mind the voluminous intertestamental literature, which was valued and preserved but never accorded canonical status by the Jewish people. Their belief, reflected in the work of Josephus and others, was that prophecy ceased in the time of Ezra, some sixty years or more *after* Haggai and Zechariah. See Beckwith, especially ch. 4.

[69] The three traditional parts of the Hebrew Bible are the Law, the Prophets and the Writings.

[70] Hosea–Malachi make up 'The Book of the Twelve', or (among Christians) the 'Minor Prophets'.

by them. Second, by rebuilding the temple *they were preparing the way of the* LORD, making ready the stage on which the great kingdom of God drama of the future would be enacted. It was to Jerusalem and the temple[71] that the Lord Jesus himself eventually *did* come to announce that the kingdom had drawn near, and then to secure its future triumph by his own death and resurrection. It was from here that the good news of the kingdom has now gone out to the whole world, and it is to here that Jesus will one day return to take his power and reign. The rebuilding in the early Persian period can rightly be seen as preparation for all of this. Finally, however (and here we come to the heart of the matter), the rebuilding in Zechariah's day was not just *preparation* for the kingdom of God drama; it was an actual *participation* in it. Zechariah understood that, in these apparently small and insignificant events, the kingdom of God was breaking into this world; or, to put it another way, the end of the world was already beginning to happen! The apostle Paul was later to express the same breathtaking truth in the way he spoke about what happens when a person – any person – is born again: 'if anyone is in Christ, he is a new creation', or literally 'there is new creation'.[72] In other words, when someone becomes a Christian, the new creation which the prophets had spoken about is already present, to be seen and wondered at, in that 'small' event that has happened in the here and now. The kingdom of God has broken in and manifested itself in that one person's conversion.

This is why the powerful, symbolic language of Zechariah's visions and oracles was justified. It was not a flight from reality, but a way of investing the here and now with its true significance in the light of the coming of God's kingdom. Of course, the full manifestation of that kingdom is still future for us, as it was for Zechariah. There is a very definite 'not yet' aspect of it that must be recognized. Its coming is what we pray for rather than see directly. But this aspect of Zechariah's message is still true, and mightily encouraging. In a nutshell it is this: don't despise the 'day of small things' (4:10), because the kingdom of God is a *big* thing, and nothing associated with it can ever be insignificant. To be caught up in its coming, to be doing the work of the kingdom, here and now, however apparently mundane that work might appear to be, is an awesome privilege.[73]

[71] The so-called 'second temple' of Zechariah's day was later replaced by the far more splendid temple built by Herod the Great (40–4 BC). But the relationship is essentially one of continuity; the foundation stones of the earlier temple can still be seen in Jerusalem underneath those of Herod's temple.
[72] 2 Cor. 5:17.
[73] Cf. the way the apostle Paul speaks about the privilege and responsibility of being a minister of the new covenant: 2 Cor. 2:12 – 5:21.

But first, a serious problem must be faced: the unfitness of sinful human beings to engage in such a holy calling. It is in this that Zechariah's priestly background comes through most clearly in the book.

iv. Cleansing

As we have seen, the opening six verses of the book make it clear that repentance is essential. But repentance alone cannot deal with the deeper problem of uncleanness. Sinful acts and attitudes are the manifestation of an inner corruption that affects the whole person, and taints everything he or she does, including worship and service of God. Haggai had expressed it well with reference to the community to whom both he and Zechariah were called to preach: 'So it is with this people and this nation in my sight, declares the LORD. Whatever they do and whatever they offer ... is defiled.'[74] Even perfect repentance was beyond them. How then could they be heralds and agents of the coming kingdom of God?

Two hundred years earlier, the young prophet Isaiah had struggled with the same question. When he saw the exalted LORD and heard him summoning him to his service, his first reaction was one of sheer terror: 'Woe to me!' he cried. 'I am ruined! For I am a man of unclean lips, and I live among a people of unclean lips, and my eyes have seen the King, the LORD Almighty.'[75] He knew that, like all his fellow Israelites, he was unfit even to be in the presence of the Holy One, let alone to serve him.

In Zechariah this dilemma is presented symbolically by the vision of Joshua, the high priest, standing before the LORD, clothed in filthy garments (Zech. 3:1–3). Joshua's filthy clothes represent, not only his own sin, but the sin of the whole land (v. 9); that is, the whole community. None of them is clean in God's sight, and therefore qualified to worship and serve him. Nor can they do anything about it themselves; it is a problem that only God can solve.

This is the dark backdrop against which Zechariah's positive message about atonement (cleansing from sin) is unfolded. There are two aspects to it. There is a symbolic, ceremonial cleansing from sin in the present (represented by the reclothing of Joshua; 3:4–5), and the promise of a real, final cleansing for the whole community in the future: 'I [God] will remove the sin of this land in a single day' (3:9). Joshua and his associates are told that they are 'men symbolic of things to come'; the future reality is linked to the coming of someone whom God refers to as 'my servant, the Branch' (3:8).

[74] Hag. 2:14.
[75] Is. 6:5.

So the groundwork for Zechariah's treatment of this theme is laid in chapters 1 – 8, especially in chapter 3. But its full development does not come until the second part of the book, in which Zechariah speaks of a day when God will open a fountain, to cleanse his people from sin and uncleanness (13:1). We can't grasp this fully without also considering Zechariah's teaching about the Messiah, which we shall do shortly. The bottom line, though, is the good news that there is a solution to the problem of uncleanness. There is atonement for sin, but, as the whole Bible consistently teaches, it is a gift, something God provides for us, not something we can achieve by our own efforts. We can and must repent, but only God can change our hearts, and atone for the sin that (otherwise) would separate us from him forever. Without atonement, the message of the coming kingdom of God would mean nothing but condemnation. For, as the apostle John tells us, nothing impure will ever enter God's city, the new Jerusalem.[76] Only by a miracle of God's grace can sinners be cleansed and made fit to be in God's presence.

Now we are ready to draw the curtain right back, look into the very heart of the message of Zechariah, and see how God has performed that miracle.

v. The Messiah
What we might call the 'messianic' strand of Zechariah's preaching is a key element of his message about the 'now' and the 'not yet' aspects of the kingdom.

Both Haggai and Zechariah saw enormous significance in the fact that Zerubbabel had been appointed governor. For Zerubbabel was a direct descendant of king David, whose son Solomon had built the first temple.[77] Furthermore, he had played a leading role in starting the work on the new temple, even before he became governor (Zech. 4:9).[78] Moreover, his rise to prominence coincided with a

---

[76] Rev. 21:27.

[77] 1 Chr. 3, especially vv. 17–19; cf. Matt. 1, especially vv. 6b–13. There is an apparent discrepancy between Ezra 3:2; Hag. 1:1 and Matt. 1:12, where he is the son of Shealtiel, and 1 Chr. 3:19 (in the Hebrew, though not in the LXX), where he is the son of Pediah, Shealtiel's brother. The most likely explanation is that he was the product of a levirate marriage, in which case he would have been the natural son of Pediah, but the legal son of Shealtiel. See Deut. 25:5–6; Wright, 'Zerubbabel', p. 1280.

[78] See also Ezra 3:1–2. The first governor (Zerubbabel's predecessor) was Sheshbazzar (Ezra 5:14; cf. 1:8–11). Both Sheshbazzar and Zerubbabel are said to have laid the foundation of the second temple (Ezra 5:16; Zech. 4:9). It has been argued either that Zerubbabel is to be identified with Sheshbazzar, or that Ezra 1 – 6 is tendentious, and that work on the temple did not begin at all until the time of Zerubbabel (e.g. Oesterley and Robinson; Bedford). However, it seems clear (1) that Ezra 1 – 6 utilizes source material rather than being a 'free' composition, and (2) that Zerubbabel and

revival of the Levitical priesthood in the person of Joshua, as we have seen.

Against the backdrop of earlier prophecy, all this was highly significant. Isaiah had spoken of a day, beyond the tragedy of the exile, when a shoot would come up from the stump of Jesse (the line of David, which had been cut off), and of a Branch from his roots that would bear fruit.[79] Jeremiah had adopted the expression 'the Branch' as a technical term for the future Messiah:

> 'The days are coming,' declares the LORD,
>   'when I will raise up to David a righteous
>   Branch,
> a King who will reign wisely
>   and do what is just and right in the land.
> In his days Judah will be saved
>   and Israel will live in safety.'[80]

Furthermore, he had declared that God was just as committed to his covenant with the Levites (the priestly line) as he was to his covenant with David:

> For this is what the LORD says: 'David will never fail to have a man to sit on the throne of the house of Israel, nor will the priests, who are Levites, ever fail to have a man to stand before me continually to offer burnt offerings, to burn grain offerings and to present sacrifices.' The word of the LORD came to Jeremiah: This is what the LORD says: 'If you can break my covenant with the day and my covenant with the night, so that day and night no longer come at their appointed time, then my covenant with David my servant – and my covenant with the Levites who are priests ministering before me – can be broken and David will no longer have a descendant to reign on his throne.'[81]

Sheshbazzar are distinguished in those sources and not just in the narrative in which they are embedded. See especially Ezra 5:6–17 (correspondence between the provincial authorities of Trans-Euphrates and Darius I), in which Sheshbazzar is clearly a past figure while Zerubbabel (by implication) is still building the temple. On the sources see Williamson, pp. xxiii–xxiv; and on the implications for the separate identity of Sheshbazzar see Wright, 'Zerubbabel', p. 1280. Andersen has argued (convincingly in my judgment) that the various statements about the 'founding' of the temple in Ezra and Haggai-Zechariah are complementary rather than contradictory, and that the historicity of Ezra 1 – 6 should not be lightly dismissed.

[79] Is. 11:1.
[80] Jer. 23:5–6; cf. 33:15–16.
[81] Jer. 33:17–21.

No wonder, then, that the appointment of Zerubbabel as governor, with Joshua the high priest at his side, was greeted with such enthusiasm by Zechariah and his contemporaries. Zerubbabel was only a governor, to be sure – not a king. But his rise to leadership gave strong encouragement to those who were looking for the fulfilment of Isaiah's and Jeremiah's prophecies. This is the context in which the 'messianic' language that Haggai and Zechariah use with reference to Zerubbabel must be understood.

If we had only Zechariah 1 – 6 we might think that Zechariah believed Zerubbabel himself to be the promised Messiah. He describes Zerubbabel as a man empowered by the Spirit, chosen by God to build the temple (4:6–9), and one of the two anointed ones (literally 'sons of oil') who serve the LORD of the whole earth (4:14), a possible allusion to the passage from Jeremiah 33 to which I have just referred. And in chapter 6 the person who will build the temple of the LORD is referred to as 'the man whose name is the Branch', and it is said that 'he will be clothed with majesty and will sit and rule on his throne' (6:12, 13) – evidently as a king.

In spite of all this, however, there are good reasons to believe that Zechariah did not think that Zerubbabel himself was the Messiah. The first is that Zerubbabel, the Persian-appointed governor of Yehud, clearly fell far short of being the ideal king that Isaiah and Jeremiah had predicted, and Zechariah seems to be quite aware of this fact. The day of Zerubbabel is a 'day of small things' (4:10), not the final reality. The second reason is that in chapters 7 – 14 Zechariah speaks of another figure, a king, who will come to Jerusalem 'on that day', in the future (9:9–17, esp. vv. 9, 16). His career is described only in outline, as though it is a part waiting to be played by a figure whose full identity is yet to be revealed. In chapter 9 he appears as 'righteous and having salvation, / gentle and riding on a donkey'. In chapters 10 – 11 his rule is contrasted, by implication, with that of false shepherds, who have exploited and scattered God's flock. Chapters 12 and 13 speak about the smiting of a good shepherd, a man intimately connected with God himself, so much so that, in God's own words, he is 'the man who is close to me' (13:7). While the connection is never made explicitly, the conclusion we are naturally led to is that the king and the smitten shepherd are one and the same person. What unfolds in these chapters, therefore, is the outline of a fascinating drama: the arrival of an ideal king, his conflict with false shepherds, his rejection and his death. And, somehow associated with all this, the opening of a fountain to cleanse the citizens of Jerusalem from sin and uncleanness (13:1) – the fulfilment of the promise of 3:9. In many ways the career of this 'good shepherd' closely parallels that of the Suffering Servant of the LORD in Isaiah 40 – 55.[82]

We can see, therefore, that in the context of the book as a whole, Zerubbabel is not presented as the Messiah, if by that we mean the complete fulfilment of earlier prophecies about an ideal king. Zerubbabel is a very important figure, with a number of significant messianic qualities: he is a descendant of David, a leader chosen by God and empowered by his Spirit. His specific divine calling is to rebuild the temple. But after him, in a 'day' not yet present but foreseen by Zechariah, will come another, greater person, an ideal shepherd-king, who will bring salvation. And when he comes, and only then, will the promise of full atonement for sin be realized. Zerubbabel, then, is *a* 'messianic' figure, but not *the* Messiah. He is a forerunner of the Messiah, just as his temple is a forerunner of the magnificent 'house of the LORD' in the last two verses of the book (14:20–21).[83]

What were the implications of this message for the current situation of Yehud in Zechariah's own day? If what we have just said is true, Zechariah should not be seen as the spokesman for a revived nationalism, aimed at inciting rebellion against the Persian authorities. His point was not that the present situation was unsatisfactory, and that Zerubbabel should be hailed as the Messiah and be proclaimed king in defiance of Persia. His preaching, rightly understood, was not politically driven at all. Rather, it was theologically driven. It showed that the present situation, while not ideal, should be welcomed and viewed positively, as a sign that the ancient promises were still in force, and in God's time – *on that day* – the Messiah would come, and God's will would be done perfectly on earth as it is in heaven.

vi. The people of God

We have just seen how closely aligned Zechariah's messianic theology is with that of Isaiah. So too, is his understanding of the people of God.

In one sense Zechariah's message is quite narrowly focused. It is about Jerusalem and its people, both now and in the future. But

---

[82] The career of the Suffering Servant is unfolded in a series of poems commonly referred to by scholars as the 'Servant Songs'. It was Bernhard Duhm who first identified 42:1–4; 49:1–6; 50:4–9 and 52:13 – 53:12 as the four Servant Songs. Most scholars today still follow his lead, but with some difference of opinion about the precise limits of the passages. I take the four Songs to be 42:1–9; 49:1–7; 50:4–9 and 52:13 – 53:12, and regard 61:1–3 as a fifth and final Song that brings the whole series to a climax.

[83] Cf. Childs, p. 478: 'the foundation of the earthly temple built by Zerubbabel adumbrates the heavenly temple of the new age (Ezek. 40ff.)'.

because his vision of the kingdom of God is so all-inclusive, his preaching can never, in the end, be merely nationalistic or racially based. On the contrary, he understands that God's intention is not simply to bless Jerusalem for its own sake, but so that it might become a source of blessing to the whole world.[84] I have already dealt with this above when we looked at the theme of the city of God. I mention it again here simply to underline it, because it is of such importance for us as contemporary Christian readers. Zechariah understood that because God is the Lord of the whole earth, his people must ultimately be a vast, multicultural, multi-ethnic community drawn from all nations, united finally by their common acknowledgment of him as the only true God. The coming of God's kingdom is not the hope of Israel alone, but of the whole world. The people of God will finally be all who have come to the cleansing fountain, and the new Jerusalem will be their home forever (Zech. 2:11; 8:20–23; 14:16).[85]

But while Zechariah's understanding of the people of God is inclusive in this important sense, he is not a universalist. The closing verses of the book make it clear that not all will acknowledge the LORD as king, or join those who worship him. In the end there will be only two kinds of people: those who acknowledge God's kingship and those who don't. And only the former can properly be called his people. For them there will be worship and celebration (14:16); for the rest, plague and punishment (14:18–19). Zechariah's inclusivism is not a sentimental kind that turns God into a kind of benign, indulgent Santa Claus, but a robust one, that takes the revealed truth about God seriously, and boldly sets before us the unavoidable choice that confronts us all. Will we acknowledge God's right to our worship and obedience, and so take our place – humbly and thankfully – among his people, or will we continue to defy him and face his wrath? For God's kingdom *will* come, and his will *will* be done. How we respond to that fact is up to us, and God will hold us accountable for the choice we make.

4. The unity of Zechariah

In spite of all I have just said about the message of the book, it has long been held by the majority of Bible scholars that it is not a unity.

---

[84] This is a principle reflected throughout Scripture, beginning with the establishment of Eden as the source of life-giving rivers (Gen. 2:10–14), and continuing with the promises to Abraham (Gen. 12:1–3), and the election of Israel as a 'kingdom of priests', set in the midst of the whole earth (Exod. 19:5–6). The same idea is developed extensively in the New Testament.

[85] Cf. Is. 66:18–24.

The issue is a complicated one, and many different proposals have been made about which parts of the book are from Zechariah himself and which are not. A detailed discussion would take us too far from our present purpose and is unnecessary, as good summaries can be found in any standard Bible dictionary or encyclopedia.[86] However, since I have so far been treating the book as a unity, some words of explanation are called for.

The essence of the matter is that many scholars think that some of the material in the book reflects a different time (or times) from those in which Zechariah himself lived, and therefore must have been added later.[87] What most agree on is that chapters 9 – 14, in particular, were written long after the temple was completed. Zerubbabel and Joshua had passed from the scene and rapacious new leaders ('bad shepherds') had taken their place. Most scholars have been impressed by the fact that chapters 9 – 14 are markedly different in style from chapters 1 – 8, that Zechariah himself is no longer mentioned, and that Greece is explicitly referred to in 9:13. They therefore conclude that chapters 9 – 14 are not from Zechariah at all, but from an anonymous prophet who lived much later, after the conquests of Alexander the Great (356–323 BC), when Greece had replaced Persia as the imperial power that dominated the Middle East. It was a far darker period for the people of Jerusalem and it was harder to be positive about current events; all hope was placed in a supernatural intervention of God, to judge the world and establish a new, perfect age.[88]

On the face of it, all this makes a great deal of sense, and it has become so widely accepted in scholarly circles that until quite recently it was hard to find any serious study of the book as a whole. Even commentaries on Zechariah have commonly been published

[86] E.g. for a conservative treatment see Wright, 'Zechariah', pp. 1275–1276; and for a more mainline critical treatment see Meyers, Myers and Petersen, vol. 6, pp. 1061–1068. The acuteness of the problem is reflected in the fact that the latter deals with Zech. 1 – 8 and Zech. 9 – 14 in two separate articles by different authors! For a treatment that concisely reviews the traditional critical study of Zechariah, and moves beyond it to address the meaning of the text in its canonical form, see Childs, pp. 472–487.

[87] As in so many other issues of a similar kind, the work of Julius Wellhausen, in the late nineteenth and early twentieth centuries, was foundational. For Wellhausen himself on the (dis)unity of Zechariah see Wellhausen, pp. 5391–5395. For a good, brief summary of his views and their influence on subsequent study of Zechariah, see Cook, pp. 123–125; and cf. Floyd, pp. 260–263, for his impact on the study of the post-exilic prophets in general.

[88] A significant variant of this basic view is represented by Hanson, pp. 240–262, 280–388. He argues that the two parts stem from (roughly) the same time, but are opposed to one another ideologically: chs. 1 – 8 reflect the perspective of the priestly establishment, and chs. 9 – 14 that of a disillusioned, disempowered minority.

as two separate volumes, on chapters 1 – 8 and 9 – 14 respectively, sometimes by different authors.[89] In the last few years, in line with broader developments in biblical studies, some scholars have again attempted to make sense of the book as a whole, while still accepting the view (explicitly or implicitly) that it is not all by the same author.[90]

The view I have adopted here, and which will be reflected in what follows, is that, while another person or persons may well have had a hand in producing the book in the form we now have it, it is essentially from Zechariah himself, and expresses his own 'kingdom of God' theology in its various aspects. There are two main reasons for this. The first is that the arguments *against* its unity are not nearly as convincing as many have supposed them to be. For example, if (as the book quite clearly claims) Zechariah received revelation from God, there is no reason in principle why he may not have foreseen, especially in outline, events that lay beyond his own time. Furthermore, as far as the explicit reference to Greece is concerned (9:13), this is hardly surprising, even if one did not believe in divinely given revelation. As we have already seen, Darius I ruled an empire that extended from India in the east to Greece in the west, and the conquest of Greece was one of his chief ambitions. It was never realized. His long-planned attempt to invade the Greek mainland culminated in a humiliating defeat in the battle of Marathon in 490 BC. But Greece loomed large in everyone's mind in the early Persian period. It is no wonder, then, that Zechariah should have seen it as a potentially hostile power on the western horizon. For the record, Greece is also referred to in the books of Isaiah, Ezekiel and Daniel.[91] Furthermore, the fact that the heading 'An Oracle' at 9:1 and 12:1 does not name Zechariah is not at all remarkable. 'Many subsections of prophetic books have their own superscriptions, sometimes with reiteration of the prophet's name (e.g. Is. 2:1; 13:1; Jer. 7:1; 11:1; 18:1; Hab. 3:1) and sometimes without (particularly in the case of oracles against foreign nations, e.g. Is. 15:1; 17:1; 19:1; 21:1; 22:1; 23:1; Jer. 48:1; 49:1, 7, 28).'[92] And as for the admittedly different style of chapters 9 – 14, this may have as much to do with the different occasion and purpose of the material as difference of authorship. We all recognize that an author may produce various kinds of literature, and may write differently

[89] E.g. on Zech. 1 – 8 the works of Petersen (1984), Meyers and Meyers (1987) and Love, and on Zech. 9 – 14 those of Lamarche, Meyers and Meyers (1993) and Petersen (1995).
[90] E.g. Conrad and Sweeney.
[91] Is. 66:19; Ezek. 27:13; Dan. 8:21; 10:20; 11:2.
[92] Floyd, p. 262.

in different periods of his career.[93] There is some evidence of editorial activity, but not enough in my judgment to warrant assigning any sizeable parts of the book to a second author.[94]

The second reason is because the task we have set ourselves is to understand the message of the book of Zechariah as part of the Bible (i.e. as Scripture), and those who have transmitted it to us as Scripture quite clearly *intended* us to read it as a unity. They have not placed it in the canon of Scripture as two separate books, but as one, and introduced it as 'the word of the LORD [that] came to the prophet Zechariah' (1:1). This means that we shall be able to understand its rich, multifaceted message only when we read it as one, interconnected whole.

Of course, in the final analysis, the proof of the pudding is in the eating. Perhaps the strongest argument for reading the book as a unity is that it lends itself so well to it. To anyone willing to approach it as a *reader* rather than an excavator, it yields a coherent, powerful message that looks much more like the vision of one very enlightened mind rather than a patchwork of discordant pieces.[95] That, at least, is something we have already seen in outline, and which the following chapters will attempt to show more fully. Already, however, we can begin to see how this part of the Bible speaks to us today, how it is God's word for us now.

[93] E.g. 'early' and 'late' Shakespeare, or Goethe.

[94] In most places where his name appears, Zechariah himself is speaking in the first person: *I had a vision ... he showed me Joshua ... Again the word of the LORD Almighty came to me ...* and so on. But in the three headings we noted earlier he is spoken *about* in the third person: 'the word of the LORD came *to the prophet Zechariah*' (1:7; my emphasis), or just *to Zechariah* (7:1). These headings appear to have been written by someone we might call the editor of the book – the person who arranged its contents in the way it now appears. Of course, Zechariah could have done this himself, but it is more likely in my judgment that it was done by someone else. Also, as many scholars have noticed, the visions of chapters 1 – 6 have small oracles attached to them, or even embedded within them (e.g. 2:6, 7–13; 4:6–10a). Most scholars take this as evidence of further editorial activity, but the truth is that we simply don't know who put them there, and they are so closely linked in thought with the visions that there are no certain grounds for concluding that they are later additions. It should be noted that for the Christian reader there is nothing in the recorded words of Jesus or the apostles to tip the decision about unity one way or the other. There are a number of quotations from Zechariah in the New Testament (which I shall refer to shortly) but none contains any reference to the human author. In this respect the situation for Zechariah is different from that for Isaiah (on which see my comments in Webb 1996, pp. 33–37).

[95] Redditt, pp. 38–43, is broadly representative of this alternative view. He himself would not use the term 'patchwork', but does regard the book as having been compiled from materials (from various sources and by different hands) that remain inconsistent with one another.

5. Zechariah, Jesus and us

Our first impression, as we begin to read the book of Zechariah, may be of remoteness – of distance from us. However, we need to bear in mind two things. First, if the theme of the people of God is developed in Zechariah in the way we have said it is, then we ought not to view Zerubbabel and his contemporaries as representatives of an alien race, but as our spiritual ancestors, who knew and served the same God we do. And second, to think that the book of Zechariah deals only with things behind us would be a serious mistake, which we need to free ourselves from at once. As we have seen, the whole book is governed by the vision of the coming kingdom of God, and the 'day' that the last chapter speaks about – when 'the LORD will be king over the whole earth', and 'there will be one LORD, and his name the only name' (14:9) is still ahead of us, not behind us. That is why Jesus taught us to pray, 'Your kingdom come'. The same vision that fires the book of Zechariah is to fire our lives as well.

In many ways, nothing has changed. Those who recognize God as king are still a minority, and have to live out their lives in a world that, for the most part, does not. Progress in the work of the kingdom is still often slow and discouraging, and beset with difficulties and opposition. The call to repentance still needs to be sounded, not just to the world at large, but to the church. In a world where we often seem powerless, we still need, again and again, to have our vision of God enlarged, and to be reminded that it is 'not by might nor by power, but by [his] Spirit' (4:6) that his work is done and his kingdom purposes advanced. In other words, there are many levels at which the message of Zechariah resonates, more or less directly, with our own situation.

But a great many things *have* changed. In particular, we now read Zechariah from the other side of the great, world-changing crisis of the birth, life, death, resurrection and ascension of Jesus Christ. The time for building temples of the kind Solomon and Zerubbabel built is long since over, since the reality to which they pointed has now been realized in the person Jesus Christ. The work of the kingdom goes on, but in a different way – through the worldwide preaching of the gospel – and the temple raised up in this way consists of living stones, men and women who have been united to Christ by faith, and indwelt by his Spirit. Given the radical newness of all this, we might, perhaps, expect the New Testament writers to ignore the book of Zechariah as no longer relevant. In fact, they do just the opposite: they turn to it as a resource for teaching us the true significance of what has been accomplished for us in Christ and of the situation in which we now find ourselves. How often Zechariah is referred to in the New Testament is hard to determine precisely (especially in the case of indirect references), but one well-known authority lists eleven direct quotations and sixty-four allusions,[96] most of them in the Gospels and the book of Revelation.[97]

The quotations in the Gospels are especially significant because of the very special moments in Jesus' ministry they are associated with. When Jesus rides into Jerusalem at the beginning of the last, fateful week of his life, Matthew raises Zechariah 9:9 like a banner:

This took place to fulfil what was spoken through the prophet:

> 'Say to the Daughter of Zion,
>   "See, your king comes to you,
> gentle and riding on a donkey,
>   on a colt, the foal of a donkey." '[98]

The apostle John does the same; but in his Gospel there is an added touch – Jesus *deliberately* entered the city this way *so that* Zechariah's prophecy would be fulfilled:

Jesus found a young donkey and sat upon it, as it is written,

> 'Do not be afraid, O Daughter of Zion;
>   see, your king is coming,
> seated on a donkey's colt.'[99]

This is the midpoint of John's Gospel, where Jesus, having been rejected by his own people as their Messiah (1:11), turns his face towards the cross, which from here on casts its shadow over everything.[100] Both Gospels continue to refer to Zechariah (sometimes very pointedly) as events unfold: the betrayal for thirty pieces of silver,[101] the piercing of Jesus' side on the cross, releasing a flow of

---

[96] Aland et al., pp. 888, 900.

[97] The only quotation outside the Gospels and Revelation listed by Aland et al. is Eph. 4:25 (Zech. 8:16), but this is at best a verbal parallel. No citation formula is used.

[98] Matt. 21:4–5.

[99] John 12:14–15.

[100] See especially the two quotations from Isaiah in John 12:37–41. The first, in v. 38, is from Is. 53.

[101] Matt. 27:9–10. The use of the thirty pieces of silver to buy a potter's field is said to fulfil what was spoken by Jeremiah (cf. Jer. 18, 32). But the connection with Zech. 11 is obvious. The event appears to have been seen as a fulfilment of what had been said (or done) by both prophets, but Jeremiah, as the major figure, is the one named.

blood and water,[102] and the scattering of the disciples when Jesus is smitten.[103] It is a scenario powerfully reminiscent of Zechariah 9 – 14: the arrival of an ideal king, conflict with false shepherds, piercing, the opening of a fountain to cleanse from sin and uncleanness. There can be little doubt about the conclusion we are meant to draw: Jesus is treading a path preordained for him, and already revealed in outline in the inspired Scriptures of the Old Testament, especially the book of Zechariah.[104]

Here we come to the very heart of Zechariah's theology. Like Isaiah he understood that the kingdom of God would come, finally, only through the atoning death of the Messiah. Only in this way could the people of God be cleansed from their sins, totally and forever, and be made fit to enter their inheritance on the final day. There is a deep connection here with Isaiah's teaching about the Suffering Servant. Only after the suffering, death and glorification of the Suffering Servant of God is free pardon and forgiveness offered to all who will come to God to receive it.[105] And Isaiah,[106] like Zechariah (14:16–21), ends with the people of all nations, a new people of God, worshipping God as King in the New Jerusalem. These two great prophets combine in their witness to the inseparable link between the kingdom of God and a suffering Messiah. Both, in their own way, see Christ's glory and speak of him.[107]

But even that – amazing though it is – is not the complete picture of how Zechariah is taken up in the New Testament. At the climax of the whole Bible, in the book of Revelation, it springs into prominence again, once more at a most significant moment:

> Look, he is coming with the clouds,
>   and every eye will see him,
>   *even those who pierced him*;
> and all the peoples of the world will
>   mourn because of him.
>   So shall it be! Amen.[108]

Revelation, too, is by the apostle John, and his reference here to the One whom men pierced is the eschatological counterpart to his

[102] John 19:37.
[103] Matt. 26:31; cf. Mark 14:27.
[104] Cf. Newman, p. 51: 'With Zechariah (among others) supplying the prophetic script, Jesus' entry into the city on a donkey and his subsequent temple action (whatever else it signifies) would have consciously evoked messianic expectations.'
[105] Is. 53; 55.
[106] Is. 66:19–24.
[107] John 12:41; cf. vv. 13–15 of the same chapter.
[108] Rev 1:7; my italics

reference to the piercing of Jesus in his Gospel.[109] A second 'seeing' of Christ by those who crucified him will take place at his second coming, when not just they but all people will mourn because of him. But in this context, it is only believers (like John and his readers) who are regarded as cleansed (vv. 5–6). The mourning of the rest of humanity at this point is not met with forgiveness. The time for that is past. Those who will not see Jesus as their crucified Messiah will see him one day as their arriving Judge. So the ultimate issues of the kingdom of God, life and death, salvation and damnation, are seen to turn critically on people's response to Jesus Christ. That is the powerful, sharp edge to the message of Zechariah, and of the Bible as a whole. The message of the kingdom of God is the gospel of Jesus Christ. The coloured horses of the apocalypse in Revelation 6:1–8 recall the coloured horses of Zechariah's visions. As in Zechariah they are associated with God's anger against the nations and the exercise of his worldwide sovereignty, and the rider of the white horse carries the name the Word of God – one of John's titles for Christ.[110] We are left in no doubt, then: it is in Jesus that God's sovereignty over the rebellious nations is finally expressed, in universal judgment.

How, then, does the book of Zechariah speak to us today? It does so in two main ways: first, by acquainting us with some of our spiritual forebears whom we might not otherwise know – people like Zerubbabel, Joshua and Zechariah himself – people who were far from perfect, but who believed that God was king and lived by faith in his promises. It challenges us to let the vision of the coming kingdom of God fire our hearts, as it did theirs, and to worship and serve him in our own age and generation, as they did in theirs. But more important by far, it teaches us of Christ, his person and his work, and shows us in a particularly powerful way his crucial place in God's purposes for us and for the whole world. It focuses the longing we have for God's kingdom to come, and his will to be done, on the person of Jesus the Messiah. It translates the prayer 'Your kingdom come' into the cry 'Amen. Come, Lord Jesus.'[111]

---

[109] 'Eschatological', from the Greek *eschatos* (latter, last), means 'having to do with the last things, or the last days'.

[110] Rev. 19:11; John 1:1–14. As in Zech. 1:8, one mounted horseman is singled out from the rest. Kline (1990, pp. 4–6) argues that the mounted Angel of the LORD of Zechariah's vision is a pre-incarnation manifestation of Christ. He notes that 'the messianic king once again appears as a mounted figure' in Zech. 9:9, this time riding a donkey.

[111] Rev. 22:20

6. One final comment

a. The nature of prophecy

It has not been possible to provide here the kind of introduction to Old Testament prophecy as an oral and literary phenomenon that might be expected in a longer, more technical, commentary. For those who are interested, the chapter on prophecy by Richard Patterson in *A Complete Literary Guide to the Bible*, edited by Ryken and Longman, is excellent. Patterson deals with the characteristic forms of prophecy as an essentially oral genre, but then goes on to offer sound advice on how to read it in the final, literary form in which we now have it in the canon. He notes Leland Ryken's characterization of prophecy as 'visionary literature', which 'transforms the known world or present state of things into a situation that at the time of writing is as yet only imagined'.[112] Patterson himself prefers 'proclamation' as perhaps the most appropriate designation of the prophetic genre, but recognizes that it moves beyond preaching to inscripturation, and has a visionary dimension that transcends the boundaries of the prophet's own time.

All this is highly relevant to the following exposition, which seeks to do justice to the structure and unity of Zechariah's message in its final, literary form, without ignoring the historical context in which that message originated.

[112] Patterson, p. 166.

Part 1
Kingdom prelude

Zechariah 1 – 6

1. A call to return to the LORD (1:1–6)

Zechariah's ministry begins when he is commanded by the LORD to remind the people of Jerusalem of their recent history. The earlier prophets had warned their forefathers that God was angry with them, and that they should turn from their evil ways before his judgment fell on them (2–3). But they had been stubborn, and refused to do what those earlier prophets had said (4b). Now those former generations were gone. So too were the prophets who had preached to them, but history had borne out the truth of what they had said (5–6). The ruined state of Jerusalem, and the fact that the former kingdom of Judah had been reduced to a small province of the vast Persian Empire showed that the warnings the prophets had given were no idle threats. The generation that experienced the terrible events of 587 BC did eventually repent (6b), but only after they had reaped the bitter consequences of their deeds.[1] There is a moral in this story, of course: 'Don't be like your forefathers! Learn this lesson from history: God's anger is a reality to be reckoned with. He punishes those who refuse to repent' (4a).

The rather abrupt, confrontational character of this opening volley of Zechariah's preaching alerts us to something about the Old Testament prophets that we must grasp at once, or we shall never understand them. They were not philosophers, who gave

---

[1] See the book of Lamentations, especially 1:18; 5:19–22. The NIV sets the last part of v. 6 off as a separate paragraph, suggesting a change of subject: *Then they* [Zechariah's audience, unlike their forefathers] *repented*. But the way the quotation marks are continued (again, an editorial decision by the translators) suggests the opposite, namely that this is a continuation of the story about the forefathers: *Then they* [the forefathers] *repented*. So the NIV ends up being confusing. In fact, there is no break at all in the Hebrew, and no change of subject. The expression 'they repented' means 'the forefathers [who have just been mentioned in the first half of the verse] repented'. See Childs, p. 476.

people their own thoughts about life. Nor were they religious entertainers, who built their reputations and careers on giving people what they wanted to hear. They were messengers, who delivered messages they had received from God. They did not deal in abstract theories about the nature of reality or in general principles of morality. They addressed people in concrete situations, declaring the will of God to them, and calling for an obedient response. They were agents through whom God conducted his relationship with the people he had chosen to use in the outworking of his purposes for the entire world. It always was, and still is, a serious matter to be confronted by *the word of the LORD* (1), and it was not always easy to be a prophet charged with the responsibility of preaching it.

This eruption of God's word into Zechariah's life, and the life of his community, happened, we are told, in *the eighth month of the second year of Darius*; that is, in late October or early November of the year 520 BC.[2] It came just as the world was beginning to breathe a little easier again after the upheavals that had accompanied Darius I's rise to power.[3] Some changes were bound to follow as Darius consolidated his position and began to put his own stamp on imperial affairs; whether this would prove to be good or bad for Yehud and its people remained to be seen. What seemed to be called for, surely, was a word to steady and settle the community, assuring them of God's control of all things, and his good intentions for them as his people. There is nothing wrong with this in principle, and indeed Zechariah would soon be given some positive things to say to his people. But what he was told to speak to them about first was God's anger – with their *forefathers* (2), but, by implication, with them as well.

God's anger has never been a popular topic, which is why false prophets and preachers generally avoid it. Jeremiah's quarrel with the false prophets of his day was that they dressed the wounds of God's people too lightly, saying 'peace, peace', when there was no peace.[4] The deeper problem was that they were saying what was merely popular instead of what was true, the visions of their own minds instead of messages they had received from God.[5] False prophecy, at its deepest level, is a form of idolatry, because it takes away the truth about God and puts a lie in its place. It misrepresents God by remaking him into the kind of god we can feel comfortable with, a kind of Santa Claus god who gives us what we want without requiring us to change.

[2] See the table in Baldwin 1972, p. 29.
[3] See the introduction, p. 22.
[4] Jer. 6:14; 8:11.
[5] Jer. 23:16–18.

The truth proclaimed by the biblical writers could hardly be more different. God is generous and gracious – more so than we can ever fully grasp – but he is also sovereign and just, and entirely consistent in treating us as accountable for how we respond to him. He is a God of judgment as well as grace, as seen again and again in the biblical record of his dealings with the world, and Israel in particular. Consider, for example, his expulsion of Adam and Eve from the garden after they defied him, the judgment of the great flood, the scattering of the builders of the tower of Babel, and the overthrow of Sodom and Gomorrah.[6] Consider too his many judgments on Israel through the course of her history in the Old Testament period, not least the horrors of the siege and fall of Jerusalem, and the exile of its people, so recent in the memory of Zechariah's community.[7] Nor is the picture of God fundamentally different in the New Testament. Jesus warned his disciples not to fear men, who could kill only their bodies, but to fear God who, after the killing of their bodies, had the power to throw them into hell.[8] He told them to pluck out their eyes if need be, rather than run the risk of being thrown into hell, a place of judgment where 'their worm does not die, and the fire is not quenched'.[9] The fullest revelation of the wrath of God is in the death of Jesus, where he suffered the full extent of that wrath for us. There was no other way we could be saved from it, for God could not, and would not compromise his own holiness.[10] It was the most astonishing act of grace to us, but the New Testament is clear that it is God's only and final offer:

> If we deliberately keep on sinning after we have received the knowledge of the truth, no sacrifice for sins is left, but only a fearful expectation of judgment and of raging fire that will consume the enemies of God. Anyone who rejected the law of Moses died without mercy on the testimony of two or three witnesses. How much more severely do you think a man deserves to be punished who has trampled the Son of God under foot, who has treated as an unholy thing the blood of the covenant that sanctified him, and who has insulted the Spirit of grace? For we know him who said, 'It is mine to avenge; I will repay,' and again, 'The Lord will judge his people.' It is a dreadful thing to fall into the hands of the living God.[11]

[6] Gen. 3:23–24; 6:5–7; 11:1–8; 19:24–25.
[7] 2 Kgs. 25:1–21.
[8] Luke 12:4–5.
[9] Mark 9:47–48.
[10] See Is. 53, especially vv. 4–6, 10.
[11] Heb. 10:26–31.

The New Testament gospel has the truth of God's righteous anger at the heart of it, just as surely as the preaching of the Old Testament prophets. Indeed, the message of the cross makes no real sense without it.

Zechariah began his prophetic ministry by reminding the people of how the *earlier prophets* had warned their forefathers to turn from their *evil ways* and *evil practices* (1:4). The context suggests that the prophets he had in mind were men like Isaiah, Jeremiah and Ezekiel, whose ministry fell mostly or entirely in the time leading up to the fall of Jerusalem. A survey of the books that record their preaching indicates that they denounced two main sins again and again: idolatry and hypocrisy.

Idolatry is putting something else – something that is not God – in his place, and giving it the honour only he should have. We have already noted that false prophecy, which abounded at this time, was a subtle form of idolatry. But there were also many other, cruder forms. Israel's history began with Abraham being called out of idolatry,[12] and the first sin his descendants committed after God had brought them out of Egypt was to turn back to idolatry again. Moses' long stay on Mount Sinai unnerved the Israelites. They felt abandoned and vulnerable in the desert, so they persuaded Aaron to assume the leadership and make them a golden calf to worship – a god they could see – and began to attribute their deliverance from Egypt to it instead of to the LORD.[13] It was the beginning of a long history of apostasy that, again and again, aroused God's anger against them and threatened to bring their relationship with him to an end.[14] After Solomon, the apostasy of the golden calf was repeated by the first king of Israel (the northern kingdom), who erected two such idols, one in Bethel and one in Dan, and urged his people to worship in these places instead of going to Jerusalem.[15] It was a clear case of political expediency taking precedence over faithfulness to the LORD, and it set the northern kingdom on a downward course from which it never recovered. In the south, determined efforts were made by several of the kings to prevent Judah going the same way.[16] But even here, the drift towards apostasy proved unstoppable. In the face of the ever growing threat from Assyria, Manasseh decided it was prudent to give at least token

---

[12] Josh. 24:2.

[13] Exod. 32:1–4.

[14] See especially the repeating pattern of apostasy and punishment at the hand of enemies in the book of Judges (Judg. 2:10–19).

[15] 1 Kgs. 12:25–33.

[16] Especially by Hezekiah in the eighth century, and Josiah in the seventh (2 Kgs. 18:1–7; 2 Kgs. 22).

recognition to the imperial gods and introduced pagan rites into the very centre of the nation's life – the temple of the LORD in Jerusalem.[17] According to the writer of 2 Kings, it was such a flagrant act of rebellion that even the subsequent reforms of Josiah could not avert God's wrath from Judah.[18] The prophets consistently denounced idolatry in all its forms, and warned of the judgment it must inevitably bring.[19] Ezekiel in particular, in exile in Babylon, identified the pollution of the temple with idols as Israel's crowning sin, which had driven the LORD from his sanctuary and exposed it to destruction.[20] Idolatry was certainly one of the *evil practices* of the forefathers. It was a violation of the first requirement of the covenant God had made with Israel at Mount Sinai: 'you shall have no other gods before me'.[21]

The other great sin of those earlier generations that the prophets had spoken against was hypocrisy: worship divorced from any serious commitment to obeying God in everyday life. Israel never, as far as we can tell, abandoned worship altogether – including the worship of the LORD. Rather, they corrupted it with idolatry, and divorced it from life, so that it became a form of superstition, a way of 'keeping God happy' and securing benefits from him, rather than of recognizing his kingship. The prophets rightly understood that the God who had revealed himself at the exodus was a God who was opposed to oppression and committed to justice. His justice was the essence of his 'godness' (his holiness); it was the quality, par excellence, that distinguished him from all other gods, and from sinful human beings.[22] Justice was the foundation of his throne.[23]

Furthermore, he demanded justice of his people; that is, that they treat one another as he had treated them. The Ten Commandments laid two essential duties on the Israelites: to love God with all their hearts, and to love their neighbours as themselves.[24] To profess love for God (by worshipping him), and to fail to love one's

[17] 2 Kgs. 21:1–18.

[18] 2 Kgs. 23:26–27.

[19] See especially Amos 5:4–6, 25–27; 8:13–14; Hos. 2:12–13; 4:6b–19. Cf. Is. 40:18–20; 44:9–20.

[20] Ezek. 5:11; 8:1 – 11:15 (esp. 8:6).

[21] This is literally 'no other gods over against me (i.e. in my presence)' (Exod. 20:3). What is specifically forbidden in the following couple of verses is the manufacture and worship of idols.

[22] Is. 5:16.

[23] Ps. 89:14.

[24] This was how Jesus summarized the teaching of both the Law (of Moses) and the Prophets (Matt. 22:34–40; Mark 12:28–31). Of the Ten Commandments, the first four explain about how to love God, and the last six about how to love one's neighbour.

neighbour (by not acting justly) was the purest hypocrisy, and it aroused God's anger. The following passage from Isaiah is typical of the passionate way in which the prophets spoke for God on this core issue ('Sodom' and 'Gomorrah' are derogatory terms for Jerusalem):

> Hear the word of the LORD,
>   you rulers of Sodom;
> listen to the law of our God,
>   you people of Gomorrah!
> 'The multitude of your sacrifices –
>   what are they to me?' says the LORD.
> 'I have more than enough of burnt offerings,
>   of rams and the fat of fattened animals;
> I have no pleasure
>   in the blood of bulls and lambs and goats.
> When you come to appear before me,
>   who has asked this of you,
>   this trampling of my courts?
> Stop bringing meaningless offerings!
>   Your incense is detestable to me.
> New Moons, Sabbaths and convocations –
>   I cannot bear your evil assemblies.
> Your New Moon festivals and your appointed feasts
>   my soul hates.
> They have become a burden to me;
>   I am weary of bearing them.
> When you spread out your hands in prayer,
>   I will hide my eyes from you;
> even if you offer many prayers,
>   I will not listen.
> Your hands are full of blood;
>   wash and make yourselves clean.
> Take your evil deeds
>   out of my sight!
> Stop doing wrong,
>   learn to do right!
> Seek justice,
>   encourage the oppressed.
> Defend the cause of the fatherless,
>   plead the case of the widow.
>
> Come now, let us reason together,'
>   says the LORD.

'Though your sins are like scarlet,
    they shall be as white as snow;
though they are red as crimson,
    they shall be like wool.
If you are willing and obedient,
    you will eat the best from the land;
but if you resist and rebel,
    you will be devoured by the sword.'
            For the mouth of the LORD has spoken.[25]

Nothing could be plainer. To worship God without practising justice is to have blood on your hands, and to be no better, as far as God is concerned, than the people of Sodom and Gomorrah whom he overthrew with fiery judgment. It is to be guilty of the worst kind of hypocrisy.[26] It is sin, deep-dyed and crimson red. It can be forgiven, if it is genuinely repented of, but to persist in it is to court certain disaster. It was the second great *evil practice* of the forefathers that brought the wrath of God down on their heads.

But what of the people of Zechariah's day? Zechariah clearly means them to understand that their own behaviour is just as bad as their forefathers'. Yet in this important opening passage there is no direct reference to any specific sin they are guilty of. There is no evidence in any of the biblical books dealing with this period that idolatry was still a problem. The experience of exile seems to have cured the Israelites of that particular sin, once and for all! There is some evidence of the kind of hypocrisy the earlier prophets had denounced creeping back, but it seems to have been something that emerged later rather than at this point,[27] and there is certainly no reference to it here. So why the stern warning of their need to repent?

To find the answer, all we need to do is recall the close relationship between Zechariah and Haggai, and attend carefully to what we have been told in verse 1 about the time when Zechariah was told to deliver this particular message. It was *in the eighth month of the second year of Darius*, just two months, or not much more, after

---

[25] Is. 1:10–20. Many similar passages could be quoted, especially from the other eighth-century prophets (Amos, Hosea, Micah). Jeremiah's famous temple sermon (Jer. 7:1–15) is an equally passionate denunciation of the same sin at a slightly later time.

[26] Cf. Jesus' stern denunciations of the Pharisees as 'hypocrites': Matt. 23:15–29; cf. Matt. 6:2–16; Luke 13:15. Note especially Matt. 15:7: 'Isaiah was right when he prophesied about *you*' (my italics; cf. Mark 7:6).

[27] See my comments in the introduction about how the 'repentance' theme develops through the book of Zechariah (pp. 32–33). For the way this problem became worse later see Mal. 1:6–14; 2:10–16; Neh. 5:1–13.

Haggai had begun his own ministry by rebuking the people for their slackness about rebuilding the temple:

> In the second year of King Darius, on the first day of the sixth month, the word of the LORD came through the prophet Haggai to Zerubbabel son of Shealtiel, governor of Judah, and to Joshua son of Jehozadak, the high priest:
> This is what the LORD Almighty says: 'These people say, "The time has not yet come for the LORD's house to be built."'
> Then the word of the LORD came through the prophet Haggai: 'Is it a time for you yourselves to be living in your panelled houses, while this house remains a ruin?'
> Now this is what the LORD Almighty says: 'Give careful thought to your ways. You have planted much, but have harvested little. You eat, but never have enough. You drink, but never have your fill. You put on clothes, but are not warm. You earn wages, only to put them in a purse with holes in it.'
> This is what the LORD Almighty says: 'Give careful thought to your ways. Go up into the mountains and bring down timber and build the house, so that I may take pleasure in it and be honoured,' says the LORD.[28]

Zechariah's call for repentance makes perfect sense in this context. The sin of the people is their failure to get on with building the LORD's temple, and they are already experiencing his anger with them in the form of failed harvests and grinding poverty. Zechariah is saying something extremely important here about 'kingdom of God' living. To grasp it properly, though, we must step back again for a moment and do a little more background work.

In many ways the failure of the community to press on with work on the temple was entirely understandable. We are given a summary in the book of Ezra of the many difficulties they had faced over the previous eighteen years: 'the peoples around them set out to discourage the people of Judah and make them afraid to go on building. They hired counsellors to work against them and frustrate their plans during the entire reign of Cyrus king of Persia and down to the reign of Darius king of Persia.'[29]

As many of us know from bitter experience, it is hard to keep going with something long term, even if you believe it is what God wants you to do, in the face of the kinds of things mentioned here: discouragement, intimidation, false accusation, and constant

---

[28] Hag. 1:1–8.
[29] Ezra 4:4–5.

frustration. They have the potential to wear down even the most stouthearted individual or community. So difficult in fact did the situation become in the eighteen years in question that work on the temple was eventually brought to a standstill, and nothing at all had been done on it for the two years immediately before Haggai and Zechariah began to preach.[30]

Before we let our sympathy for these people run away with us, however, it is vital that we remind ourselves of the importance of the task they had been called to. We saw in the introduction that the temple was absolutely central to the Old Testament prophetic vision of the future kingdom of God. This was God's building project, and he had a great deal invested in it. It was God himself, Isaiah tells us, who had raised up Cyrus as his instrument to set this work in train.[31] He had brought him against Babylon precisely so that these people could be free to go back to Jerusalem to engage in it.[32] In short, he had reconfigured the entire Middle East in order to get this job done! It was vital for the proper honouring of his name before the world, and the manifestation of his kingship on earth.[33] In other words, it was 'kingdom of God' work, and these people had been brought back to Jerusalem for the very purpose of engaging in it. Such work was bound to be opposed, for it was to be done in a world that, on the whole, did not acknowledge God's rule. But how had the returnees behaved when this opposition had intensified to a point where progress was brought to a halt? Had they given themselves to prayer and fasting, laying their circumstances before God and calling on him for boldness to continue?[34] Not at all. According to Haggai they had given up and turned to other things, living in their own 'panelled houses', while 'this house', God's temple, remained a ruin.[35]

It is not entirely clear what is meant by 'panelled' houses.[36] Presumably nothing too elaborate is on view, given the harsh economic circumstances.[37] More than likely the people were simply

[30] Ezra 4:24.
[31] Is. 44:24–28.
[32] Ezra 1:1–4.
[33] Is. 40:1–5; 66:18–24.
[34] Cf. the prayer of the Jerusalem church in Acts 4:23–31, and its result!
[35] Hag. 1:4.
[36] See Baldwin 1972, p. 40, who prefers 'roofed in'. The relevant Hebrew word (*sāpan*) means both 'to cover in' and 'to panel'. Its root provides the noun for 'ceiling' (cf. AV, RV).
[37] 'Haggai probably implies that the people had completed their homes rather than that they had gone to the lengths of adorning them with wood panelling, but it could be that the governor's residence was being reconstructed with some of the elegance of Solomon's palace' (Baldwin 1972, p. 40).

putting the finishing touches to their homes, and making them as comfortable and attractive as their limited means allowed. And what, we may well ask, is wrong with that? Isn't it what anyone would do – at least any normal person? So why does Zechariah, like Haggai, tell them to repent of it, and return to the LORD?

We seem to have a difficulty. But actually it is a breakthrough, for now we have come to the very essence of what Zechariah is saying in this important introduction to his preaching. The sin of the people, as Haggai's words had made clear, lay not so much in what they were doing as in what they were not doing. It wasn't the 'sin' of home improvement, or interior decorating – as though these things were wrong in themselves[38] – it was the sin of immersing themselves in these things *while the LORD's house remained a ruin* (Hag. 1:4). It was the sin of behaving just like ordinary people, who have no interest in the kingdom of God. In other words, it was of being normal! And the point of Zechariah's strong language is that this was just as bad as the sins of idolatry and hypocrisy that the forefathers had been guilty of. It aroused God's anger just as much, and was every bit as deserving of his judgment. But (and here was the real danger) it was far harder to recognize as sin, and so much easier to excuse. It took the stern words of the prophets to make them see it for what it was.

A striking example of the same kind of thing at the personal level is described for us in the last chapter of John's Gospel. Jesus has just been crucified, buried, and raised from the dead on the third day.[39] He has appeared to his disciples (including Peter), and breathed on them, symbolically imparting the Holy Spirit to them for the work he has called them to do.[40] Soon the day of Pentecost will come, and the church will be launched on the mission to take the gospel to the ends of the earth.[41] Peter's response at this hugely significant moment is an unexpected, yet entirely understandable one: 'I'm going out to fish,' Peter told [the other disciples], and they said, 'We'll go with you';[42] 'but that night', John tells us, 'they caught nothing'.[43] There was nothing wrong with fishing as such; it just wasn't what Peter and his companions were meant to be doing at that time, and to go and do it was to turn aside from God's calling on their lives. The rest of the chapter is about how Jesus went after

---

[38] Any more than the story of the tower of Babel in Gen. 11:1–9 is about the sin of high-rise development!
[39] John 19:16b – 20:18.
[40] John 20:19–23.
[41] Acts 1:8.
[42] John 21:3.
[43] Ibid.

them and, ever so gently, reclaimed them for the work he wanted them to do.[44]

Peter and his companions were exhausted – physically and emotionally. Everything had become just too intense for them. They just wanted to be normal for a while. But the reality is that they, and we, are not meant to be 'normal' people, and we won't be happy trying to be so. As Peter himself later put it, we are 'a chosen people, a royal priesthood, a holy nation, a people belonging to God, that [we] may declare the praises of him who called [us] out of darkness into his wonderful light'.[45] The danger is that when we face opposition and discouragement, and when being who we are and doing what God has called us to do becomes just too difficult, we shall lapse back into normality, as the people of Zechariah's day did. It was to people who had fallen into precisely this sin that the LORD's first message through Zechariah was directed: *'Return to me,' declares the LORD Almighty, 'and I will return to you,' says the LORD Almighty* (1:3).

It was a demand, *Return to me* – repent, come back into a right relationship with me and begin to live lives, once again, that truly honour me. But it was also a promise: *I will return to you*. The promise, like the demand, is first of all about restored relationship, the turning of the LORD's face towards the community again in blessing, instead of anger.[46] But it also had another dimension to it, for Ezekiel had spoken of a day when the LORD would return to Jerusalem and fill it, and especially the temple, with his glory,[47] a promise that had been reaffirmed by Haggai just one month previously.[48] The next *word* received by Zechariah, beginning in 1:7, is essentially about the Lord's continuing commitment to this promise. That is one reason why the passage we have just been looking at is such a fitting introduction to the series of eight visions that follow, and to which we now turn.

2. Vision 1: The man among the myrtle trees (1:7–17)

We are introduced to the visions by being told that *on the twenty-fourth day of the eleventh month* of the same year, approximately two months later, the *word of the LORD* came to Zechariah again.

[44] John 21:4–23. Cf. the memorable words that refer to the LORD's reclamation of Samson in the book of Judges: 'But the hair on his head began to grow again after it had been shaved' (Judg. 16:22). Samson too had wanted to be normal.
[45] 1 Pet. 2:9.
[46] See Hag. 2:19b.
[47] Ezek. 43:1–5; 48:35.
[48] I.e. in the seventh month of the second year of Darius (Hag. 2:1–9; cf. Hag. 1:15).

It was during that night, according to verse 8, that Zechariah saw the first vision, and also, we presume, all the others, since they follow in quick succession and no other time of reception is mentioned. Whether they are best seen as eight separate visions, or one vision in eight parts, we are meant to understand that they are all part of one visionary experience and, as we shall see, they are deeply connected to one another. It must have been quite a night for Zechariah, requiring a rather strong cup of coffee (or the ancient equivalent) to get him up and going again the next morning![49]

We are also clearly intended to understand that these were no ordinary visions, the kinds of things we are accustomed to call dreams, brought on by simple indigestion or anxiety. They are collectively called *the word of the LORD* that came to Zechariah (1:7). That is, they did not originate in his own mind but outside it. They were (together with the interpretation that accompanied them) a revelation from God, not just for Zechariah himself, but for the people he was called to preach to.[50]

What he sees is a man mounted on a red horse, with three groups of horses behind him: red, brown and white respectively (8).[51] We may presume, I think, that these horses, too, had riders. The 'man' on the red horse – also referred to as *the angel of the LORD* (11) – is their leader, and the other three groups of horsemen have come to report to him. All are standing among some myrtle trees in a ravine. Zechariah naturally wants to know what the vision means, and asks an angel (who also appears in the vision) to explain it to him (9). Before he can do so, however, the leading horseman himself explains that the others are patrols whom the LORD has sent throughout the earth (10). They have now returned, and report to him that the whole world is *at rest and in peace* (11). Surprisingly, this is greeted with dismay by their leader, who immediately cries out to the LORD, asking him how long he will withhold his mercy from Jerusalem (12). The LORD responds with *kind and comforting words* (13), which Zechariah is told he must proclaim to the people (13–14a). The remaining verses spell out what these comforting words are, namely that the LORD is no longer angry with Jerusalem, but with the nations that have abused her. He will judge them for what they have done. He will return to Jerusalem. His house (the temple) will be built in it, and all the surrounding towns will again overflow with prosperity (14b–17). In short, this vision contains

---

[49] Likewise, probably, for his wife, if he had one and she shared his bed that night!
[50] Cf. Is. 1:1.
[51] The words for *red, brown* and *white*, are all plural, indicating groups of horses rather than three single horses.

good news for the people of Jerusalem and the whole province of Yehud, and Zechariah has been commissioned to preach it to them.

So then, the main thrust of the vision is clear. Many of the details are less so, but we must do our best to understand them also. Otherwise we shall miss much of the richness of what is here for our instruction and encouragement.

The word translated *ravine* in the NIV is literally 'the deep'; that is, the watery depths of a sea or a river.[52] This is the meaning it has elsewhere in the Old Testament,[53] and later in the book of Zechariah itself (Zech. 10:11: 'the surging sea will be subdued, / and all the *depths* of the Nile will dry up'). If that is the meaning here, it could be that this part of the vision recalls the great moments of Israel's past, at the Red Sea and the Jordan River, when the LORD came to Israel's rescue, bringing them through the depths and giving them victory over their enemies.[54] The myrtle trees, too, may be significant, because in the book of Isaiah (with which Zechariah has important connections, as we have seen) myrtle trees are associated with God's promise to bring new life to Israel, and ultimately to the whole world. So, for example, Isaiah 41:19 (my italics):

> I will put in the desert
>   the cedar and the acacia, the *myrtle* and the olive.
> I will set pines in the wasteland,
>   the fir and the cypress together...

And Isaiah 55:13 (my italics):

> Instead of the thornbush will grow the pine tree,
>   and instead of briers the *myrtle* will grow.

It could be that no more is on view than a location close to Jerusalem with which Zechariah and his community would have been familiar. But given the highly symbolic nature of Zechariah's visions in general, it is likely that the myrtle trees by the ravine (or the deep) are meant to signify deliverance from an ordeal of some kind and the promise of a new beginning. That certainly fits well with the message of comfort Zechariah is told to preach in verses 14–17.

Another potentially confusing feature of this vision is the presence of *two* 'angels', or 'messengers' (for that is what the Hebrew word means). One of them speaks directly to Zechariah (9b, 14). The other, called *the angel of the LORD*, *rides* the red horse (8a) and

---

[52] Heb. $m^e\d{s}ul\^a$.
[53] E.g. Ps. 68:22; Neh. 9:11.
[54] So Kline 1990, pp. 9–10.

stands (is located) among the myrtle trees, in front of the other horsemen (8b, 10).[55] The first angel serves as a kind of companion and interpreter to Zechariah, and appears in seven of the eight visions (1:9, 13, 14, 19; 2:3; 4:1, 4, 11; 5:2, 3, 10; 6:4).[56] The second appears only in this first vision, and in the fourth (1:11, 12; 3:1, 5, 6).[57] This *angel of the* LORD is a rather mysterious figure, who appears many times in the Old Testament, from Genesis onwards.[58] Sometimes he speaks and acts so like God that we must assume, I think, that he *is* God, manifesting himself in human form.[59] At other times he is clearly distinguished from God. Here in Zechariah's first vision, as we have seen, he is the leading horseman. But he is also an intercessor. He is the one who cries, *how long?*, appealing to God to turn his anger away from Jerusalem (12). The identity of this angel is one of the unsolved mysteries of the Old Testament. Some have suggested that he is Christ, appearing to the Old Testament believers before his incarnation.[60] This is possible, but probably more than we can be sure of. All we can say with certainty is that he appears to have a special closeness to God, and an authority to speak in his name which surpasses that of the prophets, or even of the other angels. He is also, as we see here, one who is identified intimately with God's people, and intercedes for them. One of the things this opening vision impresses on Zechariah and those he will preach to is that the rebuilding of Jerusalem and the temple is not simply their business; it involves the angels as well. It may happen on earth, but it is part of the business of heaven.

The second puzzling feature of this vision is the horses. The significance of their colours is unclear.[61] Perhaps their simple variety is the key; these horses represent the many different kinds of horses engaged in such work. That would certainly sit well with the fact that, with the leading horse, they make up a set of four (one, plus

[55] *Standing* (10), as the context makes clear, is not to be taken literally. The angel of the LORD remains on the horse throughout the scene.
[56] In 5:2–3 he is referred to only indirectly, as *he* (NIV). The only vision he does not feature in at all is the fourth (ch. 3). Angels play a similar role in the visionary experiences of Ezekiel and Daniel. They are characteristic of the later prophetic literature of the Old Testament, and especially of the apocalyptic literature of the intertestamental period. They also feature in the book of Revelation in the NT.
[57] He is also referred to once in the second part of the book, at 12:8.
[58] We first meet him in Gen. 16, where he appears to Hagar, after she has fled into the wilderness (vv. 7, 9, 11).
[59] E.g. Judg. 6:11–16. Cf. Gen. 22:11ff.; 31:11–13.
[60] E.g. Kline, 'How long?' (1991, pp. 29–30).
[61] See the discussion (including a review of the many suggestions that have been made) in Baldwin 1972, pp. 138–140. Many ancient commentators thought that the colours represented different countries. Kline (1990, p. 7) suggests that 'the palette selection of red(s) and white was designed to create the impression of flames and light'.

three groups), corresponding to the four points of the compass.[62] The general significance of mounted horsemen of this kind would have been immediately apparent to anyone who lived in Zechariah's world, since the Persian rulers are known to have used mounted horsemen regularly to patrol their vast empire and report on its condition. They played a key role in surveillance and political intelligence.[63] The sight of the passing horsemen reminded subject peoples of who ruled their world, and that they were being watched. But the mounted horsemen of this vision speak of another King and a different kingdom.

Here we meet the first great truth that undergirds the good news of this first vision. *Comforting words* (13) are of no value whatever if the one who speaks them has no power to put them into effect. But Zechariah is shown that that is not the case here. The God who promises to restore Jerusalem is the LORD of the whole earth, and it is he, not the Persian emperor, who will ultimately determine what happens in it. His horsemen patrol the entire world. Nothing happens without his knowledge, and nothing will finally escape his righteous judgment. The horses we see here will appear again a few chapters later, this time pulling chariots (military vehicles) and going out from between mountains of bronze (6:1–2). In other words, the reconnaissance taking place here is in preparation for war. The nations, in their pride, think it is they who rule the world. But it is not so, and in due course they will learn this to their cost. The judgment foreshadowed in this first vision is put into effect in the last one. Though judgment may be delayed, it will certainly come, for the LORD – the God of Israel – is the sovereign LORD of the whole earth, and nothing can withstand his purposes. His kingdom will come, and his will will be done. His promises are not idle, and neither are his threats.

But we must press into this a little more closely to be sure we understand exactly what is being said. What is it about the nations that causes God to be angry with them? It is the same kind of issue we had to grapple with in the first six verses of the chapter, where it was the sin of Zechariah's own community that was on view. Now it is the sin of the world at large that we must think about, for that too arouses God's anger (15). On one level the answer to this question is obvious: God is angry with the nations because of their mistreatment of his people. He was angry with his own people and used the nations to punish them, *but they added to the calamity* (15b). That is, they used excessive force and brutality,

---

[62] Some of the colours are different in 6:2, but again there is a set of four. Cf. the 'four winds of heaven' in 2:6.

[63] Meyers and Meyers 1987, p. 128.

exceeding their mandate and committing war crimes for which God will hold them accountable, even if no human court ever does.[64] This is something we all understand, I think. Even now, as I write these words, a well-known political figure is standing trial for atrocities committed in a recent conflict in the Balkans[65] – recalling the postwar trials of Nazi war criminals. Such things matter to God, and should to us too. An incapacity to be aroused when we should be is just as bad as being inflamed by unwarranted anger.[66]

There is something else here, however, that is even more serious, though it may not be as obvious to us. It has to do with the report the patrols bring back and the way the angel of the LORD responds to it (11–15a):

> *And they reported to the angel of the LORD, who was standing among the myrtle trees, 'We have gone throughout the earth and found the whole world at rest and in peace.'*
>
> *Then the angel of the LORD said, 'LORD Almighty, how long will you withhold mercy from Jerusalem and from the towns of Judah, which you have been angry with these seventy years?' So the LORD spoke kind and comforting words to the angel who talked with me.*
>
> *Then the angel who was speaking to me said, 'Proclaim this word: This is what the LORD Almighty says: "I am very jealous for Jerusalem and Zion, but I am very angry with the nations that feel secure."'*

The greater sin of the nations, and the chief cause of God's anger at them, is that they are *at rest and in peace*, and *feel secure*. The angel of the LORD is particularly distressed about this state of affairs and asks *how long* God will allow it to continue, especially since the *seventy years* appointed for Israel's punishment have now come to an end. He almost certainly has in mind the prophecy of Jeremiah:

> This whole country will become a desolate wasteland, and these nations will serve the king of Babylon for *seventy years*. 'But when the *seventy years* are fulfilled, I will punish the king of Babylon and his nation, the land of the Babylonians, for their guilt,' declares the LORD, 'and will make it desolate forever.' ...
>
> This is what the LORD says: 'When *seventy years* are completed

---

[64] Cf. Is. 47:5–7.
[65] I refer to the trial of the Serb leader Slobodan Milošević.
[66] Note Eph. 4:26: 'Be angry but do not sin' (RSV).

for Babylon, I will come to you and fulfil my gracious promise to bring you back to this place.'[67]

In fact, a very significant fulfilment of this prophecy had already taken place in the fall of Babylon and the decree of Cyrus that had permitted those exiles who wished to do so to return to Jerusalem some eighteen years previously. How, then, are we to understand God's anger at the nations for being *at rest and peace* and feeling *secure*?

This is another point at which we must remember that Zechariah and Haggai prophesied at the same time. Just four months earlier Haggai had prophesied of a great disturbance that God would bring upon the whole earth, and he had repeated it two months later – very close to the time of Zechariah's visions:

> This is what the LORD Almighty says: 'In a little while I will once more shake the heavens and the earth, the sea and the dry land. I will shake all nations, and the desired of all nations will come, and I will fill this house with glory,' says the LORD Almighty ...
> ... I will shake the heavens and the earth. I will overturn royal thrones and shatter the power of the foreign kingdoms.[68]

Actually, the world was not entirely at rest and peace at the time of Zechariah's visions. Most of the disturbances that had attended Darius's rise to power had subsided, and his grasp on power was firm. But Egypt was still in rebellion – a problem still to be dealt with.[69] What troubled the angel of the LORD was not so much the rest or unrest of the world in this sense, but its complacency, its smugness. Many wrongs still remained unrighted; foreign powers still ruled over Jerusalem and its people, and *there was no sign of the*

---

[67] Jer. 25:11–12; 29:10; my italics. For a good discussion of the meaning of the 'seventy years' see Kline, 'How long?' (1991, pp. 22–25). Kline himself thinks that they were 'a literal, if slightly rounded, number for the critical period of captivity (605–538), from the deportation in the time of Daniel to the decree of Cyrus permitting the exiles to return' (p. 23). They have been understood as 'a conventional expression for a span of divine displeasure (cf. Is. 23:15). Others see a reference to the period from the fall of Jerusalem in 587 to the time of Zechariah's night visions (520), or to the revelation he received two years later (and thus almost exactly seventy years after 587), in which these "seventy years" are again mentioned (Zech. 7:5)' (p. 30). To these might be added the fact that it was seventy years from the destruction of the first temple in 587/586 BC to the completion of the second in 516 BC (Ezra 6:15). However, since none of the specific periods suggested fits all the contexts in which the expression is used, it would appear best to see the seventy years as a symbolic way of referring to the period of Jerusalem's punishment as determined by God.

[68] Hag. 2:6–7, 21–22.

[69] See the discussion in the introduction, p. 22.

great shaking that Haggai had spoken about. The promised judgment of the nations had not happened; they continued to disregard his kingship with impunity. The good news of this vision is that it will not always be so. The patrols have come back. God is fully apprised of the situation, and fully intends to fulfil the words he has spoken. Preparations for the final conflict between the kingdom of God and the kingdoms of this world are already in hand. The mighty shaking will surely come – in its time.

It is important to realize that the future judgment of the world is a reality, and is good news for the people of God. For it means that oppression, cruelty and injustice will not prevail in the end, however long they may appear to do so.[70] God has already set a day 'when he will judge the world with justice by the man he has appointed. He has given proof of this to all men by raising him from the dead'.[71] The final proof of God's intention to judge the world is the resurrection of Jesus Christ from the dead. People everywhere have been put on notice. Preparations are in hand; the judge has already been appointed. His kingdom will come and his will will be done, here on earth, as it is in heaven. The truly astounding thing about this world facing judgment, however, is not its overt hostility to God and his people, but its sheer indifference. That is how it was in Noah's day, and in Zechariah's. It is how it is in our own day, and (according to Jesus) how it will be right to the end:

> As it was in the days of Noah, so it will be at the coming of the Son of Man. For in the days before the flood, people were eating and drinking, marrying and giving in marriage, up to the day Noah entered the ark; and they knew nothing about what would happen until the flood came and took them all away. That is how it will be at the coming of the Son of Man.[72]

The good news for the people of God is that there will be an end. The cry 'How long?' and the prayer 'Your kingdom come' will not go unanswered.[73] The challenge is to live now in the light of that truth.

Which brings us, finally, to the positive *comforting words* with which this passage ends (13–17). What we have noted so far is conveyed indirectly, by the symbolism of the vision. What now follows is the message Zechariah is explicitly commanded to

[70] See Rev. 18, especially v. 20.

[71] Acts 17:31.

[72] Matt. 24:37–39.

[73] According to Rev. 6:10–11 the cry 'How long?' will continue to go up until the day of final judgment.

proclaim to the people (14, 17); it is the positive counterpart to the truth that God will judge the world. In a nutshell, the comforting truth for the people of God is that, unlike the world, they are no longer the objects of God's anger, but of his mercy (15–16). Indeed, he is *very jealous* for them (14). Unfortunately, 'jealousy' has negative overtones for us today. It suggests selfishness, envy, and malicious resentment of what others have. But the jealousy of God, as the Bible describes it, is something utterly untainted by any such mean-spiritedness. It is his intense, protective concern for what is rightly his own: his name, his land, his city (Jerusalem), his house (temple) and his people. They are his, and he will defend and protect them against all assailants, and avenge every wrong committed against them. He is utterly, even fiercely, committed to their welfare. Note the way he refers here to *my house* (16), and *my towns* (17) – which includes their inhabitants. Jealousy, in this sense, is another name for love: the kind of love a deeply devoted, honourable man has for his wife. And there is great security in knowing that you are the object of such love; indeed, to be so loved – especially by God – is the true comfort we all need and long for.

Jerusalem and *Zion*, in verses 14 and 17, are alternative names for the one place: the city God had chosen to be the centre of his kingdom on earth.[74] That 'chosenness' was symbolized particularly by the temple, the place, above all others, of his presence with and among his people.[75] What Zechariah is told to proclaim is that the LORD *will again comfort Zion and choose Jerusalem* (17b). That is, the time of her punishment (temporary abandonment) is over, and the time for God to reaffirm his choice of her has come.[76] The NIV is not quite as accurate as it could be here, for literally verse 16 speaks of something that has already happened as well as of something promised: 'I *have returned* to Jerusalem with mercy, and my house *will be rebuilt*.'[77] The *measuring line ... stretched out over Jerusalem* (16b) probably indicates that Jerusalem is destined to become the

---

[74] Ps. 132:13. See the introduction, pp. 33–35. 'Zion' was the name of the Jebusite fortress (citadel) of the city in pre-Israelite times (2 Sam. 5:7), but subsequently became an alternative name for the city itself, especially in Psalms.

[75] 1 Kgs. 8:27–30; cf. Exod. 25:8.

[76] Cf. Is. 40:1–2; and especially Is. 54:7.

[77] The first verb, *šaḇtî*, is perfect; the second, *yibbāneh*, is imperfect. In verse (poetry) such alternation of verb forms would be unremarkable, but in the context of Hebrew prose (as here) it requires explanation. The relationship between verb forms and tense in Hebrew is hotly disputed, but the sense of the preceding perfects (*I was angry ... but they added*, 15) supports the reading for *šaḇtî* I have proposed. Cf. AV, 'I am returned', and RSV, 'I have returned'. For the *measuring line* see 2:1, and my comments there.

glorious city of Ezekiel 40 – 48, or at least the forerunner of it.[78] What *comforting words* these are for Zechariah's contemporaries! God is not merely watching them from a distance, to see whether or not they live up to his expectations. He is already in their midst, a theme that will be developed strongly in the fifth vision (4:1–14).[79] Nor do they have to try to mollify him by good deeds, as though they are under constant threat from his anger. His anger has already turned away from them; he has returned to them *with mercy* (16). The task of building the temple, to which they are called, is God's work, and its completion is guaranteed by his own commitment to it. Their present hardships and difficulties are only temporary; what lies ahead is blessing that will *overflow* to the surrounding towns of Judah (17), and ultimately to the whole world. Then the 'chosenness' of Jerusalem and its people will be evident to all people everywhere, and they will be drawn to it like thirsty men to an oasis (8:18–22; 14:6–9).

But now we are getting ahead of ourselves, for the theme of worldwide blessing is yet to emerge explicitly. This first vision is about two things: first, God's anger at the nations who have mistreated his Jerusalem and its people, and second, his own intense (jealous) determination to bless and prosper them, especially by ensuring that their work of rebuilding his temple is brought to a successful conclusion. It is bad news for an indifferent world, but good news indeed for people who have repented of living as if God doesn't matter, and put their hand again to the work of his kingdom.[80] Both aspects of its message will be developed further in the visions that follow.

3. Vision 2: Four horns and four craftsmen (1:18–21)

This second vision is the briefest of the eight, and perhaps the most enigmatic, even though, as in the first vision, a certain amount of explanation is provided by the interpreting angel.

Zechariah sees *four horns* (18), which he is told represent *the nations* that have scattered the people of Judah, Israel and Jerusalem (19b, 21b). This part of the vision is relatively easy to understand, since horns are weapons that aggressive, powerful animals use to attack their prey. The *four* horns represent all the nations that have

---

[78] Ezekiel's climactic vision in those chapters begins with his seeing a 'city', and 'a man ... with a linen cord and a measuring rod in his hand' (Ezek. 40:3). See also 2:1 and my comments there.

[79] Cf. Hag. 2:4 ('Be strong ... and work. For I am with you').

[80] See Ezra 5:1–2.

acted like this towards Israel.[81] They have behaved like animals, goring, tearing, terrorizing her, and scattering her people far and wide.[82] It began in the second half of the eighth century, with the attacks of Assyria on the northern Israelite kingdom, climaxing in the fall of Samaria in 722 BC. It continued in the late seventh and early sixth century with the similar attacks by the Babylonians on the southern kingdom, culminating in the fall of Jerusalem and the destruction of the temple in 587 BC. It is not just one attack that is on view, but a whole history of subjugation and brutalization, summarized as the scattering of *Judah, Israel and Jerusalem* (19). Nor was it just the great imperial powers who participated in this predatory behaviour. Edom, in particular, is condemned in the Old Testament for the way it took advantage of Judah's collapse to move in, seize its lands, and sell its people into slavery.[83] This was especially bitter for the Israelites, since the Edomites were closely related to them as descendants of Esau, Jacob's brother.[84]

Such things leave deep scars on people's minds that are not easily healed, which is why conflicts, such as we have today in Israel, Northern Ireland and the Sudan, drag on for so long. This is especially so where aggrieved parties have enough power to inflict pain on their enemies, but not enough to redress their situation completely. The people of Jerusalem in Zechariah's day were utterly powerless to call the nations to account for what they had done. The return some eighteen years previously had been some compensation, to be sure. But the reality was that the vast majority of the Israelites were still scattered, and that all of them lived under a foreign regime that had inherited and retained all the spoils of its predecessors. Nehemiah, some seventy years on, described their situation as follows: 'see, we are slaves today, slaves in the land you [God] gave our forefathers so they could eat its fruit and the other good things it produces ... its abundant harvest goes to the kings you have placed over us. They rule over our bodies and our cattle as they please. We are in great distress.'[85]

So the question that continually gnawed at the minds of the

[81] Cf. the similar symbolic significance of the number 'four' in the 'four winds of heaven' in 2:6; 6:5; the four horses/horsemen of 1:8, and the 'four chariots' of 6:1.
[82] Cf. Kline 1992, pp. 22–23: 'Zechariah introduces into the meaning of the lifting up of the horns the specific connotation of ferocity, hostility and tyranny by qualifying the action as an animal-like attack against Judah that devastated it and rendered it helpless.' Cf. Jer. 50:7, 11. He notes the way horns figure prominently also in the depiction of hostile imperial powers in the visions of Daniel (Dan. 7:7–8, 20–25; 8:5–12).
[83] See the book of Obadiah, especially vv. 9–14.
[84] Gen. 25:19–28; 36:1–40; Obad. 10.
[85] Neh. 9:36–37.

people, and pushed its way out in prayers such as this was 'Who will call the nations to account for what they have done?' There was so much unfinished business in God's moral government of the world. If God is king, how can the world remain as it is?

The answer this vision gives is astonishing, and at first appears to make no sense at all. Zechariah sees four *craftsmen* (20) or, as we might say today, tradesmen.[86] It is a humble term. It does not refer to rulers, or military leaders, or scholars, but to people who work with their hands, skilfully, to be sure – but not with hands that grasp the instruments of power. It is used of the weavers, engravers and carpenters who worked on the tabernacle in the days of Moses,[87] and on the temple in the time of Solomon.[88] It is also used of the workmen who were engaged by the later reforming kings Joash and Josiah to make repairs to the temple.[89] Finally, and very significantly for our present purposes, it is used in Ezra 3:7 of the workmen who had been hired to do the initial rebuilding of the temple just eighteen years before Zechariah began his ministry. In spite of this, however, some have found it difficult to believe that they could be quite as ordinary as this; after all, according to verse 21b they have come to *terrify* and *throw down* the horns (power) of the nations. Surely, then, they must be powerful figures themselves. The attempt to invest them with such power is apparent in certain translations, such as the New Revised Standard Version, in which they are called four *blacksmiths* – conjuring up an image of strongly built men with huge hammers, anvils and fiery forges. But this translation is entirely unwarranted, and (as we shall see) unnecessary. Long before the NIV, the AV had nicely captured the disarming unpretentiousness of the term: Zechariah saw four 'carpenters'.

At the heart of this vision, therefore, there is a strange conjunction of weakness and power. There are four horns (power) and four craftsmen or carpenters (weakness). The task of the craftsmen is to overthrow the power of the nations, and the correspondence of the 'four' and 'four' implies that they are equal to the task! But how can this be so?

The answer lies in the term 'craftsmen', and in the context provided for this vision by what immediately precedes it. The first vision concluded with the promise 'I [the Lord] will return to Jerusalem with mercy, *and there my house will be rebuilt. And the measuring line will be stretched out over Jerusalem*' (1:16; my

---

[86] Hebrew, *ḥārāšîm*.

[87] Exod. 28:11 (where the word translated 'engrave' [NIV] is from the same root as 'craftsmen'); 35:35; 38:23.

[88] 1 Chr. 22:15; 29:5.

[89] 2 Kgs. 12:11; 2 Chr. 24:12; 2 Kgs. 22:6; 2 Chr. 34:11.

italics). Then comes the vision of the four craftsmen, followed by a vision that opens with Zechariah seeing a young man with a measuring line in his hand (2:1). In other words, the promise of 1:16 is programmatic for the next two visions, and therefore this present vision must have something to do with the rebuilding of the temple – which provides a perfectly natural reason why craftsmen appear at this point.[90] They have come to engage in the rebuilding of the temple. But the vision Zechariah sees sets these simple tradesmen in a staggering new light. They are not as weak and ordinary as they appear to be. On the contrary, they are chosen instruments to manifest God's rule in the world and to judge the nations. This is truly astounding, but before we dismiss it as unbelievable nonsense we should consider, for example, the case of Noah (a marine carpenter!), who performed a similar role in his day. 'By faith Noah, when warned about things not yet seen, in holy fear built an ark to save his family. *By his faith he condemned the world* and became heir of the righteousness that comes by faith.'[91]

Noah was not just a boat-builder; he was also a preacher.[92] But it is his simple act of building the ark that is emphasized here. It was by doing *that* that he condemned the world. Of course, it was God who brought the flood. But here is the point: Noah *participated in that judgment* by his simple act of building the ark. He put the world on notice, so to speak: he consigned some to salvation, and others to destruction. In the New Testament Paul speaks in similar terms about his own ministry of proclaiming the gospel (a message that appeared foolish and weak): 'For we are to God the aroma of Christ among those who are being saved and those who are perishing. To the one we are the smell of death; to the other, the fragrance of life. And who is equal to such a task?'[93]

Paul's answer is that his adequacy for such a task comes from God. God is the judge, but those he chooses to preach the gospel are his instruments for putting that judgment into effect.

The danger for Zechariah and his contemporaries was that they might underestimate the significance of the work God had called them to do. There seemed to be so many bigger, more urgent matters in the world that needed attention, and that required far

---

[90] There may be a secondary allusion in the *four horns* to the horns of the bronze temple altar (Exod. 27:2; 30:2; 1 Kgs. 1:50; cf. Ezek. 43:15). The four craftsmen symbolically subdue the nations by binding them to the corners of the Lord's altar. So Conrad, p. 77. Cf. Kline (1992, p. 24), who picks up the 'altar' aspect of the horns, but interprets it rather differently.

[91] Heb. 11:7; my italics.

[92] 2 Pet. 2:5.

[93] 2 Cor. 2:15–16.

greater resources than anything they themselves possessed. The really big issues in God's administration of his world would have to be dealt with by mighty men, on the battlefield and in the halls of political and economic power. If God chose to use human beings to deal with these issues, he would surely choose the mighty. The work of Zechariah and the others in rebuilding the temple was at best a sideshow. So how could they give themselves to it with the enthusiasm and commitment it required?

The revolutionary message of this vision is that the judgment of the world is already being put into effect wherever God deploys his workmen. Through them God brings his kingdom into this world, a kingdom that will eventually sweep away and replace every earthly power. In other words, precisely because it is the work of his kingdom it can never be a mere sideshow while the main game happens elsewhere. It *is* the main game! To be sure, God also uses other means of judging the nations. By his sovereign providence he raises them up and brings them down, and he will call them all, finally, before the bar of his judgment on the last day. But that is not something somehow unrelated to, and separate from, what he does when he deploys people in the work of his kingdom here and now. Indeed, it is precisely by doing this that he most clearly shows his hand as the world's ruler and judge, and begins to put the final judgment into effect.

It is vitally important that we be clear about this in our own time, when there are so many wrongs that need righting in our world, and so many urgent and good causes that clamour for our attention. Of course, the time for building temples of brick and mortar is over, for the reality they symbolized has now come in the person of Jesus the Messiah, crucified and risen.[94] Jesus announced a new building programme,[95] and initiated it himself by preaching the kingdom of God and training and equipping his disciples to do the same. He went to the cross that there might be a gospel to preach. But the preaching of that gospel will always seem weak and pointless to those whose minds have not been schooled by the Scriptures to see the world the way God does.[96] It is true that God is not indifferent to the many unrighted wrongs in our world – far from it! – and neither should we be. The many government bodies and other

---

[94] Note especially the teaching about this in John's Gospel. God has come to 'tabernacle' among us in the person of the Word made flesh, Jesus Christ (1:14). Jesus himself is the true place of worship, and the source from which the living waters flow (4:1–26). He is the true temple that, unlike the temple of Herod, cannot be destroyed (2:19–22).

[95] Matt. 16:18.

[96] 1 Cor. 1:18–25.

organizations dedicated to addressing them are means by which God works to restrain evil and promote good in a world that continues to rebel against him.[97] They are expressions of his love, even for those who do not recognize his rule and, by their own choice, remain outside his kingdom. Christians can and should be involved in public affairs, promoting justice by all reasonable means at their disposal; it is an indispensable part of loving our neighbour and being like our heavenly Father.[98] But the great danger is that, in doing these things, we might come to regard evangelism as a rather quaint, diversionary activity for Christians who have lost the plot, so to speak, and withdrawn from 'real' engagement with the world in which they live. Nothing, in fact, could be further from the truth. For the preaching of the gospel in the power of the Holy Spirit is the God-ordained means by which the powers of darkness are directly confronted, the church is built, and his kingdom advanced in this world.[99] It is the means by which people, as Paul put it, are rescued from the dominion of darkness and transferred into the kingdom of God's own son.[100] It is not a diversion from the real work of the kingdom, but the work of the kingdom par excellence. It is *the* mission of God, and of the church he founded.[101] Whatever else we do, we must engage in and support this supremely important work.

In short, we cannot pray 'Your kingdom come' without at the same time being committed to keeping the 'craft', the 'trade' of gospel ministry at the very centre of our life and vision, both as individuals and as the church. May God make us good carpenters in his building project!

4. Vision 3: A man with a measuring line (2:1–13)

We have already seen that this vision and the previous one are both closely related to the promise of 1:16: 'I will return to Jerusalem with mercy, and there my house will be rebuilt. And the measuring line will be stretched out over Jerusalem.' Zechariah has seen craftsmen coming to work on the temple. Now he sees *a man with a measuring line* (1).[102] In verse 4 he is described more particularly as

---

[97] Rom. 13:1–7; 1 Tim. 2:1–2.
[98] Mark 12:28–31; Matt. 5:13–16, 43–48.
[99] 2 Cor. 10:3–5.
[100] Col. 1:13.
[101] Matt. 28:16–20.
[102] The Hebrew expression for 'measuring line' is not the same in 2:1 as in 1:16, but there is no doubt that the same kind of instrument is on view. The two expressions are synonymous.

a *young man*. Zechariah asks him where he is going, and the man replies that he is going to measure Jerusalem *to find out how wide and how long it is* (2). As the following verses reveal, his more particular purpose appears to have been to measure the city in preparation for the rebuilding of its walls. In other words, his measuring has a practical purpose in view: he is a surveyor.

A little surprisingly, Zechariah puts his question directly to man himself, rather than to the interpreting angel (as he did in the first vision, 1:9). This leaves the angel with no apparent role to play, so he withdraws – or at least begins to, only to be intercepted by *another angel* who comes to meet him (3). This second angel tells him to run and tell the young man, in effect, that the kinds of walls he has in mind will be unnecessary, for *Jerusalem will be a city without walls*; the LORD himself will be *a wall of fire around it* (4–5). With that, the vision itself ends. It is followed immediately, however, by three short oracles (prophetic messages) closely related to it (6, 7–9, 10–13). The message of verses 4–5 was delivered by one of the angels to the young man Zechariah had seen in the vision. The three that follow are addressed to people who inhabit the real world Zechariah lived in, and were presumably delivered by Zechariah himself as God's prophet. They draw out the full significance of the vision, and apply it to the present situation of his hearers. The first urges Israelites still in exile to flee from their places of captivity and return to Jerusalem with all speed (6). The second calls on those still in Babylon in particular to do so, because God's judgment still rests on that city, and the calamities yet to fall on it will show that Zechariah has indeed been commissioned by God (7–9). The third calls on the people of Jerusalem to rejoice, because God is coming to live among them. This will prove to all that God has chosen them to be his people, and lead to a great influx of others – from *many nations* – who will also come to Jerusalem and become God's people (11a). This too will show that Zechariah has been sent by God (11b). The chapter ends with a solemn call to *all mankind* to *be still before the LORD* because *he has roused himself from his holy dwelling* (in heaven, 13). That is, he has already begun to put these promises into effect. An urgent response is called for, because God is on his way: his kingdom is coming!

There, in a nutshell, is the message of the whole chapter. But now we must attend more closely to some of the details. The big issue is the matter of coherence: what precisely is the connection between the vision and the oracles that follow it? And what exactly do some of the details of both the vision and the oracles mean?

Let us begin with the *young man* of verses 1–4. He is not named, and without further warrant we must allow him to remain anonymous. It does not really matter who he is; it is what he is doing that is significant, and it appears to be eminently sensible. He appears to have taken the promise of 1:16 to heart and is beginning to act on it. The LORD has said that the measuring line will be stretched over Jerusalem, which, at the very least, must mean that it will not stay in its present state of disrepair. So, in general terms at least, the will of God is plain, and the *young man*, with the energy and enthusiasm appropriate to his years, sets out to act in accordance with it. If Jerusalem is to be restored, the first step is to measure it up so that appropriate plans can be made and the work be set in train. Furthermore, even without a specific revelation to justify it, what the young man is setting out to do is nothing more than what common sense would dictate. The environment was hostile, as we have already seen. There were enemies intent on frustrating the attempts of the community to rebuild the temple. So what could be more prudent than first to secure the city by restoring its walls? Then the temple reconstruction could proceed in a protected environment and have a better chance of success. The young man is surely to be commended for his zeal and good sense.

That may be so, and indeed the message he is given in verses 3–4 is not so much a reprimand as a further revelation, to enable him to understand the will of God more fully. God is more committed to the protection and future prosperity of Jerusalem than he himself can ever be. But (and here is the point) that security and prosperity will not be achieved by man-made walls, or indeed by any human activity at all, but by the promised presence of God. He himself will be *a wall of fire around it* and *its glory within* (5).[103] In other words, now is not the time to be rebuilding the walls. The priority at present is to rebuild the temple (as the following visions will confirm), and God himself will defend the city while that work goes ahead. In fact, another seventy-five years will pass before the walls are rebuilt, and God will raise up the right man to do it at that time.[104] It is not required now. There is a striking contrast between the well-intentioned activity with which this chapter begins (1), and the call to *be still before the LORD* with which it ends (13). It is a lesson we all need to learn again and again: God's work must be done his way, and in his time.

The following three oracles present Jerusalem as the place to which all must come, beginning with the scattered exiles of Israel

---

[103] Cf. the protecting presence of God in the pillar of fire by day and cloud by night at the time of the exodus from Egypt (Exod. 14:19–20).
[104] See Neh. 1 – 6, especially 6:15–16.

(6)[105] and ending with *many nations* (11). It is the place of God's presence and therefore the only place of real security. It is contrasted, in verses 7–9, with Babylon, the city doomed to destruction.[106] Historically the fall of Babylon had already taken place. It was conquered by Cyrus the Great in 539 BC – which is why the original exiles had been able to leave there and return to Jerusalem.[107] But in this forward-looking prophecy Babylon has become a symbol of all that is hostile to God and his people. It represents the 'city of man', which rejects the rule of God and persecutes his people. This symbolic significance of Babylon goes back to the story of the tower of Babel (the forerunner of Babylon) in Genesis 11,[108] and runs right through to Revelation 18, where Babylon stands for Rome – and hence the pagan world – the enemy of God and people of God. Babylon is the world in its determined, organized hostility to God, a world on which God has already passed judgment. To leave Babylon, therefore, and go to Jerusalem, is to break solidarity with a world that rejects God and flee to him for mercy and protection. It is to be like the pilgrim in John Bunyan's famous story, or like Abraham, setting out from Ur.[109] It is to cast in your lot with God and his people – to set out resolutely for the new Jerusalem, the city of God.

Zechariah affirms two things here that are always held in a delicate balance in Scripture. The first is the special place of Israel in God's purposes, represented here by *Judah* and *Jerusalem* (8, 12); the second is his intention, finally, to include people of *many nations*, and to own them as *my people* just as surely as he ever owned Israel (11).[110] Again we are in touch with a theme that arcs right across the biblical revelation. It is a programme announced in the promises made to Abraham, who was called to 'leave' (be separated from) others, to live in a special, covenant relationship

---

[105] *The land of the north* (6) is, metaphorically, 'the land of the enemy'. Because the terrain directly east of Israel is virtually impassable (at least by armies), the enemies that preyed on Israel in the eighth to the sixth centuries (Assyria and Babylon) always approached from the north. See Jer. 1:13–16.

[106] *Daughter of Babylon* (7) is a poetic expression meaning 'the people of Babylon' (Baldwin 1972, p. 109; Meyers and Meyers 1987, p. 164). Cf. *Daughter of Zion* in v. 10. Cities, and therefore their populations, are typically referred to (metaphorically) as women in the OT.

[107] See the introduction, p. 24.

[108] The tower of Babel was built on the plain in 'Shinar' (Gen. 11:2), and it was to 'Shinar' ('Babylonia', NIV) that Daniel was later brought as a captive by Nebuchadnezzar (Dan. 1:2). Cf. Zech. 5:11.

[109] Heb. 11:8–10.

[110] Cf. v. 4, where the new Jerusalem is depicted as overflowing because of the *great number* of men and animals in it – a microcosm of the new creation. Cf. also the 'great multitude' of Rev. 7:9.

with God, so that finally, through him, all peoples on earth might be blessed.[111] The programme is realized in the person of Jesus Christ, the true seed of Abraham, in whom all the promises of God are fulfilled.[112] It is vital that we realize, however, that that fulfilment in Christ does not obliterate the special place of Israel in God's purposes; on the contrary, it brings it to perfect realization. Only by bowing the knee to the true seed of Abraham, the one perfect Israelite, can any person be saved. There is no Saviour but Israel's Messiah, and no God but Israel's God. As the apostle Peter put it, so brilliantly and starkly, 'Salvation is found in no-one else'.[113] Zechariah expresses that same truth here in terms of pilgrimage to Zion. There is only one place to which all must come in order to be saved. Only there will God dwell with his people and be a wall of fire around them. There is no other way to escape destruction. The Messiah himself will come clearly into focus (as we shall see) in chapters 9 – 14.

Only two matters remain for brief comment before we pass on. First, this vision and the oracles which follow it confirm that the promise of 1:16 will indeed be fulfilled. The present, ruined city, will in due course, be replaced by a new one. But the new Jerusalem of the future will far surpass anything that the *young man* of verse 4 could have imagined as he set out on his surveying expedition. Indeed, we can hardly fail to see in the way this vision opens a reminder of the closing chapters of the book of Ezekiel.[114] There Ezekiel is transported in a vision to a very high mountain and sees a magnificent city, the new Jerusalem, laid out before him. And he sees a 'man' (in this case a divine being) with 'a measuring rod' in his hand, who takes him on a tour of it, and shows him all its perfections.[115] Zechariah 2 shows that what Ezekiel saw will indeed be realized,[116] but not by human effort. God himself will bring it about (13). Even the later rebuilding of the walls by Nehemiah – important though that was – was only a shadow of what still lay in

---

[111] Gen. 12:1–3.

[112] Gal. 3:16; 2 Cor. 1:20.

[113] Acts 4:12.

[114] Ezek. 40 – 48.

[115] Ezek. 40:3. The expression 'measuring rod' is different from the *measuring line* of Zech. 2:1, just as the man 'like bronze' of Ezek. 40:3 is different from the *young man* of Zechariah's vision. The point is that the similarities are just as conspicuous, and significant, as the differences.

[116] In fact, the fulfilment envisaged by Zechariah surpasses, in some important respects, what was seen by Ezekiel. I have in mind especially the inclusion of people drawn from *many nations* in the citizenry of the new Jerusalem – a theme strongly Isaianic rather than Ezekielian. See especially Is. 2:1–4; 66:19–24.

the future.[117] What the people of Jerusalem needed to give themselves to immediately was the rebuilding of the temple.

Second, we are twice told that the fulfilment of what Zechariah prophesies here (the judgment of 'Babylon' and the return of the LORD to live among his people in the new Jerusalem[118]) will show that Zechariah was indeed a true prophet, commissioned by the LORD Almighty himself (9b, 11b).[119] Clearly, the people of Zechariah's own day regarded him as a true prophet, for they obeyed his call to arise and build.[120] So did those who preserved his words for us as holy Scripture. But the final vindication of all God's faithful prophets will be on the last day, when everything God has spoken through them will be realized. It will also be the moment of final vindication for all who have received it as God's word and lived by it.

5. Vision 4: Clean garments for the high priest (3:1–10)

This vision and the next (in ch. 4) stand at the centre of the series of eight, and are markedly different from the others. As we have seen, all eight visions constitute one *word* or revelation given to Zechariah near the beginning of his ministry (1:7). The first three focus on the community as a whole and all have to do, in one way or another,

---

[117] E.g. Jerusalem did not overflow with population in Nehemiah's day (as anticipated in Zech. 2:4). On the contrary, a certain percentage of the community had to be compelled to move into it (Neh. 7:4; 11:1–2). Baldwin (1972, p. 106, following Jeremias, pp. 58–84) notes that 'the prophecy [of Zech. 2:4] was nearer to fulfilment in the time of Jesus, when at festival times the city overflowed with pilgrims from all parts of the known world'.

[118] The fact that a future return is anticipated here does not contradict the assertions elsewhere in the book that he has already returned to be present with Zechariah's contemporaries in their work of rebuilding the temple (e.g. 1:16, on which see my comments above). God has, likewise, already come to us in Jesus, is with us by his Spirit, and will come in glory in the future. In Zechariah's day too the kingdom of God had already come, and yet was still to come. See the introduction, pp. 35–37.

[119] The general point being made here is true, even though some of the details of the passage are unclear. V. 8, in particular, is notoriously obscure, and it is possible that the underlying Hebrew has suffered some corruption in transmission. Most likely *after he has honoured me* (literally 'after glory') refers to Zechariah's seeing of these eight visions, which were effectively his commissioning as a prophet. The reference to his being *sent ... against the nations* indicates that he was sent to announce God's judgment on the nations, represented here by Babylon (though this was only one aspect of his ministry; cf. Jer. 1:10). See the discussion of this verse in Baldwin (1972, p. 109) and other standard commentaries. Sweeney (pp. 588–589) thinks that 'after glory' (*'aḥar kāḇôd*) is a cryptic reference to Yahweh, who refused to let Moses see his 'glory' (*kāḇôd*) but permitted him to see his back (*'aḥôr*, which is a variant of *'aḥar*, 'back', 'behind', 'after'). The speaker (whom Sweeney takes to be the second angel of v. 3) is saying that he has been sent by Yahweh, just as Moses was.

[120] Ezra 5:2.

with the rebuilding of the temple. But now there is a change. In visions four and five the spotlight falls on the two leaders: Joshua the high priest (ch. 3), and Zerubbabel the governor (ch. 4). The focus shifts from the task itself to the human instruments God will use to sustain and lead the community as they do it. In the visions that follow, the focus shifts back again to the community as a whole. So we have come to an important point in the vision sequence: these two men are key players in God's declared purposes.

But at once Zechariah is shown what appears to be an insurmountable problem: Joshua the high priest is unclean.

a. The problem (3:1, 3)

Zechariah finds himself in a courtroom where a trial is about to begin. The judge is *the angel of the LORD*, who acts as God's appointee and representative. The prisoner in the dock is Joshua the high priest, *dressed in filthy clothes* (3). The prosecuting attorney is Satan, who stands on Joshua's right side, ready to *accuse him* (1b).[121] This is a serious situation indeed, for Joshua is the spiritual leader of the community who (in the normal course of events) will officiate in the rebuilt temple. But he is clearly unfit to do so.

In the rituals prescribed in the law of Moses, the high priest was the supreme intermediary between the people and God. He alone had the awesome privilege once a year, on the Day of Atonement, to enter the Most Holy Place of the temple with the blood of a sacrificial animal in order to intercede for the people, 'so that they [would] be acceptable to the LORD'.[122] He wore their names on the breastpiece of his robe, over his heart, and on two elaborately ornamented pads, on his shoulders.[123] In other words, the acceptability of the people with God depended critically on the acceptability of the high priest. He symbolically carried them into the presence of God as their representative and mediator.

---

[121] The word *śāṭān* means 'opponent'. See Num. 22:22, where the angel of the Lord stands in the road 'to oppose' Balaam (literally 'as a satan'). Here in Zech. 3 it is used with the article, literally 'the opponent'. The use of the article, plus the courtroom setting, suggest that *śāṭān* is being used in this passage as a descriptive term rather than a personal name. 'The satan' is 'the opponent' of Joshua in a legal sense. He is the prosecuting attorney, whose role is to present the evidence against the accused (cf. Ps. 109:6; Acts 25:18). However, the strong terms in which he is rebuked in v. 2 suggests that his motivations are less than honourable. The whole scene is very reminiscent of Job 1 – 2, where 'the satan' plays a similar role and displays a similar disposition. In 1 Chr. 21:1 *śāṭān* is used without the article, as a personal name – an anticipation of the full unmasking of Satan as the arch-enemy of God and his people in the NT.
[122] Exod. 28:38; Lev. 16:1–17; 23:26–32; Heb. 9:6–7.
[123] Exod. 28:6–30.

Because of the crucial importance of what they did, priests (and especially the high priest) were required to avoid all uncleanness. They were forbidden to marry a woman who had had any form of sexual contact with another man, or to touch a dead body.[124] They were to observe strict dietary laws. All Israelites were obligated to avoid the moral evils proscribed by the law (adultery, stealing, murder etc.). But the ceremonial regime required of priests symbolized something more, namely perfection: the total purity required for access to God.[125] Of course, only Jesus had that perfection in reality, but the priests of the Old Testament had a special obligation to strive for it, and to adhere, in dress and behaviour, to a regime that symbolized it. When he entered the Most Holy Place the high priest wore a gold plate on the front of his turban, inscribed with the words 'HOLY TO THE LORD'.[126]

What a contrast all this is to the *filthy clothes* worn by Joshua in Zechariah's vision! He is manifestly unfit to be in the presence of God, let alone to serve him as high priest. And that means that the whole community is in trouble, because Joshua is their mediator and representative. Nor is the problem simply that Joshua has infringed this or that commandment – ceremonial or moral as the case may be. It is not so much a matter of 'sins' (plural) of which he may be guilty, but his *sin* (singular) – the underlying condition (4b). It is the same problem that caused Isaiah to cry out with despair when he found himself in the presence of the holy One,[127] and made Peter beg that Jesus might depart from him.[128] It is not merely the problem of having done unclean things, but of being an unclean man. Joshua stands before the angel of the LORD turned inside out, with what he really is on full display, covered with shame and condemned in the court of heaven. Satan, the accuser, does not even need to present the case against him: the *filthy clothes* Joshua wears do it for him. There is surely no hope for this man, or for those he represents.

So there is the problem. How can a sinful man like Joshua be acceptable to God? How can anything he does be acceptable, or advance God's purposes? And likewise for the community he leads. In particular, how can this community rebuild the temple, or Joshua

---

[124] Lev. 21.
[125] It is noteworthy, in this respect, that the ritual prescribed in the law of Moses for the installation of priests begins with the candidate being brought to the door of the tabernacle and washed with water (Exod. 29:4; 40:12; cf. Lev. 8:6; Ps. 51:2, 7). Thereafter they had to wash their hands and feet at the laver every time they came to minister at the altar or enter the tabernacle. Cf. Kline 1993, p. 11.
[126] Exod. 28:36.
[127] Is. 6:7.
[128] Luke 5:8.

officiate in it? After the strongly positive message of the previous three visions, we seem suddenly to have reached an impasse.

But now something totally unexpected happens.

b. An astonishing reversal (3:2–7)

The LORD declares that Joshua is a saved man, *a burning stick snatched from the fire* (2b), and that he simply will not allow any charge Satan brings against him to stand. The angel of the LORD responds by ordering that his *filthy* garments be taken off, and that he be reclothed at once with *rich* ones (4). Zechariah (who himself acts with sudden boldness at this point) orders that he be given a clean turban as well, and it is done (5). So in seconds his investiture is complete.[129] And then the charge is given by the angel of the LORD, speaking in God's name. Joshua is told that if he faithfully discharges the duties of his office[130] he will have charge of God's courts (in the temple), and be given *a place among those standing here* (7). Precisely what this means is not clear. It may be a promise that Joshua will have the privilege of entering the immediate presence of God in the most holy place of the temple – an honour equal to that of the angels who stand in God's presence in heaven. Or it may refer to a heavenly reward he will receive when his ministry on earth is done. What is beyond doubt is that, far from being condemned and disqualified, Joshua has effectively been appointed (or reappointed) as high priest to serve in the temple that will shortly be completed. The essence of the matter is captured in the pronouncement of verse 4: *See, I have taken away your sin.*

This is good news indeed for Joshua. What better news could any man hear?[131] But there is a question hanging in the air that demands, surely, to be answered. If this is indeed a courtroom scene, what has happened to due process? What kind of judge is this, who on the one hand acknowledges the reality of Joshua's sin, and at the same time refuses to allow the case against him proceed? How can a man who ought to be condemned be summarily acquitted and appointed to high office? Either sheer arbitrariness, or wanton partiality is operating here (as when a corrupt judge dismisses

---

[129] Cf. Is. 61:10: 'he has clothed me with garments of salvation and arrayed me in a robe of righteousness'. The 'standing' of the angel of the LORD at the end of v. 5 is the positive counterpart of the *standing* Satan in v. 1. Satan stands to condemn; the angel of the LORD stands to justify.

[130] Cf. the similar conditional statement in 6:15b, and see my comments there.

[131] Cf. Is. 6:7b and 2 Sam. 12:13 (where David receives a similar absolution after his sin with Bathsheba).

charges against a personal friend) – or else there is another explanation.

Indeed, there is, and to find out what it is, all we need to do is read on.

c. The One who is to come (3:8–10)

In the closing verses of the chapter we are told that the explanation lies in something God will do in the future. Joshua and his associates are *men symbolic of things to come* – and especially of the fact that God will bring his *servant, the Branch* (8). Joshua's *associates* are presumably his fellow priests.[132] As we saw in the introduction, *the Branch* by this time has become a technical term for the Messiah, the ideal future king of David's line.[133]

This brings us to an astonishing promise, which bridges the gap between what Zechariah has just seen in the vision and the massive problem that faces the whole community in the real world. It is a promise that sums up the good news of the gospel in a single sentence: *I will remove the sin of this land in a single day* (9b). That is, what Zechariah has just seen done symbolically for Joshua the high priest will one day be done actually for the whole *land* (the entire community)[134] – in a single day, once and for all, when the Messiah comes. Furthermore, this promise is engraven on a stone, which is given to Joshua as a guarantee of its fulfilment. The exact nature of the stone is unclear, though the *seven eyes* (or 'facets')[135] suggest it is a gemstone, perhaps intended to be worn on the front of Joshua's turban as a constant reminder to him – as a wedding ring is worn on a bride's finger.[136] It was not the stone that was of prime significance, however, but the promise inscribed upon it. Every time Joshua and his associates entered the temple to engage in their priestly duties they would effectively be claiming this promise. So too, especially, would Joshua, when he entered the most Holy Place every year on the Day of Atonement with the blood of the sacrificial victim, to intercede for the people. One

---

[132] They are *seated* before Joshua (8), and are the earthly, human counterpart of the divine beings who are *standing* before the angel of the Lord in the heavenly court (4, 7).

[133] See the introduction, pp. 39–42.

[134] *The sin of this land* is metaphorical for *the sin of the people of this land*. In 13:2–3 the cleansing of the land itself is taken up as an issue in its own right, though there is still an intimate connection between land and people. See my comments there.

[135] See the NIV footnote.

[136] Note that it is *set in front of* Joshua (9); i.e. 'positioned over [his] forehead' (Kline 1993, p. 27). Cf. other 'promise-signs', such as the rainbow of Gen. 9:13–16, and the sign of circumcision in Gen. 17:1–14.

day, God would send his servant the Branch, and then the problem of uncleanness would be dealt with finally. It was the promise Joshua and those he served as high priest were to depend on utterly for their acceptance with God. As we have seen, the second part of the book is largely concerned with the fulfilment of this promise, from the coming of the ideal king in 9:9, to the opening of a fountain to cleanse the people of Jerusalem *from sin and impurity* in 13:1.

Chapter 3 ends with a miniature picture of paradise: *In that day each of you will invite his neighbour to sit under his vine and fig-tree* (10).[137] It is a picture of perfect peace and abundant provision – blessings too good to keep to oneself, that can be fully enjoyed only by being shared. Chapter 14 presents the same basic vision of paradise restored in terms of pilgrimage and worship – people of *all the nations* coming to Jerusalem to worship the King, the God of Israel, and to join in the celebration of the Feast of Tabernacles – the last great 'harvest-home' festival (Zech. 14:16).[138]

In summary, then, the message of this fourth vision turns on two key figures: Joshua the high priest, the spiritual leader of the community – chosen, called to priestly service, but unclean – and the coming one, the Branch, through whom that uncleanness is dealt with finally, in a single day. It is a vision about the problem of sin in the life of God's people, and God's way of dealing with it. The solution is shown to be symbolized in the sacrificial, intercessory ministry of the priests (and especially the high priests) under the old covenant, but realized only in the person and ministry of the Messiah, the perfect servant of God. Joshua had the promise of his coming, and of the *day* when he would deal with sin; we have the fulfilment of it in the cross of Jesus Christ. His cry 'It is finished!', uttered with his dying breath, was the triumphant announcement that the long-waited 'day' had finally come, and that the promised cleansing had been realized.

What does this mean for us, who are called to participate in the work of God's kingdom now? First, it means that we don't have to pretend. We are indeed sinners, unclean and unfit to serve God. Indeed, facing this truth is the first step towards cleansing and wholeness. Second, it means that we don't have to try to defend

[137] Cf. Mic. 4:4. The imagery is drawn from the idyllic description of the prosperity Israel experienced in the days of Solomon (1 Kgs. 4:25 [MT 5:5]).

[138] The Feast of Tabernacles was a joyful autumn festival, lasting seven days, and celebrating the end of the agricultural year, when the produce of the wheat and grape harvests had been gathered in (Deut. 16:13–17). At the same time, it recalled the very different circumstances of Israel's ancestors, who dwelt in temporary shelters (booths) in the wilderness, on the way to this land of plenty (Lev. 23:43). See 14:16 and my comments there.

ourselves, by explaining or excusing ourselves, or trying to shift the blame to others. Joshua is silent throughout this vision. There is nothing he can say in his own defence: he is guilty as charged. The accusation Satan levels at him is true; he is not righteous, and neither are we. But finally, and this is the heart of the matter – neither are we condemned! For everything necessary for us to be accepted by God, and to be able to serve him, has already been done for us, once and for all – on a single day – at the cross, when Jesus died in our place. It was there that due process was observed and our sin was dealt with, with the seriousness that it deserved. By that one, final and perfect sacrifice, we have been put beyond the power of Satan's accusations, and of God's own wrath against us, forever. Indeed, the only One who has the right to condemn us, now intercedes for us in heaven.[139]

This great good news has perhaps never been better expressed (outside the Bible itself) than in the following lines:

> When Satan tempts me to despair,
> And tells me of the guilt within,
> Upward I look, and see Him there
> Who made an end of all my sin.
>
> Because the sinless Saviour died,
> My sinful soul is counted free;
> For God, the Just, is satisfied,
> To look on Him and pardon me.[140]

It is a truth we must grasp firmly and learn to take our stand on if we are to rise up and serve God as we should.

6. Vision 5: The gold lampstand and the two olive trees (4:1–14)

This vision begins somewhat unexpectedly, with the interpreting angel awakening Zechariah from sleep (1). It is the only vision introduced in this way. While all the visions were seen during the night (1:8), they were not (or at least, not all) seen simply in the form of dreams. The 'waking' associated with this fifth vision may be an indication of its special significance. Certainly it is the one in which the great matter in hand – the rebuilding of the temple – features most prominently.

Zechariah sees a *gold lampstand* with *seven lights* on it (2).

---

[139] Rom. 8:33–34; 1 John 1:8 – 2:2.
[140] From the hymn by Charitie L. de Chenez (1841–1923), written in 1863.

Immediately the lampstand that Moses was commanded to make for the tabernacle comes to mind. It was made of pure gold, and had seven branches, three on either side of the main upright stem, each supporting a small oil lamp.[141] Solomon's temple had ten such lamps, five on each side of the holy place – the larger of the two inner rooms.[142] Nothing more is heard of these ten lamps; however, in the rebuilt temple of the period after the exile, they appear to have been replaced by just one again.[143] Each of the lights was trimmed daily, using specially prepared olive oil, so that the seven-branched lamp was kept burning continually as a sign of the LORD's constant presence.[144] It is natural that we should think of this lamp here in the context of temple reconstruction. However, the lamp Zechariah sees seems to be of a rather different kind. It has a *bowl* at the top from which oil flows continually, via seven *channels*, to the *seven lights* arranged around and slightly below it – probably in a circle (3). Beside the lamp Zechariah sees two *olive trees*, one on either side, with two *branches* from which *golden oil* is poured – presumably into the bowl at the top of the lampstand (3, 11–12).[145]

Zechariah is naturally curious about the significance of this unusual lamp, and asks (three times) for explanations (4, 11, 12). When he says *what are these* (plural), in verse 4, he may mean the two olive trees, since he repeats the question, specifically naming them in verse 12. Or possibly, he may have in mind (as well) the *seven lights*, because the angel appears to know he wants to know about them and gives him an explanation of them in verse 10b. But first he is told what the vision as a whole means. It contains, in symbolic form, a message – a *word of the LORD* – for Zerubbabel, which the angel speaks to Zechariah in verses 6–7. This is immediately followed by a second message – another *word of the LORD* – which comes directly to Zechariah in verses 8–10a. Both messages concern Zerubbabel, and taken together they say two basic things: first, Zerubbabel will be empowered by the Spirit of the LORD (6), and he will succeed in bringing the work of rebuilding the temple to completion (7–10). Some have seen the *mighty mountain* that will be levelled in verse 7 as the huge pile of rubble remaining from the destruction of the previous temple.[146] More likely it represents any and every difficulty, however great, that Zerubbabel may

---

[141] Known in Hebrew as the *mᵉnôrâ*. See Exod. 25:31–40.

[142] 1 Kgs. 7:49.

[143] 1 Maccabees 1:21; cf. Baldwin 1972, p. 118.

[144] Lev. 24:1–4.

[145] The *golden oil* (NIV) is literally just 'gold', but this almost certainly refers to the golden colour of the pure olive oil.

[146] E.g. Sweeney, p. 608.

encounter.[147] The *capstone* (literally 'head stone', 7) is the last stone – the stone that will complete the building. Zechariah is told that Zerubbabel will *bring out* the capstone (in ceremonial style), amid cries of *God bless it! God bless it!* by the people (7b). That is, they will invoke God's blessing on the completed temple, much as the crowds might cry 'God save the King' at a coronation.[148] So at the heart of this vision is a strong endorsement of Zerubbabel as the divinely chosen temple builder. As governor he no doubt had many other responsibilities as well, but for Zechariah none was as significant as this one: *The hands of Zerubbabel have laid the foundation of this temple; his hands will also complete it* (9a).[149] Indeed, the fulfilment of this word would be one of the clearest signs that Zechariah was a true prophet (8b).[150]

But this leaves a lot of fairly obvious questions still unanswered – which is why Zechariah continues to seek clarification: what is the meaning of the two olive trees, and of the two branches and golden pipes that pour out the golden oil (11–12)? And what are we to make of the lampstand itself, with its seven lights (2–4)? Let us think about the lampstand first. It can hardly represent Zerubbabel, as that would leave us with a problem about the identity of the two olive trees. (We shall return to this shortly.) Nor, given its distinctive design, can it simply represent the temple lampstand, or the temple as a whole. Furthermore, in spite of the fact that its *seven lights* are the seven *eyes of the* LORD, *which range throughout the earth* (2, 10b) the lamp as a whole cannot represent God, since it is clearly dependent on outside resources (the oil from the two olive trees). We are therefore driven to the conclusion that the lampstand represents the community – the people who are involved with Zerubbabel in the work of rebuilding the temple. It is a community 'alight' with the presence of the all-seeing, all-knowing God, who

---

[147] Cf. Is. 40:4; Matt. 21:21; Mark 11:23.

[148] See, e.g., 1 Kgs. 1:39. According to v. 10 they will rejoice when they see the *plumb-line* in the hand of Zerubbabel (NIV). But this translation is unlikely to be correct. What is in his hand is not 'the plumb-line' (*ha'ᵃnāk*; cf. Amos 7:7), but 'the tin stone' (*hā'eḇen habbᵉḏîl*) or 'the stone of separation' (since *bᵉḏîl* is from the root *bdl*, to 'separate'). The most likely translation is the one provided by the JB, 'the chosen stone', the same stone as in the previous verse. 'The cause of rejoicing, therefore [in both v. 7 and v. 10], is the placing of this last ceremonial stone, the crown of all their work, on the height of the temple walls by Zerubbabel' (Baldwin 1972, p. 123).

[149] Cf. Ezra 5:16, where (in a letter to Darius) Sheshbazzar is said to have laid the foundation. It appears that Sheshbazzar was given the credit for the project in his official capacity as the governor at the time, while Zerubbabel was the person who took the lead in the actual execution of it at the start. See the discussion of this issue in the introduction, pp. 39–42, especially note 78.

[150] Cf. Zech. 2:9, 11, and my comments on those verses.

dwells in their midst.[151] At one level, visions four and five are about
the two leaders of the community, Joshua and Zerubbabel. But at
another level they are about broader, deeper questions that have to
do with the community as a whole and its relationship with God.
Vision four was about how God intended to deal with the sin
(uncleanness) of his people. This one is about how God will sustain
the life of the community while it does the work he has given it to
do. For it is a very small, fragile community, in a largely hostile
environment. How will it be sustained? How will the 'lamp' be kept
burning? This brings us back again to verse 6, which gives the
answer in one unforgettable sentence: *'Not by might nor by power,
but by my Spirit,' says the LORD Almighty*. God will sustain the life
of the community by his Spirit.

There are two ways, at least, in which we can see this in
operation in the situation described by the vision. First, there are
the two leaders represented by the two olive trees to the right and
left of the lampstand. Zechariah is told that *These are the two who
are anointed to serve the Lord of all the earth* (14). Given all that
has gone before, they must be Joshua and Zerubbabel. They are
literally 'sons of oil'. As servants of God they are accountable to
him and draw their own authority and strength from him. But as
'olive trees' in this vision, they are also the source of the oil that
fuels the lamp. That is, they are one very important means by
which God nourishes and strengthens the community. There is no
explicit use of the language of 'anointing' here (despite the NIV
translation),[152] but the conjunction of designated leaders, oil and
the Spirit, makes an allusion to it transparent; and anointing – as we
know from elsewhere in the Old Testament – has to do with two
things: appointment and empowerment. So, for example (and
classically), when Saul, Israel's first king, is rejected by God,
Samuel is despatched to anoint David as his successor.[153] That
anointing, 'in the presence of his brothers', marked him as the
one chosen by God to be king.[154] It was confirmed later by a
more public anointing when he was officially installed in office.[155]
But it was followed immediately by the Spirit of the LORD coming
on David in power, 'from that day' forward, to equip him for the
work he was to do.[156] In a similar way here, Joshua and Zerubbabel
are two anointed leaders, called by God and empowered by his

[151] Cf. the seven 'golden lampstand' communities (churches) of Rev. 1:12 – 3:22.
[152] I.e. the verb *māšaḥ* (to anoint), or the noun *māšîaḥ*, 'anointed one, messiah'.
[153] 1 Sam. 16:1.
[154] 1 Sam. 16:13.
[155] 2 Sam. 2:4.
[156] 1 Sam. 16:13.

Spirit.[157] As such they are one means by which the Spirit is already at work in the community. The second is not so obvious from the vision itself, but emerges clearly from the broader context. As we saw from the way the book starts, Zechariah associates his own ministry closely with that of the 'earlier prophets' (1:4; cf. 7:7). But the messages of these prophets were words 'that the LORD Almighty had sent by his Spirit' (7:12). So too, we are clearly meant to infer, were the words of Zechariah himself (and those of Haggai). The preaching of these prophets was another important means by which the Spirit of God was at work sustaining the life of the community.

But here we must be careful to attend to the text clearly. For it does not say, 'by my Spirit-anointed leaders', or 'by the Spirit-inspired preaching of my prophets', but simply *by my Spirit* (6). The distinction – and it is an extremely important one for us to grasp – is between the means God uses, and God himself. Zechariah is a leader raised up by God, but Zechariah is not God. The eight visions to which this one belongs are *the word of the LORD* that came to Zechariah (1:7), but these eight visions are not God. The Spirit of God, however, *is* God. It is vital that we always distinguish clearly between God himself and the instruments he uses. Otherwise we shall fall into subtle forms of idolatry, and even cultism. In the former the Bible is treated as God, and knowledge of the Bible becomes an end in itself (and a cause of pride) rather than knowledge of (relationship with) God himself. In the latter, leaders are treated as God; that is, they are regarded as having infallible knowledge, and therefore absolute authority over the beliefs and behaviour of their followers. It is rare for such distortions of true religion to occur in full-blown form; this happens only in the most extreme sects and cults. But tendencies in these directions are quite common, and are always dangerous. Zerubbabel and the whole community he led had to know that they needed God if they were to do his work in his way. The resource for doing the work of the kingdom of God is the Spirit of God.

The same principle is established, in the New Testament, at the very beginning of the church's life and mission. Jesus personally chose the men who were to lead the Christian movement after his return to heaven, and spent a great deal of time training and teaching them. They were God-appointed leaders, who already had the word of God (the gospel). Surely they had all the authority and resources they needed. But no – Jesus told them to wait for something: 'you

---

[157] See the discussion of the 'messianic' significance of this passage in the introduction, pp. 39–42.

will receive power when the Holy Spirit comes on you'.[158] And so they gave themselves to prayer until the promised gift was received on the day of Pentecost.[159] The result was a powerful proclamation of the gospel and the launching of the worldwide mission of the church. What is often unnoticed, however, is that in Acts chapter 4, something very similar happens again – to the same (if somewhat enlarged) group of people. In a context of intensifying persecution Peter and John and the other believers gather to pray. Again they are filled with the Holy Spirit and speak the word of God boldly, and the work of evangelism and church building moves forward once more.[160] In other words, while the day of Pentecost was a unique moment in the history of the church, it was the beginning of something that continued, and it established a principle that was to undergird the whole work of the kingdom of God in the future: the church would be built and the world evangelized as the gospel was preached in the power of the Holy Spirit. Believers needed to be filled with the Spirit of God in order to do the work of God. That is why Paul himself – an apostle appointed by God, and a man who knew the gospel if anyone did – writes to the Ephesian Christians, 'Pray also for me, that whenever I open my mouth, words may be given me so that I will fearlessly make known the mystery of the gospel ... Pray that I may declare it fearlessly, as I should.'[161] He is asking them to pray that God will give him, again and again, the same fearlessness (boldness) that was given to the first, Spirit-filled believers in Jerusalem in Acts 4.[162]

Why, though, should Zerubbabel in particular be given this word about the Spirit? He was not called to proclamation, but to building in a quite literal sense. The first, and most obvious, reason is that he was engaged in the work of the kingdom of God, and empowerment by the Spirit is essential for doing the work of the kingdom of God, whatever form it may take at a particular time. But there is another possible reason, especially in view of the way Zerubbabel is presented to us as a leader. In Haggai we are told four times that Zerubbabel was the governor.[163] In Zechariah he is the temple builder, and is presented as the driving force behind the whole temple-building project from beginning to end (4:9). In other

---

[158] Acts 1:8.
[159] Acts 1:12–14; 2:1.
[160] Acts 4:23–33; 5:12–16.
[161] Eph. 6:19–20.
[162] He uses the same word *parrēsia* as is used of Peter's preaching in Acts 2:29, and of Peter and John and the other believers in Acts 4:29, 31. Note how Paul has just referred to the Word of God as the 'sword of the Spirit' (Eph. 6:17).
[163] Hag. 1:1, 14; 2:2, 21.

words, he was an extremely capable man. The other outstanding leaders of the Persian period, Ezra and Nehemiah, were also very able people. But they are both shown as, above all, men of deep dependence on God. Perhaps the most impressive thing about them is their genuine piety, expressed especially in prayer.[164] In contrast, all we know for sure about Zerubbabel is his impressive leadership ability. And it is to him in particular that this word is given: *'Not by might nor by power* (i.e. not by merely human resources, however impressive) *but by my Spirit,' says the* LORD *Almighty.*

It remains only to underline one thing before we pass on to the next vision. I have already stressed it in the introduction, so there is no need to dwell on it again here.[165] But it is this: this fifth vision also contains an important message for the whole community. They must not despise *the day of small things* (10), for the kingdom of God can never be anything other than an overwhelmingly great reality, and participation in it by obedient service to God is always the most wonderful privilege, however apparently insignificant the particular task of the moment may appear to be. This vision not only reminds them of the immense significance of what they are called to do, but of the great resources that have been provided to enable them to do it: leaders raised up and empowered by God, the word of God preached to them by his prophets, and – above all – God's personal presence among them by his Spirit.[166] God, who had called them to rebuild the temple, would surely sustain them as they did it. He would keep the lamp burning.

7. Vision 6: The flying scroll (5:1–4)

With this vision and the next we come to another distinct phase in the progression of the eight-vision sequence. In the previous two, as we have seen, the main focus has been on the two leaders, Joshua and Zerubbabel. Now the primary focus shifts back again to the whole community, and from the task of rebuilding the temple to matters of general lifestyle. The lamp will not go out, but will it burn brightly and clearly? Or will it give off smoke and smells caused by the presence of contaminants, things offensive to God and incompatible with his holiness? The issue is not the same as in Vision 4. There it was sinfulness (uncleanness) as a general human

---

[164] Note the great prayers of Ezra and Nehemiah in Ezra 9 and Neh. 1:4–10. Cf. too, Daniel, who lived on into the early Persian period (Dan. 6:10; 9:3–19).
[165] See the introduction, p. 37.
[166] Cf. the promise of Jesus in the Great Commission, 'Surely I am with you always' (Matt. 28:20), a promise that was made effective through the subsequent sending of the Holy Spirit (John 14:6–18; 16:5–11).

condition that affects all that people do and creates a potential barrier to them having any relationship with God or serving him acceptably. The answer was a gracious, sovereign act of God to remove the uncleanness and replace it with righteousness (i.e. a right standing with God) – purely as a gift: 'See, I have taken away your sin, and I will put rich garments on you' (3:4). It was good news for sinners who have repented and want to serve God. Here, however, the issue is *un*repentance – the continued presence in the community of people who persist in conduct offensive to God. His response to this problem, as we are about to see, is eradication (Vision 6) and removal (Vision 7).

The sixth vision opens with Zechariah seeing *a flying scroll, thirty feet long and fifteen feet wide* (1–2), which, he is told, is *the curse that is going out over the whole land* (3).[167] Verse 4 is a little more precise: it doesn't just 'go' out; it is 'sent' out, by God – and for a very specific purpose: *according to what it says on one side, every thief will be banished, and according to what it says on the other, everyone who swears falsely will be banished* (3). This scroll apparently had writing on both sides, like the scroll Ezekiel saw when he was called to announce God's impending judgment on Jerusalem.[168] In the case of Zechariah's scroll the writing prescribed the appropriate punishment for thieves and perjurers: banishment from the community.[169] So totally were they to be removed that no trace of them would remain. Even their houses would be utterly destroyed, both *timbers* and *stones* (4). It could be that death rather than banishment is what is on view[170] – as happened to Achan (a thief) in the time of Joshua[171] – but if so, this is hinted at rather than directly stated. The bottom line is that the scroll represents

---

[167] The Hebrew word *'ālâ*, translated here as *curse*, is actually quite a neutral term, meaning a solemnly sworn commitment to do something, usually in the context of a covenant. In many contexts it is translated simply as an 'oath' or 'sworn agreement' (e.g. Gen. 24:41; 26:28; Deut. 29:12 [MT 11]; 1 Kgs. 8:31 etc.) In others, however (as here), it has the decidedly negative sense of a *curse*, a sworn commitment to punish someone (e.g. Deut. 29:20 [MT 19], 21 [MT 20]; 30:7; Is. 24:6 etc.).

[168] Ezek. 2:9–10.

[169] The word translated *banished* in the NIV generally refers in the OT to being 'released' from an oath. This may be because an obligation entailed in the oath has been fulfilled (e.g. Gen. 24:8, 41), or because the person has been found not guilty of a crime, and is therefore 'released' from the punishment involved in not keeping the oath (e.g. Num. 5:19, 28; Judg. 15:3; Prov. 11:21 etc., where the same term is used in the MT) – a meaning entirely inappropriate in Zech. 5:3. The NIV translation suggests (correctly, I think) that nqh is used here with heavy irony: the thief or perjurer is 'released' from covenant obligation to the God of Israel by being expelled from his covenant community. Cf. the way excommunication is spoken of in 1 Cor. 5:4–5.

[170] The Hebrew verb nqh is sufficiently general to allow for either.

[171] Josh. 7; cf. Acts 5:1–11.

God's intention to root out, eradicate, such people from the community.

The fact that the scroll has writing on both sides, and the nature of the offences it is directed against, both suggest a strong connection with the law of Moses – especially the Ten Commandments.[172] So too does the fact that it is sent out by *the LORD Almighty*, the same God who gave Israel the law.[173] The Ten Commandments summarized Israel's covenant obligations to the LORD, Yahweh, who had delivered his people from slavery in Egypt.[174] They were written on two stone tablets, and spelled out the behaviour expected towards God himself (the first four commandments) and towards other people (the last six): the vertical and horizontal aspects of the covenant relationship.[175] The specific commandments relating to stealing and perjury (the seventh and ninth respectively) both deal primarily with duty to one's neighbour. Stealing deprives him of his property. Perjury (swearing falsely) has the potential to deprive him of much more, perhaps even his life, since it is particularly associated with the processes of a court: trial before a judge.[176] However if, in swearing to tell the truth, one has invoked the name of the LORD (Yahweh), as would presumably be normal in Israel, then perjury would also entail misusing his name, which is the third commandment.[177] So these two offences neatly encapsulate both aspects of covenant obligation, and involve deliberate violation of both. Stealing and perjury are both, by their very nature, deliberate. Furthermore the offenders on view here, literally 'the thief' and 'the false-swearer' (both with the definite article) are not people who have lapsed temporarily from an otherwise moral life, but people whose conduct is of such a settled and persistent kind that 'thief' and 'perjurer' properly express their basic character. The solemn message of this vision is that such people have no place in a community ruled by the LORD Almighty. He himself will root them out.

---

[172] According to Exod. 32:15 these too, at least in their rewritten form, were written 'on both sides [of the two stone tablets], front and back'. See Kline 1995, pp. 4–5.

[173] The LORD Almighty or Lord of Hosts (i.e. Lord of armies, the warrior God), is one of the titles for Yahweh, the God of Israel, in the OT. It is especially common in Isaiah, Jeremiah and Zechariah. It also occurs in certain parts of the psalter (e.g. Pss. 24, 46, 48, 69, 84).

[174] Exod. 20:2.

[175] Exod. 20:1–17; Deut. 5:6–21.

[176] See Deut. 17:8–13; cf. 1 Kgs. 21:8–15. The general principle expressed in the commandments also covers lesser offences such as 'spreading slander' against one's neighbour (Lev. 19:16), but that is not the primary meaning of the commandment, as the immediately preceding verses make clear (Lev. 19:12–15).

[177] Exod. 20:7.

So the basic significance of the scroll is clear. But two further aspects deserve brief comment. First, its size. It is big – much bigger than a normal scroll, such as a reader could easily pick up and put down.[178] It is much more like a huge billboard, confronting and uncompromising – and appropriately so, because the matter it deals with is weighty. Let persistent offenders beware, and also a community unaware or unconcerned about their presence within it![179] Finally, the scroll is *flying* (1), which suggests swiftness and imminence. It approaches like a bird of prey seeking its quarry, and there is no escape from it. It 'goes out' *over the whole land* (3),[180] and 'enters' houses (4). No area of life is beyond its reach; there is no place to hide from it. This is one of the most terrifying warning passages in the Old Testament.[181] There is no room for complacency. God's law cannot be disregarded with impunity. Repentance is an urgent matter!

Much more could be said, but since the next vision is closely related to this one I shall go on to that one now, and then make some summary reflections on both of them.

8. Vision 7: The woman in a basket (5:5–11)

Now Zechariah sees something else *appearing* (5).[182] It is a *measuring basket*, and Zechariah is told by the angel that it is (represents) *the iniquity of the people throughout the land* (6).[183] Then the cover is raised and Zechariah sees a woman sitting inside the basket, apparently with the upper part of her body now sticking out through the open lid (7)! The angel immediately announces, *This is wickedness*, pushes her back down into the basket, and clamps the lead cover shut (8). It is not entirely clear from this whether the angel means that the woman represents wickedness, or that the

---

[178] It is not certain whether or not the precise dimensions of the scroll (20 cubits by 10, NIV footnote) have any particular significance. Given the general 'temple' context of Zechariah's visions, however, it is perhaps noteworthy that these were the dimensions of the porch of Solomon's temple (1 Kgs. 6:3). It was probably from here that the law was read to the people every seventh year at the Feast of Tabernacles (Deut. 31:9–11; 2 Kgs. 23:2). See the discussions in Baldwin 1972, p. 126; and Sweeney, pp. 615–616.

[179] Cf. Rev. 2:14–16.

[180] I.e. the entire province of Yehud. Cf. *this land* in 3:9.

[181] Cf. the equally chilling warning passages in the NT, especially Heb. 6:4–8; 10:26–31.

[182] Literally, it 'goes forth' (Heb. *yṣ'*), like the scroll of v. 3.

[183] The word translated *the iniquity of the people* (one word in the MT) is literally 'their eye' (*'ênām*), but this makes no sense. A very minor emendation of the Hebrew produces *'ᵃwônām* (their iniquity), which is supported by the LXX and the Syriac. The text has apparently suffered a minor corruption in transmission.

whole thing – the basket with the woman inside it – represents wickedness.[184] What follows, however, seems to indicate the latter. For now Zechariah sees *two women, with the wind in their wings*.[185] Like the scroll of the previous vision they are possessed of the power of flight. As Zechariah watches, they lift the basket up *between heaven and earth* (9), putting it temporarily into limbo, with no obvious place to belong. When Zechariah (naturally enough) asks where they are taking it (10), the angel gives an answer in which every word is pregnant with significance: they are taking it *to the country of Babylonia to build a house for it*, and *when it* (the house) is ready, they will *set* the basket *there in its place* (11). It is an intriguing vision, somewhat bizarre, but not confusing if we attend to its details carefully.

The *measuring basket* Zechariah sees is, in Hebrew, an 'ephah', a container used for measuring grain.[186] An ephah of grain was equivalent to approximately 36.5 litres or 5 gallons.[187] No normal-sized woman could sit in an ephah, even if (for some unaccountable reason) someone wanted to put her there.[188] So the image of the woman in the ephah is doubly grotesque – an absurd distortion of reality, as evil always is of course. But there is another significance to the ephah much more recognizable as belonging to the real world in which both we and Zechariah live. For the ephah represents the world of trade, and this grotesque ephah the wickedness all too often associated with it. A particularly striking example of this occurs in the book of Amos. In a typically passionate denunciation of injustice, Amos speaks about those who attend the religious festivals like good, observant Israelites, but whose minds are really elsewhere. They say:

---

[184] The pronoun *this* (zō't) is feminine, as is the word *wickedness* (rišʿâ), but this does not settle the matter, as the feminine pronoun is commonly used in Hebrew to refer in summary fashion to a whole state of affairs that has just been described.

[185] If a woman is associated with wickedness in the first half of the vision, two women are God's agents for removing it in the second. (Cf. how the woman appears as both the temptress [ch. 7] and the epitome of wisdom [ch. 31] in the book of Proverbs.) However, the character of the two women who remove the ephah here is ambiguous. What they do is good, but Kline (1995) thinks that they themselves are evil on the grounds that they have wings *like those of a stork* (9), an unclean bird (Lev. 11:19; Deut. 14:18). 'Unclean agents are used by the judge of Israel to remove the defilement from his holy land to unclean Babylon' (p. 14). It should be noted, however, that the eagle (also an unclean bird, Lev. 11:13) is viewed positively in other contexts (e.g. Deut. 32:11; Is. 40:31).

[186] Lev. 19:36; Ruth 2:17; 1 Sam. 1:24. Actually the word 'ēpâ is a quantity term, like 'litre' or 'gallon', but is here used of the container used for measuring the quantity.

[187] See any standard Bible dictionary or encyclopedia.

[188] Note that she has to be *pushed* back into it in v. 8.

'When will the New Moon be over
   that we may sell grain,
and the Sabbath be ended
   that we may market wheat?' –
  skimping the measure,
    boosting the price
    and cheating with dishonest scales,
  buying the poor with silver
    and the needy for a pair of sandals,
    selling even the sweepings with the wheat.[189]

'Skimping the measure, / boosting the price' is literally 'making the ephah small, and making the shekel great'. Such sharp practices are not only hypocritical; they are unjust. They defraud the customer of his rights, cheat him of what is his (in this case food, an essential commodity), and the poor often suffer the most. Here is one of the most obvious connections with the previous vision, for the dishonest businessman is a thief, exactly the kind of person God has sworn to banish from among his people (5:3–4). And the *wickedness* he exemplifies is precisely the kind of evil that aroused God's anger against a former generation (1:2–4). It cannot therefore be allowed to persist in this one, for its continued presence puts the whole community in jeopardy.[190] Hence the removal operation that follows.

Here we must attend again to that pregnant, final verse. The ephah is taken to *the country of Babylonia* (literally 'the land of Shinar', 11), which has the same symbolic significance here as in 2:7. It is the negative counterpart of Jerusalem, the kingdom of man versus the kingdom of God – the human race organized in defiance of God. No place better symbolizes that than 'the land of Shinar', the place where the tower of Babel was built at the beginning.[191] No wonder, then, that this vision concludes with the ephah being *set there in its place*. That is where it truly belongs. But there is more to this than first meets the eye, for the ephah is not just relocated to Babylon, but a *house* is built for it there, and the word *place* is literally a 'stand' or 'pedestal'. In other words, it appears that the ephah is not simply placed in the *house*, but set up on a base there, like an idol! So what happens here is the (ironic) opposite of what happens in the opening three visions. There a 'house' (same word) is built for the LORD (Yahweh) in Jerusalem; here another house (temple) is built for the ephah (wickedness) in Babylon. The

[189] Amos 8:5–6.
[190] Cf. 1 Cor. 5:6–8; Rev. 2:14–16.
[191] Gen. 11:1. See my comments on 2:7–9.

message is clear: not only is wickedness incompatible with allegiance to Yahweh; it is an alternative, false god, that (in the end) completely dominates the lives of those who become involved with it. Those who persist in wickedness (in this case ill-gotten wealth) become enslaved to it. It becomes their god, and the pursuit of it their religion. As Jesus put it, 'You cannot serve both God and Money.'[192]

What can we now say, by way of summary, about this vision and the previous one, taken together? First, it is clear that they are closely related,[193] and together represent a significant change from what has gone before. After the focus in Visions 1–5 on the temple, those who build it and those who officiate in it, the focus shifts here to the home, the street and the marketplace. This is not for one moment to undercut the importance of the temple. It symbolized God's kingship and presence, and the place where his people had privileged access to him in prayer and worship. But temples have their dangers. People can forget the reality they symbolize and begin to treat them as ends in themselves. That is exactly what had happened in the days before the exile. People had come to think of the temple as a kind of talisman, a guarantee of divine favour. As long as they did 'church' right God would be on their side, and all would be well with them.[194] But these visions sound a sharp warning against falling into that mistake again. Having God in your midst has implications for the whole of life, not just what you do in 'church'. God is against those who do evil, whoever and wherever they are. A temple offers no protection at all to wilful sinners; nor does membership of a religious community. Israel needed to hear that message again and again, and so does the church today. It is a message written indelibly into the history of the church at its very beginning in the story of Ananias and Sapphira,[195] and we would do well to remember it.

The second thing to note here is the way that in these two visions, we begin to see more clearly the overall design of the vision sequence as a whole. We have already observed how Visions 4 and 5 (about Joshua and Zerubbabel) are in effect a central pivot. We have seen how what follows this pivot balances, by way of contrast, what precedes it. It remains only to see how Vision 8, to which we now turn, completes this pattern.

---

[192] Matt. 6:24; Luke 16:13; cf. 1 Tim. 6:6–10.
[193] Kline (1995, p. 3) regards them as one vision, giving us seven in all rather than eight, with the fourth (ch. 3) as the central one.
[194] See especially Jer. 7:1–15.
[195] Acts 5:1–11.

9. Vision 8: Four chariots (6:1–8)

Now there's another complete change, setting this final vision off as the climax. Zechariah sees *four chariots coming out from between two mountains – mountains of bronze!* (1). Chariots would have occasioned no surprise to anyone who lived in Zechariah's world. They had been the standard military equipment of conquerors ever since the Philistines introduced them to Palestine in the twelfth century BC.[196] Mountains too would have been familiar in the rugged terrain of Jerusalem and its environs. But there is something decidedly different about these mountains and these chariots.

Let us take the chariots first. There were *four* of them – a number we have already met several times in Zechariah. There were four groups of horsemen in the first vision (1:8), 'four horns' and 'four craftsmen' in the second (1:18, 20), and 'four winds of heaven' in the third (2:6). So the symbolism of the number is well established, and we can take it that these *four* chariots are representative of a much larger military force – one, in fact, that operates everywhere, throughout the whole earth, as we are about to see.

But what are we to make of the two *mountains of bronze*? In the context of these visions, where temple building plays such a central role, they remind us of the two huge bronze pillars which had stood on either side of the entrance to the great temple built by Solomon, each 8.1 metres high and 5.4 metres in circumference.[197] Solomon called them Jakin (he establishes) and Boaz (in him is strength).[198] They represented the stability and power of God's kingship, for the temple was his house, the supreme place of his rule on earth. Zerubbabel's temple had no such pillars; they were an extravagance which the current economic situation did not permit. To anyone familiar with Israel's past, however, the two bronze mountains would have had clear temple and (therefore) kingdom of God significance. As mountains are greater than pillars, however, what is depicted here transcends what was symbolized in the temples of Solomon and Zerubbabel. The chariots coming out from between the two mountains represent not the mere presence of God in his earthly temple, but his going forth from his heavenly temple to wage war. What is seen here is what was anticipated in 2:13: 'Be still before the LORD, all mankind, because he has roused himself from his holy dwelling.'

---

[196] Judg. 1:19; 4:3, 13.
[197] Respectively 27 feet and 18 feet. See 1 Kgs. 7:13–22, including the NIV footnote to v. 15.
[198] 1 Kgs. 7:21; see the NIV footnote.

This is spelled out clearly in what follows. Zechariah is told that the four chariots are *the four spirits of heaven, going out from standing in the presence of the Lord of the whole world* (5). The word translated *spirits* is the Hebrew word *rûaḥ*, which has a wide range of meanings. 'Spirit', in the sense of the essential life or vitality of the person is one of them. The other main meanings are 'breath' and 'wind'. It has already occurred in the expression 'the four winds of heaven' in 2:6. The chariots are called *spirits* because of their swiftness (they go like the wind), but also because of their intimate connection with God. They go forth from his presence, with his power and authority.[199] Wherever they go his rule is experienced as a present, powerful reality. And because he is *the Lord of the whole world* they go everywhere – *throughout the earth* (7).

But here we meet a difficulty, because in verse 6 as we have it they go in only three directions. The chariots with the black horses go north; those with the white ones go west,[200] and those with the dappled horses go south. Only three points of the compass are represented, and only three colours (of horses) instead of the four of verses 2 and 3. Furthermore, verse 6 opens (in Hebrew) with a connecting word which normally occurs only in mid-sentence.[201] All this taken together seems to indicate that the opening part of verse 6 has been accidentally lost in transmission, and that in the original form of the text all four points of the compass were covered. In any case, verse 7 makes it clear that the chariots went everywhere, to enforce God's kingship in every place.[202]

One place, however, is singled out for special mention. It is what is called in verse 8 *the north country*. There is a good reason for this, which has to do with the geography and history of Palestine, where Israel had lived since the time of the conquest under Joshua. This strategic land bridge was bounded by the Mediterranean Sea on the west and the desert on the east, so the only ways an invading army could approach it were from the north or the south. But by the time Israel was established there, Egypt, to the south, was well past its prime and no longer in a position to engage in major military campaigns beyond its borders. So the enemies that threatened Israel

---

[199] *Standing* (5) is the posture of servants.

[200] Reading *'el 'aḥᵃrêhem* (to after them) as *'el 'ereṣ hayyām* (to the land of the sea; i.e. the west), as suggested by *BHS* and adopted by the NIV. Probably *'el 'ereṣ hayyām* was changed to *'el 'aḥᵃrêhem* after the first part of v. 6 was lost in order to make sense of what was left, by having the chariots leave in only two directions (north and south). Given the desert to the east and the sea to the west, these are the only two directions in which chariots could leave Palestine, even if they were going everywhere.

[201] The relative word *'ᵃšer*.

[202] Cf. Baldwin 1972, p. 131.

always approached from the north, especially the Assyrians and Babylonians, but also troublesome neighbours such as the Syrians. In the earlier prophets, especially Jeremiah, 'the north' was symbolically the land of the enemy – the place in which hostility to Israel and the God of Israel was concentrated.[203]

Here at the end of Zechariah's last vision the chariots (i.e. 'spirits') that have gone out from the presence of the LORD (5) give his 'Spirit' (same word) *rest* in the country of the north (8). That is, they pacify the north by conquering it and establishing God's rule there. This is a rest of completion, like the rest of the seventh day after the work of creation.[204] But here what is completed is the work of judgment. It is the opposite of the 'rest' which the horsemen of the first vision had found (1:11). That was the 'rest' of a world complacent in its disregard of God. This is the 'rest' of God himself, who has completely subdued the rebellious world and established his rightful dominion over it. The conclusion of this last vision anticipates the conclusion of the whole book, the day when 'the LORD will be king over the whole earth', and 'his name the only name' (14:9).

Zerubbabel and the people of Jerusalem have a specific job to do: to rebuild the temple. They have to do it in the context of a pagan world that seems invincible, and which threatens and opposes them at every turn. The good news of this last vision is that they do not have to be intimidated by that world. God is sovereign over it and he will judge it. Indeed, as we saw especially in Vision 2, there is an important sense in which they participate in his victory over the world even now by simply doing what God has called them to do. It opens their eyes to see that the hills are full of horses and chariots of fire all around them.[205]

Now that we have looked at each of the eight visions in turn it is important to pause and remind ourselves of their unity. Collectively, they are 'the word of the LORD' that came to Zechariah on the twenty-fourth day of the eleventh month of the second year of Darius I (1:7). They are eight things, but they are also one thing, one 'word' or revelation. We have already noted the centrality of Visions 4 and 5, and many points of connection and contrast between the first three and the last three. Our findings can now be summarized as follows:[206]

---

[203] Jer. 1:13–14; 4:6 etc. Cf. Is. 14:31; Ezek. 1:4. In Zech. 2:6 exiles still living in Babylon are told to flee from 'the land of the north'.
[204] Gen. 2:2.
[205] 2 Kgs. 6:17.
[206] I am indebted for this diagram to Michael Stead, one of my former students.

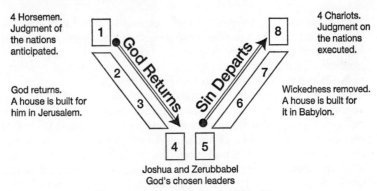

4 Horsemen. Judgment of the nations anticipated.

God returns. A house is built for him in Jerusalem.

4 Chariots. Judgment on the nations executed.

Wickedness removed. A house is built for it in Babylon.

Joshua and Zerubbabel
God's chosen leaders

The pattern of Zechariah's night visions

As the visions progress there is a movement towards the climax reached in Vision 8: the final manifestation of God's kingship in the judgment of the world.[207] The theme of the visions as a whole is the centrality of Jerusalem, the temple and the community for God's ultimate purposes for the world. He is already present among them, and through them his kingdom is even now breaking in. They are a lamp that will not go out, a sign of the coming kingdom of God.

The same message is found, transposed into a new key, in the Sermon on the Mount. The disciples gathered around Jesus were the nucleus of the new community (the church) he had come to build through his own living, dying and rising again.[208] 'You', he told them, 'are the light of the world ... A city on a hill...'[209] And that, as Jesus went on to show them, had huge lifestyle implications. That is always the case with the message of the kingdom of God. It is about God's big purposes for the world, and (if we understand it rightly) it has massive implications for how we live now.

10. The crowning of Joshua the high priest (6:9–15)

We have now come to a very significant point in our journey through the book, for this is the final passage in part 1. It begins with *the word of the LORD* coming to Zechariah again, as it had at the beginning of his night visions.[210] This time, however, he doesn't

[207] Kline (1996, pp. 20–21) shows how the theme of God's judgment of the rebellious world has surfaced repeatedly in the preceding visions.
[208] Matt. 16:18.
[209] Matt. 5:14.
[210] Cf. 1:7. The only other time this expression has occurred since 1:7 is at 4:8, in connection with Zerubbabel, the temple builder – an important point of connection with the present passage.

'see' something, but is told to 'do' something. He has had God's kingdom purposes revealed to him. Now he must act. He is a man under orders.[211]

He is told to take *silver and gold*[212] from three men who have recently arrived from Babylon (10). The fourth man, *Josiah son of Zephaniah*, may have been a smelter or craftsman, since Zechariah is told to go to his house (presumably with the silver and gold) after meeting the other three. It is unlikely that the silver and gold is simply the personal property of the new arrivals. More likely it is a gift from the Jewish community who are still living in exile in Babylon.[213] These men have come as their representatives.[214] Zechariah is told to take the silver and gold, *make a crown* with it, and *set it on the head of the high priest, Joshua* (11).[215] This is quite unexpected, since it was normally kings, not priests, who wore crowns,[216] and when Joshua was clothed in rich, priestly garments in the vision of chapter 3, a 'turban', not a crown, was placed on his head (3:5). So the meaning of the act is not self-evident; interpretation is required. In the visions it was an angel who played the role of interpreter. Here Zechariah himself is commanded to act as the interpreter by delivering an oracle as God's spokesman (12a).

The act is clearly symbolic, because after the oracle has been spoken, the crown is removed again (14a). It is not that Joshua has been installed in a new office, as would be the case at a real coronation, but that, with the royal crown on his head, he *represents* something – or rather some*one*. The essence of the oracle is that he *is* (i.e. represents) *the man whose name is the Branch* (12). Here the connections with the vision of chapter 3 are particularly strong. There Joshua and his fellow priests were told that they were 'men symbolic of things to come', especially of the fact that God was 'going to bring [his] servant, the Branch' (3:8). Joshua in particular symbolized, through the faithful exercise of his priestly ministry, the future priestly work of the Branch (the Messiah) in removing sin once and

---

[211] Cf. the very similar experience of Ezekiel after his inaugural vision (Ezek. 3:16–17).

[212] The Hebrew text has no object after the verb. NIV has supplied the words *silver and gold* from the parallel in v. 11, where what Zechariah was to take from the men is specified.

[213] Cf. Ezra 2, especially vv. 68–69.

[214] To take the gifts from them is to take it from *the exiles* (10).

[215] The word translated *crown* is plural in form, but is treated as a singular (e.g. it is used with a singular verb in v. 14). Either it is actually a singular noun that just happens to have a 'plural' ending (like *ḥokmôt*, 'wisdom', in Prov. 1:20), or the plural form is used because the crown is composite, as the two metals (silver and gold) suggest. Kline (1997, p. 5) suggests it was a two-tiered crown, with gold and silver circlets. Cf. Rev. 19:12.

[216] See 2 Sam. 12:30; Ps. 21:3 (MT 4); Song 3:11, where 'crown' is the same word as here in Zech. 6:11.

for all (3:9). Here, with a crown placed upon his head, he symbolizes the Branch (Messiah) in his future kingly work of temple-building:[217] *he will branch out from his place* [218] *and build the temple of the* LORD (12). And in order to drive the point home this is repeated, with emphasis on the 'he': *It is he who will build the temple of the* LORD (13a). But this presents us with something of a double conundrum, for in chapter 4 it was Zerubbabel who was named as temple-builder. So why is he absent here, and why is it Joshua rather than Zerubbabel who is crowned?

Let us take the puzzling absence of Zerubbabel first.[219] It is possible that he was quite literally absent from Jerusalem at this time. He may temporarily have 'returned to headquarters', so to speak, as Nehemiah did some eighty years later.[220] What is important for our purposes, however, is not the reason for his (possible) *physical* absence, but the significance of his *symbolic* absence. In the symbolic coronation Zechariah is told to perform, Zerubbabel fades into the background, and so does the temple he was commissioned to build. It is the coming one, the Branch, who now takes centre stage; and with him another temple comes into view – the future, glorious 'house of the LORD' of 14:20–21. It is *the man whose name is the Branch* (12), symbolized by the crowned high priest, who will

[217] Temple-building was an activity of kings in the ancient Near East. In Israel this was seen particularly in David, Solomon, and Cyrus the Persian, who was raised up by God for that purpose (2 Sam. 7:1–17; 1 Kgs. 5–8; Is. 44:24–28).

[218] The expression *from his place* (literally 'from underneath') is obscure, and perhaps deliberately so. The Messiah will not arise ('branch out') in a predictable way. His origins are mysterious; he will emerge from obscurity. Cf. the Servant of the Lord in Isaiah, who grows up 'like a root out of dry ground' (Is. 53:2).

[219] Wellhausen (p. 5392) proposed that it was Zerubbabel who originally figured in the passage, and that he was replaced by Joshua when hopes for a revival of the Davidic dynasty had faded (after Zerubbabel's death) – a view adopted by many subsequent scholars (see Baldwin 1972, p. 134, for references). But this is very unlikely to be correct, for three reasons. First, there is no hard evidence for it. Second, given what we now know about the conservative nature of scribal practices, it is very unlikely that such a change would have been made; and third, a coronation of Zerubbabel would have been viewed as politically seditious by the Persian authorities; it would have played right into the hands of those who were accusing the community of rebellion. In any case, it is a conjecture about the possible *origins* of the text, not an explanation of its *meaning*.

[220] Possibly to Susa in Persia, which was the imperial capital in the time of both Zerubbabel and Nehemiah. Neh. 13:6 simply says that Nehemiah 'returned to the king'. It was probably normal practice for governors to report to the king at certain intervals. In Nehemiah's case this appears to have marked the end of his first term in office, and his commissioning for a second term. Michael Stead, in an unpublished paper, has suggested that Zerubbabel's return was related to the hostile report that had been sent to Darius by Tattenai, the governor of Trans-Euphrates (Ezra 5:3–6). As governor of Yehud, Zerubbabel went to present the Jewish case. This is quite plausible in my judgment.

build *that* house – he and no other. In the crowning of Joshua the offices of priest and king merge in the person of the Messiah who is to come. Then there will no longer be two 'anointed ones' (as there were in 4:14), but only one: *he* [the Branch] *will be a priest upon his throne* (13a).[221] And so there will be *harmony between the two* (13b).[222]

With this the main symbolic act has been performed and its significance explained. But some other, lesser matters remain to be attended to before a full conclusion is reached. Zechariah is told that the crown is to be given to the men from whom the gold and silver was taken at the beginning,[223] and (eventually) to be placed in the soon-to-be completed temple as a *memorial* (14). This almost certainly means that it is to serve as a reminder of the symbolic act that has just been performed, but perhaps also as a reminder of the many exiles who (like these men) have contributed to the building project by their monetary gifts. So the crown will be a memorial of what has already taken place. But like the symbolic coronation in which it figured, it will also speak of what still lies in the future. Like the precious stone that was set before Joshua in 3:9, it has a promise attached to it: *Those who are far away will come and help to build the temple of the LORD* (15a). In view of what the symbolic act itself signified, this promise must refer to something far greater than anything that happened during the building of Zerubbabel's temple. Back in 2:11, with the final coming of the kingdom of God in view, the prophecy 'Many nations will be joined with the LORD in that day and will become my people' had been given. In effect, the promise attached to the crown here in chapter 6 restates that prophecy in terms of the Branch. *Those who are far away* are not just the scattered exiles of Israel, but people of all nations, who will come to be associated with the Branch in *his* work of building the new temple of God.[224] In other words, what happened when Zerubbabel built his temple will happen again, in a new and far greater way when the

---

[221] This is the natural sense of the Hebrew. An alternative translation, 'and there will be a priest by his throne' (implying a continued distinction between king and priest), has been proposed by several scholars, and has been adopted in some English versions (e.g. the RSV). Cf. the LXX, and see Baldwin 1972, p. 136, for references. But this requires the two occurrences of *'al kis'ô*, which occur in close succession, to be taken in two different senses. This is possible, but in my judgment unlikely. There is nothing in the syntax to indicate a change of subject.

[222] I.e. between the 'king' (symbolized by the crown) and the 'priest' (symbolized by Joshua, on whom the crown has been placed). There will be perfect harmony between them because they will be merged in one person, as they were in the person of Jesus Christ (Luke 1:32–33; Rev. 17:14; Heb. 9:11). Cf. Baldwin 1972, p. 137.

[223] There are some minor variations in the names in v. 14 as against v. 10, but clearly the same individuals are on view. See the NIV footnotes.

[224] Cf. Kline 1997, p. 20.

Branch (the Messiah) comes, and this (among other things) will show that Zechariah was a true prophet of God (15b; cf. 2:9, 11).

The closing sentence of the passage, and of the whole first part of the book is, at first sight, a rather disappointing anticlimax: 'This will happen *if you diligently obey the* LORD *your God*' (15b; my italics). Suddenly all the assurance and certainty of what has just been promised appears to be put in jeopardy by the condition now introduced. What was given with one hand now seems to be taken away with the other.[225] We are on the knife-edge, as often in Scripture, of the interface between divine sovereignty and human responsibility, and we cannot manoeuvre ourselves off it by denying either of them. The truth is that the promises of God never come without requiring a response from us, and that nothing is promised to the disobedient and unbelieving but the certainty of being overthrown by God's wrath.[226] But the truth is also that the faith to believe God's promises is itself a gift, not something we have of ourselves, and therefore the fulfilment of his promises rests with God from beginning to end.[227] Human failure does not, in the end, cancel out God's promises; it only disqualifies the disobedient from enjoying them. The bedrock reality that guarantees the future is God's total sovereignty. By his sovereign grace he enables those who are truly his to believe his promises and live by them.

The response to the preaching of Haggai and Zechariah shows that there were faithful and obedient ones in their day,[228] to be followed in turn by many others, among them Malachi, Ezra and Nehemiah. Sadly, not all were of the same stirling quality, and the long wait proved too much for many. But when Jesus the Messiah came at last, there were still 'Simeons' and 'Annas' waiting expectantly for him and living lives of godly obedience.[229] They were privileged to see the beginning of what is promised here. We wait for its completion. May the Lord, when he returns, find us just as expectant and obedient as they were.[230]

Two final comments, to complete our study of this first major part of the book. First, the symbolic crowning of Joshua concludes part 1 by revisiting the pivotal visions of chapters 3 and 4 and underlining their crucial importance. It restates their message in

---

[225] Cf. the similar, apparent conditionality attached to the promise of the second coming of Christ; he will come 'to those who are *waiting* for him' (Heb. 9:28; my italics).
[226] 2 Thess. 1:5–9; Heb. 10:26–27.
[227] Eph. 2:8.
[228] Ezra 5:1–2.
[229] Luke 2:25–28.
[230] Luke 18:8; 1 John 3:3.

terms of the promise about the coming of the Branch. It also complements all eight visions by bringing those who are still in exile clearly into view and linking them, through their representatives and through the memorial crown, with the community already in Jerusalem. Second, however, and equally importantly, it foreshadows what is to come in part 2 by shifting the focus away from Zerubbabel and the temple he is building, to the coming of the Messiah, the true builder of God's house. What is anticipated here begins to happen in 9:9 and is consummated in 14:16–21. This important passage, therefore, is in effect the hinge between part 1, which it concludes, and part 2, which it foreshadows. Jesus' bold claim 'I will build my church, and the gates of Hades will not overcome it',[231] was in effect an announcement that he was the Branch, the Messiah of whom Zechariah had spoken, and therefore the one whom the whole book of Zechariah is about!

[231] Matt. 16:18.

Part 2
Kingdom consummation

Zechariah 7 – 14

Like a garment, the book of Zechariah has different parts, and seams where the parts are joined together. In a well-made garment the seams are inconspicuous, but strong, and the same is true here. Chapters 6 and 7 lie either side of such a seam. The heading at 7:1 moves us forward two years and introduces the second major part of the book. But before we go forward, let us pause for breath and note some of the ways in which the two parts are joined at this major seam.

The most obvious link is the way the arrival of people from other places features at the end of chapter 6 and the beginning of chapter 7. In 6:10 men arrive from Babylon; in 7:2 another group arrive from Bethel.[1] In both cases these arrivals become the occasion for Zechariah to spring into action, so to speak, and present another aspect of his prophetic message. The other major link is less obvious and more long range, but it is very significant. I commented on it briefly in the introduction when I outlined the book's structure. It has to do with the way chapter 7, which opens part 2, seems deliberately to echo 1:1–6, which opens part 1. It opens with a similar heading (7:1; cf. 1:1). Like 1:1–6 it refers to the LORD's anger with the forefathers (7:12; cf. 1–2), the word he had sent them through the earlier prophets (7:12; cf. 1:4), and their refusal to pay attention (7:13; cf. 1:4). Moreover, these are not merely surface similarities. Both passages issue a strong rebuke, and call for a

---

[1] V. 2 literally reads, 'Bethel sent Sharezer and Regem-Melech' and so on. Baldwin argues (1972, p. 142) that 'Bethel' and 'Sharezer' (which follow one another in Hebrew) should be taken together as a personal name, and that this person is the sender: thus, 'Bethel-Sharezer sent Regem-Melech' etc. She thinks that the delegation came from Babylon (like the one in 6:10) on the grounds that the arrival of people from Bethel, which was close at hand, wouldn't have been sufficiently noteworthy to cause the date to be remembered. But this is a very precarious argument, not least because (as Baldwin herself notes) it requires omitting the conjunction ('and') before 'Regem-Melech.' The arrival of a delegation from Bethel may well have been significant, for reasons we shall see below.

change in behaviour. In other words, part 2, like part 1, begins with a call for repentance, and only then goes on to speak of God's jealous concern for Jerusalem and its people and his intention to bless and prosper them (8:1–3; cf. 1:14–17). So while chapter 7 is a new beginning, it doesn't take the book off in a radically new direction. It is intimately connected with what has gone before, and what follows is a further unfolding of the same basic message. Part 2 builds on the foundation that has already been laid in part 1.

It is important to note, though, that chapter 7 does not stand alone as the introduction to part 2. Chapters 7 and 8 are closely linked in a number of ways, as we shall see. The most obvious connection is the way the issue of fasting, which surfaces at the beginning of chapter 7 (vv. 2–3), is developed through the rest of that chapter, and then revisited from a new perspective in chapter 8 (vv. 18–19). The axis that holds the two chapters together is the movement from mourning to celebration, from fast days to joyful festivals. The way chapter 8 ends (8:20–23) anticipates the way the whole book ends (14:16–21). So chapters 7 and 8 together encapsulate the movement of the entire second half of the book.

1. A call for true fasting (7:1–14)

The *fourth year* of Darius I (1) falls midway between the second year, in which Zechariah began his ministry (1:1), and the sixth year, in which the work of rebuilding the temple was completed.[2] It was a time when the disturbances that had attended Darius's rise to power were over. So too was the excitement that many must have felt at that time. The challenges to Darius's rule had not produced the mighty 'shaking' of the world that Haggai had spoken about.[3] That remained a future hope (see Zech. 14:3–9, esp. v. 5); but for the present there was work to be done, especially the rebuilding of the temple. By the time chapter 7 opens most of the early difficulties have been overcome. The work is well advanced, and questions are beginning to emerge about what differences the completed temple will bring. In particular, will the pattern of religious observance remain the same, or will it change? Indeed, are changes already called for in recognition of the fact that the act of rebuilding itself has radically altered the circumstances of the community? This is the kind of issue brought to a head at the beginning of chapter 7 by the arrival of a delegation from Bethel (2).[4]

[2] Ezra 6:15.
[3] Hag. 2:6.
[4] Interestingly, the name Bethel means 'house of God' (see Gen. 28:10–22, esp. v. 17).

a. The question: Should we continue to fast? (7:1–3)

Bethel was about 20 kilometres (12 miles) north of Jerusalem, in what had formerly been the northern kingdom of Israel. The *people of Bethel* were closely related to the Jerusalem community both historically and religiously, so it was natural that they should look to its leaders for guidance concerning their religious affairs – especially since the temple was being rebuilt there. The question their representatives bring is about fasting: *Should I mourn and fast in the fifth month, as I have done for so many years?* (3). The leader of the delegation, speaking in the first person, makes the inquiry on behalf of the whole community.

Regular days of fasting had apparently been observed throughout the period of the exile by those who were still in Palestine, probably at the site of the ruined temple.[5] It is possible that the five poems of the book of Lamentations were composed specifically for use on these occasions.[6] The fast of the *fifth month* was in fact only one of several such fast days. Verse 5 refers to the fasts of the *fifth and seventh months*, and 8:19 mentions, in addition, those of the *fourth* and *tenth* months. All these fasts recalled events related to the fall of Jerusalem in 587 BC.[7] The fast of the *fifth month*, which marked the destruction of the temple, is probably singled out here because it was the most important one. Whatever applied to it would automatically apply to all the others as well. The question put by the men from Bethel was natural in the changed circumstances of the time. Now that construction was well under way, and the temple site was no longer an abandoned ruin, was it appropriate to continue observing these fast days? Was the time for such mourning over? They probably expected the *priests* and *prophets* (3) to confer with one another and come up with a simple ruling: yes, or no. In fact, they get much more than they have bargained for! Their question acts as a trigger for a quite elaborate, four-part reply that flows right through to the end of chapter 8. Each part is introduced by the statement that *the word of the LORD . . . came* to Zechariah (7:4; 7:8; 8:1; 8:18). In other words, Zechariah functions as God's inspired spokesman, and the answer he gives has all the penetrating power of the Word of God.[8] As we shall see, it pierces to the very heart of the

---

[5] See Jer. 41:5, referring to the period immediately after the temple ('house of God') had been destroyed by the Babylonians.

[6] Webb 2000, p. 59.

[7] The city wall was breached in the fourth month (Jer. 39:2), the temple was destroyed in the fifth (2 Kgs. 25:8), Gedaliah the governor was murdered in the seventh (2 Kgs. 25:25; Jer. 41:1–3), and the siege began in the tenth (2 Kgs. 25:1–2; Jer. 39:1).

[8] Heb. 4:12; Rev. 1:16.

matter, and exposes the deep underlying issues that must be faced if any kind of religious observance at all is to be meaningful and pleasing to God. I shall take each part of the answer in turn. The first two take up the rest of chapter 7.

b. False fasting (7:4–7)

The first part of the 'answer' is a series of three hard-hitting counter-questions that must have sent shock waves though everyone, not just the people of Bethel, but those in Jerusalem as well, and not just the common people, but also their leaders. They all found themselves in the firing line: *all the people of the land and the priests* (5). When they had fasted all those years[9] had they really done it for the LORD (5)? Wasn't their fasting actually just as self-centred as their feasting (6)? And didn't Zechariah have to speak to them like this because they were in fact no better than those to whom the earlier prophets had preached *before* the disaster of 587 BC (7)? What they called 'fasting' was not true fasting, and what they called 'mourning' was not genuine sorrow. The problem was not with the outward aspects of what they had been doing, or even with the words they had been saying, but with the motivation behind it. It had not been *for* the LORD. That is, they had not come before God in order to submit themselves to him, but simply to try to get things from him. In short, there had been no genuine turning towards God in repentance.

The second part of the answer brings this right down to the nitty-gritty of everyday life by explaining what *real* fasting would involve.

c. The kind of fasting God requires (7:8–14)

The kind of fasting God requires is not to abstain from food, but to abstain from sin – especially the sin of mistreating our fellow human beings: *Do not oppress the widow or the fatherless, the alien or the poor. In your hearts do not think evil of each other* (10). Or, to put the same things positively: *Administer true justice; show mercy and compassion* (9b). If their fasting had truly been 'for God' it would have resulted in changed behaviour – behaviour that reflected God's own character, and his own passionate commitment to justice. Without this the question of whether or not certain religious observances should be continued is of no consequence at all. Without the kind of repentance that affects behaviour no religious

---

[9] For the expression *seventy years* see my comments on 1:12.

rite has any validity, for it is not honouring to God and not acceptable to him. We have heard this before, of course. The visions of the flying scroll and the woman in the basket have already made the same general point (5:1–4, 5–11). Only the focus on the issue of fasting is new. So why the repetition, and why such an elaborate response here to a simple question about fasting?

First, the repetition. Zechariah returns again and again to the issue of repentance for one very good reason: it is necessary. Zechariah is a good preacher and pastor, which means, among other things, that he understands the weakness and sinfulness of human beings and therefore their need to be reminded constantly of certain basic things. Repentance is not something that can simply be done, once and for all, and left behind. It is not merely the renunciation of this or that particular sin, but the renunciation of self and the reorientation of a person's entire life around God. And that has to be lived out, day after day, and from generation to generation. It is not just a rite of passage, but a way of life. Repetition is needed because the self is always seeking to make a comeback as the controlling centre of people's lives, and any giving in to it is a sin that needs to be renounced – again and again.

Second, a question about fasting is a superb opportunity to make this basic point again, because fasting is perhaps the last activity in which anyone would think they had given in to self. After all, fasting is a deliberate act of self-denial, isn't it? Not necessarily; even here we can be deceived. As sinful beings we have an almost inevitable tendency to move from the true centre of things to the periphery, and from the depths to the surface. In short, to lose the heart of the matter and to turn even religious observance into a cover for an unrepentant lifestyle. In other words, to become religious hypocrites. Fasting, with its outward show of self-denial, is perhaps the classic example of a religious rite that can go badly wrong if we are not constantly reminded what the heart of true religion really is. No-one in the Old Testament was more alert to this, or warned about it more clearly, than the great prophet Isaiah:

> Shout it aloud, do not hold back.
> Raise your voice like a trumpet.
> Declare to my people their rebellion
>   and to the house of Jacob their sins.
> For day after day they seek me out;
>   they seem eager to know my ways,
> as if they were a nation that does what is right
>   and has not forsaken the commands of its God.
> They ask me for just decisions

and seem eager for God to come near them.
'Why have we fasted,' they say,
   'and you have not seen it?
Why have we humbled ourselves,
   and you have not noticed?'

Yet on the day of your fasting, you do as you please
   and exploit all your workers.
Your fasting ends in quarrelling and strife,
   and in striking each other with wicked fists.
You cannot fast as you do today
   and expect your voice to be heard on high.
Is this the kind of fast I have chosen,
   only a day for a man to humble himself?
Is it only for bowing one's head like a reed
   and for lying on sackcloth and ashes?
Is that what you call a fast,
   a day acceptable to the LORD?

Is not this the kind of fasting I have chosen:
to loose the chains of injustice
   and untie the cords of the yoke,
to set the oppressed free
   and break every yoke?
Is it not to share your food with the hungry
   and to provide the poor wanderer with shelter –
when you see the naked, to clothe him,
   and not to turn away from your own flesh and blood?
Then your light will break forth like the dawn,
   and your healing will quickly appear;
then your righteousness will go before you,
   and the glory of the LORD will be your rear guard.
Then you will call, and the LORD will answer;
   you will cry for help, and he will say: Here am I.

If you do away with the yoke of oppression,
   with the pointing finger and malicious talk,
and if you spend yourselves on behalf of the hungry
   and satisfy the needs of the oppressed,
then your light will rise in the darkness,
   and your night will become like the noonday.
The LORD will guide you always;
   he will satisfy your needs in a sun-scorched land
   and will strengthen your frame.

> You will be like a well-watered garden,
> like a spring whose waters never fail.
> Your people will rebuild the ancient ruins
> and will raise up the age-old foundations;
> you will be called Repairer of Broken Walls,
> Restorer of Streets with Dwellings.[10]

In the fourth year of Darius the work of 'raising up the age-old foundations' was already well under way, but vigilance was needed lest the old sins be raised up again too. It may well be that Zechariah has this passage in mind when he tells his hearers that his own preaching on this important issue is nothing other than *the words the Lord proclaimed through the earlier prophets* (7).[11]

But he is not through yet. The people of Bethel have asked when the time for observing certain fast days will be over. The larger issue is when fasting *itself* will be over; that is, when there will no longer be any cause to mourn at all. This is what Zechariah takes up in the next two parts of his answer. The refusal of the forefathers to listen to what God said through the prophets led to scattering and desolation (13–14). But judgment is not to be God's final word. In the future this will be reversed. The movement from chapter 7 to chapter 8 is from scattering to regathering, from rebuke to promise, and from fasting to feasting.

2. The Lord promises to bless Jerusalem (8:1–23)

We have already noted that this chapter contains the third and fourth parts of Zechariah's answer, with the transition coming at the beginning of verse 18. Together they indicate that the change from mourning to celebration will come in two stages. It has already begun *now* (11) with the Lord's return to Jerusalem and the commencement of work on the temple (1–17). But it will not be complete until *those days* (23, still future) when people of many nations will come to Jerusalem to worship the Lord and become part of his covenant people (18–23). In terms of the Bible's message as a whole the Jerusalem of Zechariah's day (which was beginning to be renewed) was a type or shadow of the new Jerusalem of the future, which would be the home of all God's redeemed people.[12]

---

[10] Is. 58:1–12.

[11] Incidentally, this is indirect evidence for the pre-exilic dating of Isaiah 56 – 66 (which many scholars have argued is *contemporary* with Haggai and Zechariah). See the discussion of the unity of Isaiah in Webb 1996, pp. 33–37.

[12] See Is. 56:17–19; Rev. 21:1–4, 22–26.

This chapter has very close links with 2:10–13 and is essentially a restatement in greater detail of the promises already made there.

a. Reasons for celebration now (8:1–17)

This section is made up of seven short oracles, all introduced in the same way: *This is what the* LORD *Almighty says* (2, 3, 4, 6, 7, 9, 14).[13] It is a seven-hued rainbow speaking of God's strong commitment to Jerusalem and its people.

The first is foundational for all the others: the LORD's *jealous* concern for Jerusalem is the source of everything good she has now, and will ever have (2).[14] The next four begin to itemize her blessings: God's presence in her midst (3), long life and many progeny for her citizens (4), and the regathering of her still-scattered exiles (7). All of these have both a present and a future aspect to them. The opening words of verse 3 are literally 'I *have returned* and I *will dwell* in Jerusalem.'[15] God was already present in Zechariah's community, as we saw in chapter 4 (the vision of the lampstand), but he would *dwell* among them in a new way when the temple was completed,[16] and in a greater way still in the future – the final day – when the kingdom of God had fully come (see 14:1–9, 16–21).[17] Jerusalem was certainly not *filled* with people in Zechariah's day; but neither was it a desolate, empty place any more. Those who were present when work on the temple began were a blend of the very old and the young,[18] forerunners of the vibrant 'family' of God's people that would one day fill Jerusalem to overflowing (4–5).[19] And while many were still scattered the present community was made up,

---

[13] The only minor variation is in v. 3, which has *the* LORD instead of *the* LORD *Almighty*.

[14] On the *jealousy* of God see 1:14 and my comments there.

[15] Cf. Meyers and Meyers 1987, p. 408, and the AV, 'I am returned ... and will dwell'. See also 1:16 and my comments there.

[16] Cf. Exod. 25:8, 'have them make a sanctuary for me, and I will dwell among them'.

[17] Cf. Ezek. 48:35, 'THE LORD IS THERE'. For the fulfilment of all these OT promises about Jerusalem, see John's vision of the holy city, the new Jerusalem, coming down out of heaven from God at the end of history, when Christ returns (Rev. 12 – 22). Note especially Rev. 21:3: 'Now the dwelling of God is with men, and he will live with them.'

[18] Ezra 3:8–13, especially v. 12.

[19] In Zechariah's day the hardships of life in Jerusalem probably meant that few of those who survived the rigours of the return journey lived to a ripe old age. Vv. 4–5 depict an ideal situation in which the blessing of long life would be experienced again, and a joyous family atmosphere would once more prevail (the old enjoying the presence of the very young, and vice versa). Cf. Mal. 4:6. Old age generally did not have the negative connotations it often has today.

largely, of people who had already returned. So the blessings spoken of here were not simply distant ideals, far removed from the present experience of the people. They already had the first instalment of them, the pledge of their future inheritance, just as the Spirit in the hearts of believers now is 'a deposit, guaranteeing what is to come'.[20]

The main focus, however, is certainly on the future. What will finally be, *at that time*, will so surpass anything previously experienced that it will seem *marvellous*, a wonder – like the miraculous deliverance Israel's ancestors experienced at the exodus (6).[21] Only to God himself will it seem 'ordinary', so to speak. Then Jerusalem will be what it always should have been, *the City of Truth*,[22] and its hilltop location the *Holy Mountain* of the LORD Almighty (3). In other words, it will be a place that perfectly, in every way, expresses the character of the God who is present in it. But that final reality is always viewed, in the Old Testament, as a light that casts its reflection backwards to motivate and guide life in the present.[23] It is the goal the people of God are always longing for, and every advance towards it is a cause for celebration. The rebuilding of the temple was one such advance – a most significant one, in fact – which is why the remaining verses of this passage are largely concerned with it.

The sixth saying is the longest, and begins with a reminder of what had been said by *the prophets*, especially Haggai, when the present work on the temple had begun.[24] *Let your hands be strong* occurs twice, in verse 9 and again in verse 13. The intervening verses contrast the past experience of want and disunity (10) with the new period of fruitfulness and blessing which is beginning to dawn now that the work on the temple is under way (12). Curse will be turned into blessing and, like Abraham, the community will not only be blessed itself; it will *be a blessing* to those around it (13).[25] In fact, that is what always happens when people believe God's promises

[20] 2 Cor. 1:22.
[21] See Exod. 15, especially v. 11, where the LORD who delivered Israel with spectacular displays of power, is celebrated as the one who works 'wonders' (the same root, *pl*') as in the word 'marvellous' of Zech. 8:6.
[22] The *City of Truth* (*'îr hā'emet*) stands in contrast to the failure to administer *true justice* (*mišpāṭ 'emet*) in the present (7:9). Cf. Conrad, p. 144.
[23] Cf. Is. 2, where the vision of the future glory of Jerusalem as the place of God's temple is followed, in v. 5, by the exhortation 'Come, O house of Jacob, / let us walk in the light of the LORD.' It is likely that this passage in Isaiah has strongly influenced Zech. 8.
[24] There are many echoes of Haggai here, as noted by Conrad (who lists them all, p. 146) and several other commentators. In particular *let your hands be strong* echoes the 'be strong' (three times) of Hag. 2:4, and *Do not be afraid* (13) echoes the 'Do not fear' (same Hebrew word) of Hag. 2:5.
[25] Gen. 12:2.

and do what he has told them to do. It is the opposite of being *afraid* (13b), which leads to withdrawal and sterility.[26]

The seventh and last saying, beginning at verse 14, is about how continued blessing depends on continued obedience, and – as always in Zechariah – that means practising truth and justice towards one's neighbour (16–17). That the temple should be rebuilt was important for Zechariah, but he never thought, or taught, that the rituals associated with the temple had any magical or automatic power to secure God's favour. The temple was a visible sign of God's presence, and people with God in their midst must love what he loves and hate what he hates; and because he hates all forms of falsehood and injustice (17), so must they. The building of the temple was a task that required strength and determination. However, to continue to live lives of truth and justice when the temple was completed would, if anything, be an even greater challenge. But only by living this way would the people continue to be blessed, and be the blessing to others that God intended them to be.

b. Reasons for celebration then – in 'those' days (8:18–23)

This final part of Zechariah's answer consists of three short sayings, again introduced by the words *This is what the LORD Almighty says* (19, 20, 23). Here, for the first time, we get the expression *in those days* (23), echoing the 'in that day' of 2:11 and 3:10. Here, as there, what is on view is the time of consummation, when every promise will be fulfilled, and struggle will at last give way to unalloyed happiness and celebration. The first saying is about the joy that will be experienced by the people of Judah themselves (19). The two that immediately follow are about *many peoples ... from all languages and nations* joining with them (20–23). In New Testament terms what we have here is the final union of redeemed Jews and redeemed Gentiles as the one redeemed people of God, the climax of God's saving work from beginning to end.[27]

Several things here give a fine sense of completeness to the long

---

[26] The repeated expression *the remnant of this people* (11, 12) is a reminder that the community is still a mixed one. Not all live repentant, obedient lives (cf. 5:1–4). The promises of God apply particularly to the faithful remnant, who do. There is another sense, however, in which the entire community is a remnant (what is left of the former kingdoms of Israel and Judah). Hence the inclusive expression *O Judah and Israel* in v. 13. The same tension still exists between the inclusive and particular senses of 'church' today. Even those who are not truly converted share for a time in the blessings enjoyed by the church as a whole. But eventually they will be judged if they do not repent (Matt. 13:24–30).

[27] Cf. Rom. 11:25–27. Together they will inhabit the new Jerusalem of the last day (cf. Rev. 7:1–10; 21:1–4, 22–27).

response Zechariah has been giving to the question about fasting that was asked at the beginning of the previous chapter. The first, as we have already seen, is the way that question is directly referred to in verse 19: *the fasts of the fourth, fifth, seventh and tenth months will become joyful and glad occasions.* Fasting will be over forever; the time of feasting will have come. The second is the way the pilgrimage of *many peoples ... to entreat the LORD* (20–21) here echoes the pilgrimage of the men of Bethel – also to 'entreat the LORD' – in 7:2. As they had come to Jerusalem to seek God, and so acknowledge his rule over them, so will people from all over the world. We can now see in retrospect that the pilgrimage from Bethel was a sign of something far greater to come. It is no rambling discourse we have been following for two chapters, but a finely crafted address that has been moving towards a very definite climax. That climax is reached with almost mathematical precision in the last verse, where the seven sayings of 8:1–17, and the three of 8:18–23, find their symbolic completion in the *ten men* who grasp the hem of a single Jew, saying, *Let us go with you, because we have heard that God is with you* (23).[28]

God had been 'with' the people of Israel, in the sense of being in a special covenant relationship with them, ever since the time of Abraham.[29] But it had never been for their sake only, but that ultimately all peoples might be blessed through them.[30] To some extent this had already been fulfilled in Israel's history through the Old Testament period as people like Rahab the harlot and Ruth the Moabitess had sought and found refuge in the covenant community,[31] and as God had used people like Joseph, Solomon and Daniel to extend the blessings of his rule far beyond Israel's borders.[32] But Zechariah speaks here of a day when this will happen on an unprecedented scale, with large numbers of Gentiles responding eagerly to the revelation of God they have received through the Jewish people. This was to find its primary fulfilment in the one called 'Immanuel, God with us', the one perfect Israelite whom all people must grasp by faith if they are to be saved.[33] The history of the Christian church began with three thousand Jews themselves doing that in Jerusalem on the day of Pentecost.[34] Since then many millions, mainly Gentiles, have joined with them and have

[28] Cf. Is. 45:14.
[29] Gen. 15:18; 17:2–7.
[30] Gen. 12:1–3; 18:18.
[31] Josh. 6:25; Ruth 2:11–12.
[32] Gen. 41:56–57; 1 Kgs. 4:34; Dan. 1:21; 3:28 – 4:3.
[33] Matt. 1:22–23; Acts 4:12.
[34] Acts 2:40–41.

come to share in the covenant blessings originally given to Israel. The *days* of fulfilment Zechariah spoke of (23) have opened out into this whole gospel era and will reach their fulfilment when the full number of the elect, both Jews and Gentiles, have been gathered in.[35]

The intriguing thing is that the original question about fasting that set this whole discourse in motion is never directly answered. Should the fasts in the fourth, fifth, seventh and tenth months continue to be observed or not? The implication is that they should not, but no ruling as such is given. We are not told why, but the reason is not hard to work out. Only one fast was prescribed in the law God gave to Israel through Moses: the annual fast on the tenth day of the seventh month, the Day of Atonement.[36] People did fast on other occasions, for various reasons, but this was entirely a matter of freedom, not legal obligation.[37] The important thing was whether they lived repentant lives marked by love for God and their fellow human beings. Zechariah's answer, precisely by *not* giving the kind of response expected, steered the inquirers away from legalism (which multiplies rules and attaches undue significance to ceremonial observances) and towards a life lived in joyful expectation of the coming of God's kingdom. It expanded their horizons and focused them on the things that matter most.

The New Testament teaching on fasting moves in the same general direction, but takes it even further. No fasting at all is prescribed for Christians, since what the Day of Atonement symbolized has been fulfilled in the death and resurrection of Jesus, and his ongoing intercession for us in heaven.[38] Jesus himself fasted during his temptation in the wilderness,[39] and expected that his disciples too would fast,[40] especially after he was taken from them.[41] His main concern, however, was to warn them against overemphasizing it, or making an outward show of it.[42] Neither Jesus nor his apostles ever require fasting of Christians as a legal obligation.[43] There is nothing wrong with fasting if it is done wisely and for proper motives. Indeed, the general tendency of Scripture is to

[35] Rom. 11:15–27.
[36] Lev. 16:29, 31; 23:26–32; Num. 29:7.
[37] For a good summary review of the biblical material on fasting see Belben, p. 373.
[38] 1 John 2:1–2; Heb. 4:14–16; 6:13 – 10:18.
[39] Matt. 4:1–4. Cf. the forty-day fasts of Moses (Exod. 34:28) and Elijah (1 Kgs. 19:8).
[40] Matt. 6:16–18.
[41] Matt. 9:14–15; Mark 2:18–19; Luke 5:33–34.
[42] Matt. 6:16–18.
[43] The textual evidence is against the references to fasting in Matt. 17:21 and Mark 9:29 (see the NIV footnotes).

encourage us to do it. It is an entirely appropriate way of humbling ourselves before God and presenting our deep concerns and needs to him. But as Christians we should be careful to avoid making rules, for ourselves or for others, where this is unwarranted.[44] Zechariah's answer to the question about fasting in these two chapters is a fine example, not only of good theology, but also of good pastoral practice.

But now it is time to move on.

3. Through suffering to glory: chapters 9 – 14

In these chapters the question of fasting is left behind, and the style of writing becomes more enigmatic. The fundamental concern remains the same, however. What changes may be expected now that the rebuilding of the temple is nearing completion? Chapters 7 and 8 have been focused on lifestyle issues: What will be the social implications of having God 'in residence' again? How should we live? Should fasting continue? Chapters 9 – 14 are more focused on events: What may be expected to *happen* after the temple has been completed? What shape will the future take as it unfolds?

Much of what follows is a further development, in one form or another, of what we have already been introduced to in the first eight chapters. The same basic themes are amplified, as it were, and played in a new key. In general, the message of these chapters is positive: the kingdom of God will come; God will manifest his kingly rule over the whole world. But there is also a darker side: victory will not come without suffering and conflict. The transition from the 'now', when the temple is completed, to the 'then', when the kingdom of God is fully revealed, is like the birthing of a child. The outcome in this case is guaranteed and glorious, but the process is painful.[45] In fact, suffering is perhaps the most distinctive new element of these chapters. Everyone suffers as the end draws near: not just God's enemies, but his own people, his Messiah, and even (as we shall see) God himself. All are caught up in the final conflict between good and evil.

The style of writing is what Bible scholars commonly refer to as 'apocalyptic'.[46] The 'last things' (the end of the world, final judgment) are spoken about in a largely symbolic way, using images drawn from the present or the past, but projected on to a huge

[44] Cf. 1 Tim. 4:3; Col. 2:16.
[45] Cf. Rom. 8:22.
[46] See the discussion of Zechariah's apocalyptic language in the introduction, note 2, and pp. 35–38.

(metaphorical) cinema screen for maximum visual impact.[47] While there are the elements of a narrative (or rather an end-time drama) the focus is not on chronology (the ordered sequence of events) but on a crisis, in which various aspects of the same basic reality (the triumph of God over evil) are presented again and again, in different combinations and sequences. So we must be prepared, as we move into these chapters, for turmoil and sudden movements backwards and forwards between different elements of the final conflict, for that is the nature of the writing. We must also be prepared for terms such as 'Israel' and 'Jerusalem' to transcend, at times, their ordinary historical sense and to become symbols of the end-time people of God and city of God.[48] The final conflict we shall see played out here is not between the modern state of Israel and those who are hostile to it, but between those who belong to the kingdom of God and those who do not. Here, at last, is the great 'shaking' Haggai had spoken about.[49] What holds everything together, in the end, is the steady focus on God himself, the divine king, and his final victory over all that opposes his rule. Our surest guide to the interpretation of these chapters will be the ways in which their content is reflected in the fuller revelation of the coming of God's kingdom in the New Testament. As we have seen in the introduction, the Gospels in particular refer to Zechariah 9 – 14 in extremely significant ways.

As already noted, chapters 9 – 14 consist of two large prophetic messages, each introduced by the heading 'An Oracle', which occurs at the beginning of chapters 9 and 12 respectively.[50] The overall theme is the rule of God, manifested first in the coming of his Messiah, the (human) king, in chapter 9, and revealed finally in the coming of God himself, the divine king of the whole world in chapter 14.

4. Oracle 1: God's rule and human leaders (chs. 9 – 11)

a. The coming of the warrior God (9:1–8)

Chapter 9 opens with a virtual catalogue of nations and cities that have been hostile to Jerusalem and its people in the past, ranging

[47] Cf., in the NT, the book of Revelation.

[48] E.g. the 'Israel' of 12:1 is expanded by the end of ch. 14 to include people of all nations (14:16), and the city of God of ch. 14, while still called 'Jerusalem' (14:16), is clearly something greater than the historical Jerusalem, either past or present. The Jerusalem of history has become the new Jerusalem of Revelation 21 – 22. Cf. Rev. 18, where 'Babylon' (a name drawn from history) is used to refer to the world (the kingdom of man), which is doomed to destruction because of its opposition to God and his people.

[49] Hag. 2:6–9.

[50] See the introduction, pp. 30–31.

from *Hadrach*[51] and *Damascus* in the north (1), to *Ekron* in the south (7), and concluding with a solemn pledge by God to defend his house *against marauding forces*, so that no *oppressor* will ever again be able to overrun his people (8). There, in a nutshell, is a summary of all that follows: the conflict between God and his enemies, with his own people caught in the crossfire, so to speak. It is an uncomfortable and dangerous place to be, but they have the promise of God's guarding presence with them: *now I am keeping watch* (8b).

Let us take the enemies first. None of them are what we might call big players. They are not the great imperial powers, Assyria and Babylon, that ravaged Jerusalem in the eighth and sixth centuries, nor the Persians who held sway in Zechariah's own day. They are the smaller enemies that had troubled Israel in earlier times. The Philistines, represented here by the names of their cities (*Ashkelon, Gaza, Ekron* and *Ashdod*) were a thorn in Israel's side from the time of the judges until their subjugation by David, roughly the twelfth to the tenth centuries.[52] Syria, represented by its capital *Damascus* (1), was a problem mainly in the ninth century,[53] but also (in one crisis at least) in the eighth.[54] The Phoenician cities of *Tyre* and *Sidon* (2–3) never threatened Israel at all (at least militarily), but are ranked with the enemies of God here because of their pride in their own skill and wealth.[55] At the height of their power they were the merchant princes of the eastern Mediterranean, renowned for their seafaring prowess.[56] All of these, like Israel herself, had suffered at the hands of Assyria and Babylon. By the time this passage was written, however, all of them were effectively spent forces, and no longer posed any serious threat to Jerusalem. The general import of this opening salvo of the first oracle is that when God comes to rule the world, all his enemies will be as these nations and cities are. His people will no longer have any cause either to fear or to envy them.

The word of the LORD, in verse 1, is virtually a title for God himself. To say that God's word is *against* his enemies is to say that

---

[51] *Hadrach* is not mentioned anywhere else in the OT, but is known from Assyrian texts that record how the Assyrians fought against it in the middle of the eighth century (Baldwin 1972, p. 158). It lay on the extreme north of Palestine (on Syria's northern border).

[52] Judg. 3:31; 10:7, 11; 13:1 – 16:31; 2 Sam. 5:17–25; 21:15–22.

[53] E.g. 1 Kgs. 20:1–34; 2 Kgs. 6:24 – 7:2 ('Aram' is the ancient name of Syria).

[54] Is. 7:1–9.

[55] Cf. Ezek. 28:1–26. They posed a religious threat to Israel (the northern kingdom) through the aggressive promotion of Baal worship by Jezebel, who was a Phoenician princess and wife of Ahab (1 Kgs. 16:29–33). But this does not seem to be what is on view here in Zech. 9.

[56] See Wiseman, p. 1228.

God is against them. God and his word are inseparable. God is in his word, and to be confronted by God's word is to be confronted by God himself. It should make us tremble every time we read the word of God in Scripture, or hear it proclaimed.[57] It is an especially serious matter if we are at odds with God rather than at peace with him. The proper way for human beings to respond to God is expressed in the rather cryptic second half of verse 1, which is a kind of parenthesis – an almost 'under the breath' comment by Zechariah before he goes on. The word of God has been spoken; all men, including Israel, watch expectantly (or anxiously as the case may be) for it to be fulfilled. Their eyes are *on the LORD*. We need to be sensitive here to the poetic character of the language. What is conveyed is a kind of tense expectancy. God is about to act. It is time to watch. The *keeping watch* by God himself in verse 8 is the divine counterpart to human watching of verse 1, and forms a bracket around the whole unit. The moment we are poised at is the one that was anticipated in 2:13: 'Be still before the LORD, all mankind, because he [God] has roused himself from his holy dwelling.'

Three things require special note before we move on. First, the *never again* of verse 8 implies that what is in view here is something that will bring an end, once and for all, to the ebb and flow of the conflict between good and evil that is the day-to-day stuff of human history. The passage speaks of an intervention of God that will bring history to its divinely determined end. Second, although the dominant note in the passage is the LORD's victory over his enemies, not all of them are destroyed (7). A remnant (*those who are left*) are spared, and incorporated into the people of God – like the *Jebusites*, who survived the conquest of Canaan and continued to live among the Israelites.[58] Some will even become *leaders* in Judah (the leading tribe)! We have met this theme before in Zechariah (2:10–13; 8:20–23), and will meet it again in the last chapter (14:16).[59] In the end, the people of God will be all who acknowledge and put their trust in the God of Israel – both Jew and Gentile. Finally, the movement in these opening verses of chapter 9 is from north to south, culminating in God's *house* (his temple, 8), in Jerusalem. This provides the bridge into the next unit, as we shall see.

b. The coming of the king (9:9–10)

The NIV takes verses 9–13 together, with the transition to the last paragraph of the chapter coming at verse 14. It is better, I think, to

[57] Is. 66:2.
[58] Josh. 15:63; Judg. 1:21.
[59] Cf. Is. 66:18–21.

take verses 9–10 as a unit, with the transition coming at the beginning of verse 11 with the words *As for you*. Verses 9–10 focus mainly on the king himself, and verses 11–16 on what his coming will mean for the people of Jerusalem.

Verse 9 is undoubtedly the best-known verse in Zechariah, and one of the better-known verses of the entire Old Testament. The key issue for the interpretation of the passage is the identity of the *king* who is seen here riding into Jerusalem on a donkey amid shouts of rejoicing. We know that he is identified as Jesus in the New Testament,[60] so that provides a fixed point for our reading of the passage in its larger biblical context. It finds its fulfilment (final meaning) in the coming of Jesus the Messiah. But what of its meaning here in Zechariah 9? It is God who has been on the move in verses 1–8, and his progress has been towards Jerusalem. So it is God himself whom we are expecting to arrive there at this point.[61] But the picture of God himself riding on a donkey is incongruous, to say the least. Furthermore, God is clearly distinguished from the king. God is the speaker (the 'I' of v. 10) who announces the arrival of the king and speaks of him in the third person: *he* [the king] *will proclaim peace to the nations*. So the king is a man, a human being – but a man who is closely associated with God.[62]

The book of Zechariah has already given us the key to the identity of this king. In its context in Zechariah, this king can be none other than the one whose coming was promised in chapter 3, and symbolized in the crowning of Joshua the high priest in chapter 6. The one whom these earlier chapters had spoken of as God's 'servant, the Branch' (3:8; 6:12), now makes his entrance as the *king*, God's chosen ruler and representative. With his arrival the stage is at last set for the drama of the promised coming of God's kingdom to be enacted. The king is God's Messiah.

Several things are said about him here. He is Zion's king (*your king*, 9), in contrast to 'king Darius', who was king of Persia (with temporary jurisdiction over Jerusalem, 7:1; cf. 1:1; 1:7), and Gaza's 'king', who appears in the catalogue of God's enemies (9:5). Gaza would *lose* her king (5), but Zion's king would come to her (9). The *king* spoken of here is like no other, as Zion is like no other place.

[60] Matt. 21:4–5.

[61] Cf. Dumbrell, p. 63; and Hanson, pp. 292–324 (who understands the whole of ch. 9 as a 'Divine Warrior Hymn'). OT expectation, in general, was of the LORD's (Yahweh's) return to Zion (e.g. Is. 52:8; 62:11). Zeph. 3:14–15, which is obviously a close parallel to Zech. 9:9, is clearly about God's presence in Zion.

[62] Cf. Hanson, p. 320: 'In keeping with the fluidity running through the royal literature of the Bible and other ancient Near Eastern sources, the anointed ruler here is celebrated alongside the divine king.' Unfortunately this important point is not developed by Hanson.

It is destined to be the centre of God's kingdom on earth, and Zion's king is the one chosen by God to rule there, over a kingdom that will eventually replace all others (10b):

> His rule will extend from sea to sea
> and from the River[63] to the ends of the earth.[64]

So this king differs from other kings both in the place from which he rules and in the extent of his rule. He is also different in his character. He is *righteous* (9). All other kings, whether of Israel or the nations, were flawed, and reflected only very imperfectly the character of God. But this king is the very embodiment of God's righteousness; he is his perfect representative. He 'has' *salvation* (9b).[65] That is, he is the agent through whom God's salvation is made available. He is *gentle*, as shown by his mode of transport. He comes unarmed, riding a donkey rather than a war-horse.[66] He is the very opposite of the proud, oppressive tyrants that have all too often ruled the kingdoms and empires of this world. And finally, he proclaims *peace to the nations* (10). We are inclined to think of peace in negative terms: the absence of conflict. The peace spoken of here certainly includes that, for in announcing the arrival of this king God promises that he (God) will *take away ... chariots* and *war-horses*, and 'break' *the battle-bow* (10a). But the *peace* the king himself proclaims is something far richer than this. The underlying Hebrew word is *šālôm*, which means 'wholeness', 'well-being', the sum total of everything good and life-enhancing. It is the word that most encapsulates life in covenant with God, rich with his blessings. The king is a preacher, and what he proclaims is peace with God, and everything that flows from that. It is what Isaiah so memorably referred to as the 'good news (the gospel) of peace'.[67] So we have a most remarkable contrast in this chapter between war and peace, between the warrior God (1–8) and the gentle king (9–10), between judgment and salvation. The bottom line is that God will triumph, but the king of verses 9–10 represents an alternative to being

[63] I.e. the river Euphrates. The *River* represents (poetically) the east. The ends of the earth are, traditionally, in the west.

[64] Cf. Ps. 2.

[65] The underlying Hebrew word (*nôšā'*) is passive, and would more literally mean he 'is saved' or 'delivered'. As Baldwin comments (1972, p. 165), this implies that the king has been through an ordeal of some kind and been saved from it. The NIV translation suggests (correctly in my judgment) that his coming at this point is to share that deliverance or salvation with his people. The nearest parallel to this in the Old Testament is Isaiah's Suffering Servant. See Is. 53, especially vv. 10–12.

[66] See 6:1–8.

[67] Is. 52:7; cf. 40:9; Rom. 10:15; Eph. 6:15.

overthrown. He comes with salvation, proclaiming peace. The *king*, so to speak, is God's final offer. It would be perilous indeed to spurn it!

All of this adds enormous depth and richness to our understanding of Jesus when we bring it back with us to our reading of the Gospels. God not only 'stood behind' Jesus when he came, but was present in him. The coming of Jesus the Messiah was the coming of God himself, not (at that time) to overthrow his enemies, but to proclaim peace, to offer an amnesty. And he came first and foremost to Israel, his own covenant people. He came to Jerusalem, as Zechariah had said he would, riding on a donkey. He came to God's house (the temple), and treated it as his own.[68] The tragedy is that, when he came, his own people did not recognize him as their king.[69] They did not know the day of God's coming to them,[70] and ended up crucifying him. The ironic sign nailed to his cross said it all: 'This is Jesus, the king of the Jews.'[71] But it was not the end of the story, just as chapter 9 is not the end of the book of Zechariah. For this tragedy, dark and terrible though it was, was within the plan and purpose of God to bring salvation, not just to Israel, but to the whole world. Not all rejected him, and around that crucified king gathered a new people of God who were destined to herald the good news of his kingdom to the ends of the earth.[72] God's kingdom had drawn near. The end of the world had begun to happen.

c. God's people share in his victory (9:11–17)

In this final part of the chapter the focus shifts from the king (Messiah) himself, to those who are associated with him and share in his victory. As we have noted the change is signalled by the opening words of verse 11: *As for you.* The word 'you' is feminine singular, and refers to Zion, or more particularly the 'Daughter (i.e. people) of Zion' who will rejoice at the coming of the Messiah and recognize him as their king.[73]

God's relationship with them is spoken of in terms of a *covenant* sealed with *blood* (11). The covenant God made with Israel at Sinai was such a covenant,[74] and so is the new covenant that has been

---

[68] Matt. 21:13; cf. Zech. 9:8.
[69] John 1:11.
[70] Luke 19:44. Hence Jesus' weeping over Jerusalem (v. 41).
[71] Matt. 27:37.
[72] John 1:12–13.
[73] The *you* of v. 9a does not refer to Zechariah's contemporaries, but to the same people addressed as 'you', v. 11. Zechariah's contemporaries (especially those still in exile) are the ones referred to as *prisoners of hope* in v. 12.
[74] Exod. 24:8; Heb. 9:20.

inaugurated by the death of Jesus.[75] In fact, sacrifice (the shedding of blood) is the only basis on which there can be any relationship at all between God and sinful human beings.[76] The close connection here between the coming of the king (9–10) and the blood of God's covenant (11) is suggestive of much more than is directly stated. Chapters 12 and 13 will tell us more. For now, however, the main focus is on the glorious future of those who respond positively to the good news of peace the Messiah brings. In short, they will share in his victory, and rule with him (11b–13). God himself will *appear over them* (14), manifesting himself as their champion who fights for them, and finally he will claim them as his own forever. He will save them as his *flock*, and they will *sparkle in his land* like priceless jewels (16).[77]

Again, the language is poetic. The images are drawn from the past and the present, but the screen on which they are projected is the future. When these words were written, many Israelites were still in exile, like *prisoners* in a *waterless pit* (11b). But they are called upon to act as people who believe in the coming of God's kingdom. They are to see themselves as citizens of Jerusalem, and therefore (by faith) of the Zion that is to be. God's promise to them is that they will have more, much more, than they have lost (12b). They have only to shake off their despair and set out for home: *Return to your fortress* (Jerusalem), *O prisoners of hope* (12). The combination of *Judah* and *Ephraim*,[78] in verse 13, speaks poetically of a united people of God, who – through God's help – are able to overcome the world (represented here by *Greece*).[79]

The 'appearing' of the LORD, in verse 14, is the counterpart of the advent of the king in verse 9. Those who have the Messiah as their king will have God as their champion.[80] They will have battles to fight, but God will be with them and fight for them, as he did for Israel at the time of the exodus.[81] And the fighting will not last forever. One day it will be over; the time of *grain* and *new wine* will

[75] Matt. 26:28; Mark 14:24; Heb. 10:29.

[76] Heb. 9:16–22.

[77] Cf. Mal. 3:16–17.

[78] As in other places, especially the book of Hosea, *Ephraim*, the name of the leading northern tribe, is here used as an alternative name for Israel, the northern kingdom (see, e.g., Hos. 10:6).

[79] On the reference to possible dating implications of the mention of *Greece* here, see the discussion in the introduction, p. 44.

[80] Cf., in the NT, the similar connection between faith in Christ now, and vindication by God on the last day.

[81] God's coming *in the storms of the south* (14), is especially reminiscent of God's revelation of himself to Israel at Mount Sinai (to the south of the land of Canaan) at the time of the exodus (Exod. 19:16).

have come (17) – the time of harvest festival, and paradise restored (cf. 14:16–21). That is the heritage of the people of God, and the glorious hope that should always inspire them and nerve them to action. As we move from chapter 9 into chapter 10, however, the mood begins to change. It is as though, after gazing at a brilliantly lit mountain peak, our eyes gradually move downwards, and we become conscious again of the distance between us and that glorious summit. There is a valley in between, and it is full of shadows.

d. True and false shepherds (10:1 – 11:3)

We need to consider chapters 10 and 11 together, because they are united by a common theme. It is announced at the beginning of chapter 10 by the statement *the people wander like sheep, / oppressed for lack of a shepherd* (10:2), and is brought to a climax at the end of chapter 11 with a solemn curse (11:17):

> Woe to the worthless shepherd,
>   who deserts the flock! ...
> May his arm be completely withered,
>   and his right eye totally blinded!

Leadership is a serious business, with high accountability attached to it, and huge consequences (for good or ill) for those who are led.

Leadership is not a new issue in Zechariah. When we were looking at the eight visions of chapters 2 – 6 we saw that the pivotal fourth and fifth dealt with the two leaders of the community, Joshua and Zerubbabel. Closer to hand, the presentation of Jerusalem's future king as the ideal leader in chapter 9 is the backdrop against which the issue of good and bad leadership is canvassed in the following two chapters. Only the 'shepherd' metaphor is new.[82] Nor is this theme dropped entirely after the end of chapter 11. As we shall see, it keeps surfacing here and there throughout chapters 12 – 14. But chapters 10 and 11 provide the most sustained treatment of it.

During the time the temple was being built the community had good leadership. But it had not always been so. The scattering of Israel, culminating in the exile to Babylon, had been largely due to the bad leadership of the rulers of both the northern and southern kingdoms.[83] Now, with his eye on the future, Zechariah sees that the restored community will again be troubled by leadership problems. After Zerubbabel and Joshua will come other leaders of a very

---

[82] But note the preparation for it in the reference to *the flock of his people* in 9:16.
[83] See the introduction, pp. 22–24.

different kind. The interval between where Zechariah himself stood (in the late sixth century) and the coming of the Messiah is seen here only in broad outline. But the general picture it paints accords well with what we now know actually happened.

Not all the leaders who arose in the period after the temple was built were bad, of course. There were great men, like Ezra and Nehemiah. But, sadly, they were the exception rather than the rule. Malachi, in the mid-fifth century, was already faced with a deteriorated situation, for which he laid the blame largely at the feet of the priests.[84] Ezra and Nehemiah both implemented reforms to try to correct problems that had arisen through the failure of both the civil and religious leaders.[85] In the more prosperous times that followed the completion of the temple a new wealthy class arose who oppressed the poor and continued to enrich themselves at their expense – forcing them into debt, and even slavery.[86] Worst of all, the governors themselves became involved in these abuses, so that Nehemiah had to draw the sharpest contrast between their behaviour and his own:

> from the twentieth year of King Artaxerxes, when I was appointed to be their governor in the land of Judah, until his thirty-second year – twelve years – neither I nor my brothers ate the food allotted to the governor. But the earlier governors – those preceding me – placed a heavy burden on the people and took forty shekels of silver from them in addition to food and wine. Their assistants also lorded it over the people. But out of reverence for God I did not act like that.[87]

It is clear from the last chapter of the book of Nehemiah, however, that by the end of Nehemiah's second term, the situation was deteriorating again,[88] and much worse was to follow in the period between the close of the Old Testament and the opening of the New.[89] The best commentary on this dark period is provided by Jesus himself: 'I tell you the truth, I am the gate for the sheep. All who ever came before me were thieves and robbers ... The thief comes only to steal and kill and destroy; I have come that they may have life, and have it to the full.'[90]

[84] Mal. 2:1–9.
[85] Ezra 9 – 10; Neh. 5.
[86] Neh. 5:1–5.
[87] Neh. 5:14–15.
[88] See Neh. 13.
[89] Note Jesus' denunciation of the religious leaders of his own time as hypocrites, and blind leaders of the blind (Matt. 15:12–14; 23:13–29).
[90] John 10:7–10.

It should be remembered too that throughout the entire period in question, apart from its internal problems the community was ruled from without by foreign powers (first the Persians, and then the Greeks) who became increasingly oppressive and hostile as time went by. It was a difficult time, to say the least, when leadership of the highest order was called for. Tragically, more often than not, it was lacking. The most persistent problem was the presence of bad shepherds. Much later, the apostle Paul warned that a very similar situation would arise in the church at Ephesus: 'I know that after I leave, savage wolves will come in among you and will not spare the flock.'[91] In the latter part of his ministry, Zechariah saw similar problems ahead for the community he had ministered to in Jerusalem.

Chapters 10 – 11 are pretty much a seamless robe; the overwhelming impression is one of interconnectedness, of unity. However, if we pay attention to expressions commonly used in prophetic literature to mark beginnings (e.g. 'This is what the LORD my God says', 11:4) and endings (e.g. 'declares the LORD', 10:12; 11:6), we may discern two main parts: a message Zechariah delivers as God's spokesman (10:1 – 11:3), and two symbolic acts he performs at God's command (11:4–17). We can summarize this as follows:

A prophetic message

Opening exhortation	10:1–2
The message itself	10:3–12
Closing exhortation	11:1–3

Two symbolic actions
Act 1

Command to perform the action	11:4
Explanation	11:5–6
The act itself	11:7–14

Act 2

Command to perform the action	11:15
Explanation	11:16
Concluding woe	11:17

All this is part of the larger oracle that spans the whole of chapters 9 – 11, as we have seen. The message of 10:1 – 11:3 is that God is angry with the shepherds who have caused his people to be oppressed and scattered, and will remedy this situation by regathering

---

[91] Acts 20:29.

them himself. Zechariah is then told to act the part of a good shepherd who is rejected by those he is seeking to care for (the first symbolic act). Finally he is told to act the part of a bad shepherd who is given to the people as a punishment for rejecting the good shepherd (the second symbolic act). The more precise meaning can be appreciated only by examining each of the parts in turn.

i. 'Ask the Lord for rain' (10:1–2)

Chapter 10 opens by appealing to the community to *ask the LORD* for the rain needed to make their crops grow (1), and not to rely on *idols*, which speak deceit, and *diviners*, who see only lying visions (2).

In agricultural societies the regular coming of the seasonal rains is essential for prosperity. In a place like Palestine, where the weather is unpredictable, it could be vital for survival. The opening chapter of Haggai, for example, refers to the hardship experienced, in Zechariah's own day, in times of drought.[92] Such circumstances are a severe test of people's belief in God's sovereignty as creator, and commitment to him alone as the One they should look to and depend on. The *idols* spoken of here are *t^{e}rāpîm* – small household gods.[93] Their association with *diviners* suggests their use in predicting the future,[94] presumably to determine the most auspicious time for ploughing, sowing, harvesting and so on. All forms of divination were expressly forbidden in the law of Moses.[95] It was the complete opposite of trusting dependence on God. Its effect was to cause people to *wander like sheep* without a shepherd (2). It snared them in *deceit*. The *comfort* it gave was a cruel *lie*, because it was based on spurious claims to revelation on the part of its practitioners (2).

But why a command to *ask the LORD for rain* at this point? At first sight it is rather unexpected. The answer lies in the way the previous chapter has ended. Zechariah has pictured the ideal future situation, when the kingdom of God has come, as a paradise of plenty, in which (9:17)

> Grain will make the young men thrive,
> and new wine the young women.

But *grain* and *new wine* come only with good harvests, which depend on good rains. Of course the people Zechariah is exhorting must look to the LORD for the seasonal rains they need year by year, but over and above that, they must keep looking to him for the

[92] Hag. 1:6, 10–11.
[93] Gen. 31:19.
[94] Cf. Judg. 17:5; 18:5.
[95] Deut. 18:10–13.

fulfilment of his kingdom promises. Every harvest, and the celebration of God's goodness that comes with it, is to be an anticipation of the final 'harvest home' they will celebrate in the new Jerusalem of the future kingdom of God – as described in the closing couple of paragraphs of the book (14:16–19). Every prayer for rain is also to be a prayer for the coming of his kingdom. Ezekiel (on whom Zechariah draws a great deal in these two chapters) had spoken of the 'showers of blessing' that would usher in that final day.[96]

The failure of past leaders to encourage the people of Israel to look constantly to God in this way led to the scattering that had happened during the exile, and which was still the experience of many of them (10). Leaders like this had been false shepherds, and the implicit warning of these opening verses (and of what follows) is that there will be more of them in the future. Bad leadership is a perennial problem, and it always leads to scattering and lostness. Idolatry too is a perennial problem, even when there is no literal worship of idolatrous religious objects. As we saw when we considered the call to repentance that opens the book, idolatry, at heart, is giving other things – things that are not God – the kind of place in our lives that only God should have.[97] The apostle Paul calls greed 'idolatry', because it makes what we want to have the centre of our lives.[98] In a similar way the apostle John's warning 'Dear children, keep yourselves from idols' neatly captures the essence of all his earlier warnings against loving the world, and all that is in it.[99] If idolatry is worshipping what is not God, divination is seeking knowledge (especially knowledge of the future) without reference to God. These things never disappear entirely; they just keep emerging in new forms, as seen in the fascination with astrology in our own day. Literal idolatry and divination do not seem to have been practised by the Jewish people in the period following the exile as they had been before.[100] But the kind of faithlessness they represent certainly did continue, especially among the nation's leaders. *Diviners* (2a), like *sheep* and *shepherd* (2b), is a metaphor. A 'diviner' here is a leader who deals in lies and falsehood rather than truth: he is the opposite of a *shepherd*. Under such 'leaders' people *wander* like sheep, and are *oppressed* (2b). The question is, if

---

[96] Ezek. 34:26. Cf. Zech. 14:17: 'If any of the peoples of the earth do not go up to Jerusalem to worship the King, the LORD Almighty, *they will have no rain*' (my italics).

[97] See the comments on 1:1–6.

[98] Col. 3:5.

[99] 1 John 5:21; cf. 2:15–17.

[100] For example, there is no reference to them in the books of Ezra, Nehemiah, Haggai, Zechariah or Malachi.

such leaders are to arise in the future, what will happen to all that was promised in the previous chapter? More particularly, what will become of God's people, to whom those promises were given? The answer lies in verses 3–12.

ii. God will care for his people (10:3–12)

God is *angry* with the false shepherds and will *punish* them (3a). He himself will *care for his flock*, represented here by *the house of Judah* (3b) and the *house of Joseph* (6). Judah was the great patriarch of the southern tribes, and Joseph the corresponding ancestor of the northern tribes. *House* is probably to be understood here in the sense of a 'community', or family, bound together by common origins and common history. So the *flock* of God on view in this passage is something much bigger than the community in Jerusalem; it is the entire people of Israel, most of whom were still (in Zechariah's time) dispersed among the nations. But within that wider 'flock', the people of Judah are mentioned first because of a particular place they have in God's plans for his people. He promises to restore their strength and dignity, making them *like a proud horse in battle* (3). The *cornerstone*, the *tent peg* and the *battle-bow* in verse 4 are all images of leadership, summarized in plain language by the expression *every ruler*, which follows.[101] In short, the key role of the tribe of Judah in God's determination to care for his people is reaffirmed. It is from Judah that effective leaders will arise again, as they have in the past. God will be *with them* (5b), and make them victorious over their enemies.

This militaristic language may seem at first sight to have little to do with the previous, pastoral image of the shepherd and his sheep. But if so, that is surely because we have a far too gentle, romanticized view of shepherding. The basic task of a shepherd was to care for his sheep. That meant feeding them, but it also meant protecting them from wild predators. A good shepherd had to be able and willing to fight for his sheep when necessary. A shepherd had to be strong.[102] In this passage God's *care* for his people (3) is expressed in his promise to provide them with strong leaders, who will fight to defend them. The result of such leadership is described in what follows. The people themselves are made strong (6–7), and their wandering and lostness is brought to an end. The scattered flock is

---

[101] For the use of *cornerstone* as a metaphor for a ruler see Judg. 20:2 (Heb.); 1 Sam. 14:38 (Heb.); Is. 19:13; Ps. 118:22. For the similar use of *[tent]peg* (Heb. *yāṯēḏ*) see Is. 22:23. Cf. Baldwin 1972, p. 174.

[102] Cf. David's testimony to his own previous experience as a shepherd in 1 Sam. 17:34–37. It was the fights he had had as a shepherd that had prepared him to fight Goliath.

'saved', 'restored' (6), made *joyful* (7), 'redeemed' (8), 'brought back', 'gathered' (10) and 'strengthened' (12). Of course, it is God himself who achieves all this. He is the subject of all the leading verbs[103] in verses 6–12. As the context makes clear, however, the means by which he brings about this remarkable reversal in the condition of his people is his getting rid of bad leaders (3a), and providing good ones in their place (3b–5). In short, strong leaders, raised up and empowered by God, are essential for the welfare of God's people. Only through such leadership can his flock be properly cared for. David himself was the classic example of such a leader in Israel's earlier history. He was literally a shepherd, from the tribe of Judah. He began his career as a leader anointed by God by confronting and slaying Goliath, and so saving Israel.[104] The promise of this passage is that God will care for his people by giving them more such leaders in the future.

But now for some of the detail. The expression *I will strengthen* occurs in verse 6, and is repeated in verse 12. It acts as a frame around the intervening verses and expresses the basic promise they contain. God is the strengthener, and it is to him his people must look – both shepherds and sheep – if they are to be strong.[105] Notice too how the command *Ask the LORD*, in verse 1, is answered by the promise *I will answer them*, in verse 6. Bad shepherds do not ask God for what they need, and neither, in the end, will those whom they lead. True shepherds depend on God themselves, and cultivate that same quality in others. That is the secret of their strength. God's promise is that he will strengthen the whole people of God (6, 12), but good leaders have a crucial role to play in this.

The 'rejecting' spoken of in verse 6b is looked back to as a thing of the past, especially the disasters that overtook the two kingdoms of Israel and Judah in the eighth century. Because of their persistent faithlessness and refusal to repent, God had rejected both their kings and the people themselves, and handed them over to their enemies. He rejected them because they had rejected him:

But they would not listen and were as stiff-necked as their fathers, who did not trust in the LORD their God. They rejected his decrees and the covenant he had made with their fathers and the warnings he had given them. They followed worthless idols and themselves became worthless. They imitated the nations around them although the LORD had ordered them, 'Do not do as they

[103] The verbs which refer to the primary acts that cause other (secondary, derivative) things to happen.
[104] 1 Sam. 17.
[105] Cf. Is. 40:28–31.

do,' and they did the things the LORD had forbidden them to do…

Therefore the LORD rejected all the people of Israel; he afflicted them and gave them into the hands of plunderers, until he thrust them from his presence.[106]

They learnt to their cost that they could not reject God's rightful claims on them with impunity.

The good news of the present passage, however, is that this state of affairs will be reversed in the future (6):

> *They will be as though*
> *I had not rejected them.*

Actually this is more than a reversal; it is the erasure of the past – as though it had never happened. What good news that is for sinners! But in the majestic poetry of this passage there is another way in which the future is contrasted with the past. 'Erasure' applies only to what was negative in the past. But what of the positive things of the past, such as the exodus from Egypt, that great act of deliverance that gave Israel its being as a free nation under God? Far from being erased, this will be repeated in the future on a far grander scale. This part of Israel's past will be 'erased' only in the sense of being eclipsed by something far more glorious – a deliverance that will reverse *all* the scattering and bondage Israel had experienced throughout the whole course of her history. There are many echoes of the first exodus here: 'redemption' (8), deliverance from 'Egypt' (10), and passage through the *sea* (11). But the language is metaphorical, and the focus of the whole passage is forwards, not backwards. *Egypt* and *Assyria* (10a; repeated as *Assyria* and *Egypt* in 11b) represent all oppressors, ancient and modern, and the *sea* that the 'redeemed' will pass through is *the sea of trouble* (11), where everything threatens to overwhelm them. This *surging sea will be subdued* and they will *pass through* it (11). God will bring them home. Finally, the comprehensiveness of the deliverance on view is indicated by the piling up of terms for those who will experience it: *house of Judah, house of Joseph* (6), *Ephraimites* (7). What were formerly parts of a divided and scattered people are here drawn together again. The new exodus produces a new Israel, in which all exiles will be included.

But here, surely, we meet a problem. How will this come about,

[106] 2 Kgs. 17:14–15, 20. The northern kingdom is primarily on view, but the pairing of Israel and Judah in v. 13 makes it clear that the same language is applicable to the southern kingdom as well.

and what is the connection between this deliverance and the issue of leadership so prominent in the first part of the chapter? To find the answer we have to go back to chapter 9, which provides the context for all that follows. The highlight of chapter 9, as we have seen, is the coming of Zion's king, the Messiah, in verses 9–10. And he comes *having salvation* (9). In other words, the arrival of the Messiah will be the trigger for all that follows to begin to be fulfilled. That will be the time for false shepherds to be judged, for the dispersed flock to be regathered, and for a new Israel to be created. Not everything would be fulfilled then, for Jesus himself spoke of a yet future coming of the kingdom, for which his disciples were to pray. The essential point is that the fulfilment would come through him, and his arrival in Jerusalem would be the sign that it was beginning to happen. The ideal leader God had promised had arisen from the tribe of Judah, and the salvation of Israel was at hand. It would come only through judgment – the judgment Jesus himself would suffer for the sins of others, and the judgment God would bring on apostate Israel and its false shepherds for rejecting their Messiah. But out of that judgment would emerge a new people of God, a new Israel, with new leaders, appointed and approved by God himself. The first of them were the twelve apostles appointed directly by Jesus.[107] Jesus explained who he was and what he had come to do in 'shepherd' terms:

> I am the good shepherd. The good shepherd lays down his life for the sheep. The hired hand is not the shepherd who owns the sheep. So when he sees the wolf coming, he abandons the sheep and runs away. Then the wolf attacks the flock and scatters it. The man runs away because he is a hired hand and cares nothing for the sheep. I am the good shepherd; I know my sheep and my sheep know me – just as the Father knows me and I know the Father – and I lay down my life for the sheep. I have other sheep that are not of this sheep pen. I must bring them also. They too will listen to my voice, and there shall be one flock and one shepherd.[108]

Jesus began his mission of gathering the scattered flock first by sending his disciples to 'the lost sheep of Israel',[109] but then, after his resurrection, to 'all nations',[110] to gather the 'other sheep' as well. Here is a comprehensiveness far surpassing that of Zechariah 10, for

---

[107] Cf. the twelve tribes from Jacob's twelve sons under the old covenant.
[108] John 10:11–16.
[109] Matt. 10:6.
[110] Matt. 28:16–20.

Jesus fulfilled all of Zechariah, not just the tenth chapter![111] Chapters 8 and 14 speak, as we have seen, not only of Jewish people being saved, but Gentiles as well (8:20–23; 14:16–19). With the coming of Jesus the Messiah, the kind of leadership God approves had indeed arisen from the tribe of Judah, and those whom he commissioned shared that accreditation with him.[112] They also shared in his authority, for they were sent forth in his name, and with his promise to be with them.[113] Today that mission goes on, but not without difficulty. Battles have to be fought, and suffering endured. But the outcome is certain. The final gathering of the full number of God's people – from both Israel and the nations – will be on the last day.[114] So the fulfilment of what Zechariah prophesied is already under way, and Jesus is central to it. He has already come, *having salvation* (9:9). In him the promised kingdom has come, and will come.

Verses 3–12 of chapter 10, then, are a magnificent prophecy about how God will care for his people by providing good leadership for them. It is framed, as we have seen, by two short exhortations (10:1–2 and 11:1–3). In the second of these the land is called upon to wail because of the judgment God will bring on the false shepherds. Unfortunately, when leaders incur judgment for how they have behaved, their people and land also suffer – at least in the short term.

iii. 'Open your doors' (11:1–3)

This short poem is an excellent example of how the Old Testament prophets took forms of speech from ordinary life and used them to express their message. 'Wailing' (2, 3) is something normally associated with disasters, and especially with death. Dirges (wailing songs) were normally sung at funerals by the family and friends of the deceased.[115] The prophets, however, took this well-known type

---

[111] In this respect it is noteworthy that the book of Revelation as a whole, with its radically Christocentric focus, follows the same broad pattern as the book of Zechariah: first the 'here and now' of the historical people of God living out their commitment to the kingdom of God in a hostile world (chs. 1 – 3; cf. Zech. 1:1 – 6:8); then the hailing of the 'Root of David' as God's chosen deliverer (chs. 4 – 5; cf. Zech. 6:9–15); and then the arrival of the end (chs. 6 – 20; cf. Zech. chs. 7 – 14). The book of Daniel exhibits the same basic pattern, with ch. 7 (the Son of Man passage) marking the transition from the court tales of chs. 1 – 6 to the presentation of the final conflict between good and evil in chs. 8 – 12.

[112] The followers derive their true identity from him. This is no longer a matter of membership of a particular tribe, or even of being Israelites. Zechariah himself foresaw the day when people, even from among the *Philistines* would *become leaders in Judah* (Zech. 9:6, 7b).

[113] Acts 3:16; Matt. 28:20.

[114] Rom. 11:25–32. What is in view in these verses is not the salvation of every Jew and Gentile without exception, but all the elect from both Israel and the nations.

[115] Sometimes, as well, by professional mourners.

of song, and used it as a way of announcing judgment. Those whom God has declared he will judge are told to start wailing *now*, because of the certainty of the disaster that lies in store for them. There is heavy irony in this, not just because the 'wailers' mourn for themselves, but because the prophet, far from showing sympathy for them, expresses *satisfaction* at the fate they suffer. He identifies, instead, with God, the one who causes the disaster to happen. In effect this poem is a poetic elaboration of 10:3:

> My anger burns against the shepherds,
> and I will punish the leaders.

The opening command, *Open your doors* (1), is the negative counterpart of 'Ask the LORD' in 10:1. Those who refuse to ask the Lord for rain (his blessing) will eventually have to open their doors to *fire* (his judgment). Lebanon is commanded to open her doors so that *fire may devour* her *cedars* (1). In Old Testament times Lebanon was famous (among other things) for its magnificent, tall cedars, which were an ideal source of timber for large buildings such as temples and palaces. Through an arrangement with Hiram, king of Tyre, Solomon had been able to import large quantities of this cedar for his own building projects. It was used in the construction of the Jerusalem temple.[116] Solomon used so much of it in the construction of his own palace that it is referred to in 1 Kings 7:2 as 'the Palace of the Forest of Lebanon'.[117] So the cedars of Lebanon came to symbolize the magnificence of Solomon's kingdom, and his ability to tap the resources of other nations in order to enrich it. In the preaching of the prophets, however, they take on an additional, darker significance. They represent not only magnificence, but pride – what is 'high' with its own importance – and especially rulers who are like this.[118] Judgment on the 'cedars of Lebanon' is therefore a most appropriate way of speaking poetically of God's punishment of leaders who have not acknowledged him in the way they have ruled.

Bashan (2) was the tableland to the north-east of the Sea of Galilee, better known today as the Golan Heights. It was conquered by Israel in the time of Joshua[119] and was a prized part of Israel's territory in the golden days of Solomon.[120] In later times Israel's hold on it became more tenuous, and it was eventually lost (in the

---

[116] 1 Kgs. 5:1–10.
[117] Note the repeated reference to cedar in 1 Kgs. 7:1–12.
[118] See Is. 2:10–18, especially v. 13.
[119] Deut. 1:4; 3:1–11.
[120] 1 Kgs. 4:13.

eighth century) to Assyria.[121] It was of strategic significance as a frontier province, and was also of major economic importance. Its higher rainfall and fertility made it prime land for grazing cattle, and nearly all the references to it in the Old Testament allude to this in one way or another.[122] Of course, in order to exploit it fully in this way, much of the native forest that covered it had to be felled.[123] This is almost certainly what lies behind the 'Wail' of verse 2b:

> Wail, oaks of Bashan;
> the dense forest has been cut down!

So the dominant image in verses 1 and 2 is trees. But the poem is not about trees; it is about the *shepherds* of verse 3. In context these must be the shepherds whom the previous passage talked about – the bad leaders who will arise in the interval between the 'now' of Zechariah's own day and the 'then' of the final coming of the kingdom of God. The trees tell a tale which the prophet uses powerfully to deliver his message about these false shepherds and the fate that awaits them. God's anger will be unleashed against them and remove them. His judgment on them will be like a raging fire in the cedar forests of Lebanon, or like the axing down of the oaks of Bashan.

Finally, the focus shifts to the devastation of the land on which the leaders depended for their wealth and security. Given the *shepherd* language of the opening line of verse 3, the *rich pastures*[124] of the second line are presumably sheep grazing land, most likely in upper Galilee. The *lush thicket of the Jordan*[125] is 'the dense confusion of tamarisks and other shrubs extending on either side of the meandering river, and covering the area inundated by flood waters when the snows of Hermon melt in spring'.[126] In biblical times it provided shelter for lions and other predators that would emerge at will to prey on sheep and other domestic animals. It still harbours wild boars.[127] Probably, the destruction on view in this verse is not the kind produced by natural disaster or economic exploitation, but by war[128] – something that features strongly in chapters 12 – 14. The main point here, though, is the effect that the

---

[121] 2 Kgs. 14:25; 15:29.

[122] E.g. Ps. 22:12; Jer. 50:19; Ezek. 39:18; Amos 4:1.

[123] Some of it had been exported to Tyre for use in boat-building (Ezek. 27:5–6).

[124] Literally 'their [the shepherds'] mantle, rich covering'.

[125] Literally its 'majesty' (gā'ôn).

[126] Baldwin 1972, p. 178. See the excellent photograph in Grollenberg, p. 17.

[127] Baldwin 1972, p. 178.

[128] Cf. Is. 1:7.

coming destruction will have on the leaders who are the objects of God's anger. They will wail like *shepherds* whose pastures have been destroyed, and like *lions* whose lairs have been ruined (3). They will have no means of providing for themselves, and nowhere to hide. The twofold *wail* of verse 2 is followed at once by the twofold *listen* of verse 3, as if to indicate that no sooner is the command given than the wailing begins.[129] In other words, when the threatened judgment comes, it will come quickly. No specifics are given; the future is seen only symbolically, and in the broadest outline. But what is presented with crystal clarity is the certainty that God will judge. Shepherds who do not care for the flock will be removed.

But there is a deeper question lurking in the background. Why do bad shepherds exist at all, and why has suffering at the hands of such leaders been so much a part of Israel's experience? Surely it is not what one would expect for people whom God has rescued from slavery and with whom he has made a covenant? In order to deal with this deeper issue, Zechariah is commanded to deliver a lesson from history in the form of an enacted parable.

e. Two shepherds: an enacted parable (11:4–17)

Zechariah is commanded to perform two symbolic actions. We have already noted what they are; now we must grapple with what they mean. Thankfully (as with the eight visions of chapters 1 – 6), the actions do not stand alone, but are accompanied by a certain amount of explanation.

First, it is important to note that in the first symbolic act, in which Zechariah plays the role of a good shepherd, he is representing God. The *covenant* in verse 10 is God's covenant, not Zechariah's, and the words and actions associated with it are all God's words and actions, even though they are spoken and performed (symbolically) by Zechariah. Second, the covenant on view is God's covenant relationship with the people of Israel. This is especially clear from the expression *Judah and Israel* in verse 14 – the two main parts of 'greater Israel' during the period of the monarchy, from David and Solomon to the exile. *People of the land*, in verse 6, is a way of referring to Jewish people living in Palestine (as in Zech. 7:5 and Hag. 2:4).[130] The NIV somewhat confuses the issue in verse 10 with the expression *all the nations*. Literally this is 'all the *peoples*',[131] and

---

[129] Cf. Conrad, pp. 171–172.

[130] Cf. Jer. 1:18; 34:19; 37:2. The usage in Ezra 4:4 is different: there the 'people of the land' are non-Jewish people of Palestine who opposed the rebuilding of Jerusalem. See Andersen, p. 32.

[131] Heb. *kol hā'ammîm*.

in this context almost certainly refers to all the tribes and people groups that constituted Israel, whether in or out of their homeland – not people of other nations.[132] Third, what is portrayed in the first symbolic act is the history of God's covenant with Israel from the time he *made* it to the time he *revoked* it (10). This 'revoking' is explained in verse 14 in terms of *breaking the brotherhood between Judah and Israel*; that is, the breaking up of what had once been a united Israel. Historically this happened in stages, from the break-up of Israel into two separate kingdoms after the death of Solomon,[133] to the fall, in turn, of both the northern and southern kingdoms, and the scattering of their citizens.[134] Although a minority had returned, this was still largely the condition of Israel in Zechariah's day. The first symbolic act is an enacted parable showing how this state of affairs had come about. It tells the story of a shepherd (God) and his sheep (the people of Israel).

Zechariah is told to act as the shepherd of a flock *marked for slaughter* (4). The flock is in this condition because those who ought to be caring for them (*their own shepherds*, 5) are in fact exploiting them for their own profit – selling them to merchants whose only interest is in their meat (5)! But the conjunction *for* at the beginning of verse 6 indicates that their condition is no accident. It is not simply a case of *king* oppressing people, but of *neighbour* oppressing neighbour. The sheep are as bad as their shepherds, and their condition is God's judgment on them all – sheep and shepherds alike. They have the kinds of leaders they deserve, and the fate that awaits them is entirely appropriate for the kinds of people they are. So the shepherd Zechariah represents in this opening part of the passage is a shepherd who will preside over the destruction of the flock – not because he is a bad shepherd, nor because he desires their destruction – but because that is what they deserve. The 'handing over' of verse 6 finds an echo in the New Testament in Romans 1 in the divine 'giving over' of people to their own destructive desires and behaviour.[135] It is a judicial act in both cases.

In verses 4–6 Zechariah is told (in general terms) what he must do; in verses 7–12 he actually does it, and here the narrative is more detailed. First, a distinction is made between the people as a whole, and some who are described as *the oppressed of the flock* (7).[136] Not

[132] Meyers and Meyers 1993, pp. 270–271; cf. Baldwin 1972, p. 184.

[133] 1 Kgs. 11 – 12.

[134] 2 Kgs. 17:1–23; 2 Kgs. 25:1–21.

[135] See especially vv. 24, 26, 28.

[136] The LXX takes *'ⁿêyî* with the preceding *lāḵēn* and reads 'for the Canaanites [i.e. merchants] of the flock' (cf. 14:21). But this is unwarranted in my judgment, and obscures an important aspect of the meaning of the passage.

everyone is guilty. Some are true victims, who suffer essentially because of the wrongdoing of others. Their existence is known by the true shepherd, and for his sake the threatened judgment is not carried out at once. Instead, he takes two staffs, called *Favour* and *Union*, and – for a time – continues to pasture the flock with them. He brings relief to the flock by 'getting rid of' *three shepherds* – presumably of the predatory kind previously referred to. 'Favour' (Heb. *nōʿam*) is literally 'beauty, delight', and can refer either to the beauty of God himself, or to the grace or favour he gives to those he loves.[137] 'Union' (Heb. *ḥōḇᵉlîm*), literally 'bonds', is used here in the positive sense of 'cords' or (metaphorically) 'pledges', which bind people and things together in unity.[138] Together the two staffs symbolize the blessedness of life in covenant relationship with God. The *three shepherds* (again taken together) represent the kind of leaders who threaten such blessedness. There may be an allusion to particular leaders whom God removed suddenly – perhaps the last three kings of Judah.[139] But we can only speculate about this, and must be careful that such speculation does not divert us from the main thrust of the passage. What is clear is that even when Israel as a whole was spiralling down to deserved judgment God continued to extend many covenant blessings to her. The judgment he exercised was not precipitate, nor without concern for the innocent. But the gross and persistent nature of Israel's sin meant that the ultimate sanction of national collapse and dissolution could not be postponed forever. And when it happened, the covenant between God and his people seemed to have come to a complete end – as graphically depicted in verses 8b–11.

This is the critical moment in the parable, and it is clearly intended

---

[137] Pss. 27:4; 90:17.

[138] Formally, *ḥōḇᵉlîm* is the active (Qal) participle of *ḥbl*, 'to bind, take in pledge' (Deut. 24:6; Ezek. 18:16; Exod. 22:26 [MT 25]; Prov. 20:16; 27:13 etc.). See Meyers and Meyers 1993, p. 264.

[139] I.e. Jehoiakim, Jehoiachin and Zedekiah. In the background, as many have noted, is Ezekiel's prophecy against the shepherds (kings) of Israel in Ezek. 34. The use of the definite article '*the* three shepherds' does seem to indicate that a particular historical situation is being alluded to, but identifying it has proved to be one of the most difficult problems in the interpretation of the book. My own suggestion is the one generally favoured by those who consider the passage to be pre-exilic. I do not subscribe to this date for the passage, but the way it functions in its context suggests some reference to the national collapse that preceded the exile. If so, the *one month* of v. 8a must be taken metaphorically for 'suddenly, in a [relatively] short time'. This is reasonable, in my judgment, given that we are dealing (if I am correct) with an enacted parable rather than a straightforward historical description of events. See Baldwin (1972, pp. 181–183) for a summary of the forty or more proposals that have been made for the identity of the three shepherds, ranging from the time of Moses to the Maccabean and Roman periods.

to shock. The flock as a whole 'detests' the shepherd, his patience with them at last runs out, and he quits (8b). He refuses to care for them any more, and leaves them to *die*. The last sentence of verse 9 is particularly chilling: *let those who are left eat one another's flesh* – almost certainly an allusion to the terrible conditions experienced by the people of Jerusalem during the long siege leading up to the fall of the city in 587 BC.[140] The famine became so severe that parents ate their own children in order to survive.[141] It is a terrible thing indeed to be abandoned by God. In fact, it is the ultimate horror, a horror experienced for us by Jesus in his death on the cross.[142] But the form that horror took for the people of Jerusalem (eating their own flesh) impresses on us that it was a fate they had brought on themselves. God gave them up to what they had chosen by rejecting him. The 'breaking' of the staff called *Favour* (10–11) indicates that the covenant relationship between the shepherd (God) and the sheep (Israel) was broken, not accidentally (as if God were powerless to prevent it happening) but deliberately, as a considered act of judgment on the people for their sin. The expression *the afflicted of the flock* (11) presumably has the same significance as *the oppressed of the flock* in verse 7. It is exactly the same expression in Hebrew, and refers to the faithful remnant. However others may have interpreted the disaster, they *knew it was the word of the LORD* – that is, they recognized it as something God had done in fulfilment of the warnings he had given.[143] And those with spiritual insight in Zechariah's own day would have recognized the same thing as they saw him enact this parable before their eyes.

But the parable of the good shepherd is not finished yet; its two final parts are dramatized in verses 12–14. The first has to do with severance pay for the shepherd (12). It is probably best, in view of what follows, to see this as a resumption of the main storyline of the parable, and to take the pronoun *them* (12a) as referring to the flock in general rather than to the 'afflicted of the flock' in the previous verse. How have the sheep valued their shepherd? What do they think he is worth? The fact that real sheep never think of such things is beside the point; licence of this kind is perfectly normal in a parable. The issue developed here has already been anticipated in the sentence *the flock detested me* in verse 8.[144] The shepherd asks

---

140 2 Kgs. 25:1–21.
141 Ezek. 5:10; Lam. 2:20.
142 Matt. 27:46; Mark 15:34; cf. Ps. 22:1.
143 2 Kgs. 17:7–20 (esp. v. 13); cf. Deut. 28:15–68.
144 Also something that 'real' sheep don't do! By this point in the parable the 'sheep' image is becoming rather transparent, and 'works' only if we think primarily of the *people* who are being referred to in this way.

them either to pay him or not, as they see fit, and they respond by giving him thirty pieces of silver (12). Zechariah is told to take this money and *throw it to the potter... into the house of the LORD* (13). In short, the payment is rejected. But why? And why is the money thrown where it is?

The *thirty pieces of silver* is hardly a contemptible price; it is a considerable sum of money.[145] Nehemiah later speaks of the forty shekels tax (presumably annual) as a 'heavy burden' imposed on the people by his predecessors.[146] Thirty shekels is the amount stipulated in the Law of Moses as compensation for the death of a slave,[147] but this should probably be taken as an indication of the high value placed on human life rather than of the paltry nature of the sum itself. As payment for the services of a shepherd, it might well be considered a *handsome price* (13). If that expression is ironical here, it is not because the sum itself is trivial, but because the shepherd regards *any* amount offered to him by people who actually detest him (8b) as unacceptable. If they had really valued him as their shepherd they would have accepted his care and heeded his warnings. The *potter* of verse 13 is presumably a craftsman associated with the temple. The services of such people were needed because the temple rituals required a continual supply of suitable vessels.[148] The money is probably thrown where it is because it was in the temple that the nation's leaders had most shown their contempt for God as the true shepherd of Israel – especially by allowing, and even promoting, idolatrous worship there.[149] It was this, above all, that had caused the LORD to withdraw his protection from Jerusalem and the temple and allow them to be destroyed.[150] The breaking of the second rod *Union* (14) depicts, as we have already noted, the breaking up of the once united Israel. Historically it began after the death of Solomon, but continued in stages over the next several centuries. The final fracturing came with the fall of Jerusalem and the scattering of its people. But the breaking of this staff also symbolizes something deeper, namely the truth that true unity between people depends on union with God. Where that basic relationship is fractured, all other relationships eventually decay as well. It has been the story of the whole world, not just of Israel.

[145] It is literally 'thirty *shekels*' – about 300 g or a third of a kilogram. See Douglas, p. 1246.
[146] Neh. 5:15.
[147] Exod. 21:32.
[148] Lev. 6:28. Cf. Baldwin (1972, p. 185), who suggests that 'a guild of potters may have been minor officials at the Temple'.
[149] See Ezek. 8 – 11, especially ch. 8.
[150] Ezek. 8 – 11.

So much for the first symbolic act. The second is much more straightforward, and can be dealt with more briefly. Zechariah is told to play the part of a shepherd again, but this time a *foolish* or *worthless* one (15, 17). This shepherd does not care for the flock at all, but slaughters and devours them (16), and when they are attacked by others he *deserts* them (17). This is the kind of shepherd the flock deserve, and their suffering at his hands is a further punishment on them for rejecting their true shepherd. It is God who 'raises up' (appoints) this worthless shepherd. But for all that, his deeds are evil, and he will be held accountable for them. Hence the dire pronouncement of judgment with which the chapter ends (17):

> Woe to the worthless shepherd...
> May his arm be completely withered,
> his right eye totally blinded!

Who can this worthless shepherd be? The tense of the verb in verse 16 ('I *am going* to raise up') suggests that he is a future figure. But the way this symbolic act follows the first makes it more natural to see him as a past figure, such as Nebuchadnezzar of Babylon, whom God sovereignly used to punish his people for rejecting him. So we appear to have a dilemma; two interpretations offer themselves, and we seem bound to choose between them. In fact, however, the verb in question is a participle in the underlying Hebrew, and the tense is much more ambiguous than the NIV translation suggests. A more literal translation would be, 'See, I am raising up a worthless shepherd.' What is seen as Zechariah performs this act is the *kind* of shepherd God gives his people when they have rejected their true shepherd. Understood in this way he does not have only one incarnation, so to speak, at one point in time. He is Nebuchadnezzar, but he is also the rapacious shepherds of 10:3. He represents all the bad leaders and exploiters Israel has had to endure, and will yet endure, because of their contempt for the loving care and discipline of God, their true shepherd.[151]

This brings us, at last, to the end of the two symbolic actions, and to the end of the prophetic message of chapters 9 – 11 as a whole. There have been many twists and turns since we set out at the beginning of chapter 9. We have tried to note the connections and transitions from one part to the next as we have progressed. But the detailed and complex nature of the material has been confusing at times, making it all too easy to lose track of where we have been. So

---

[151] Cf. the 'prophet like you [Moses]' of Deut. 18:18, who likewise had many 'incarnations', culminating in the coming of Christ.

it is time now to pause and take stock. What has it all been about, and how does the enacted parable of the two shepherds, at the end, contribute to it?

At the most general level the theme of these three chapters, as of the whole book, is the kingdom (rule) of God, from his triumphant progress to Jerusalem in 9:1–13, to the review of his dealings with Israel as their true shepherd (i.e. king) in 11:4–17. But within this framework there has been an extensive exploration of the role of human leaders, especially in God's administration of his covenant relationship with Israel. This theme is introduced with the appearance of the king riding into Jerusalem on a donkey in 9:9. As we saw when we looked at that passage, he is a human figure – God's perfect representative, the ideal leader of his people. The subsequent reference to the people of God as his 'flock' in 9:16 provides the link to the contrasting treatment of *bad* leadership in 10:1 – 11:3. The rapacious shepherds of this passage, who oppress and destroy the flock, are the complete antithesis of the ideal king, 'gentle', 'righteous' and 'having salvation', of chapter 9. The two sign-acts, which come at the end of the whole section, set all this once more in the context of the rule of God, the divine Shepherd, who brings down and raises up human leaders. So the 'oracle' of chapters 9 – 11, although complex, is not a disjointed jumble. It is held together by the consistent focus on the issue of leadership, which it explores from different, complementary angles.

But before we leave it we can say a few more things about how the enacted parable of 11:4–17 contributes to the whole and completes it. First, from the vantage point we have now reached, we can see how effectively it answers the question hanging in the air at the end of 10:1 – 11:3. It shows that suffering at the hands of bad shepherds has its root cause in a failure to value and respond properly to the loving care and discipline of the true shepherd, God himself. That is how it was with Israel, and how it is for us as well. The flock that 'detests' its true shepherd (11:8) will get a predatory tyrant in his place (11:16). In the end we get the kinds of leaders we have chosen, and that is God's judgment on us. This is why the church today needs to be constantly nourished and guided by the faithful teaching of God's Word, and be led by men who will give themselves to that as their fundamental calling. That is how God rules and cares for his people, and it is the only thing that will keep the wolves at bay.[152]

Second, the 'lesson from history' presented in Zechariah's enacted parable contains a most serious warning. Detesting the good shepherd led not just to the breaking of the brotherhood between

[152] Acts 20:17–31; 2 Tim. 4:1–5.

153

Judah and Israel (the fracturing of the covenant community, 11:14); it led to a complete breakdown in the covenant relationship with God himself (11:10–11). In other words, it is impossible to be in relationship with God unless we are prepared to be ruled by him. The alternative is not just suffering under bad leaders; it is complete disaster, as Israel learned to their cost in the bitter experience of being abandoned by God to the horrors of death and exile. Rebellion against God is a serious thing, which is why the call to repentance is an essential part of the preaching of the kingdom of God. Zechariah preached repentance, as we have seen, and so did Jesus and the apostles. We can't afford to avoid it in the interests of being winsome or inoffensive. Too much is at stake.

Finally, in the context of chapters 9 – 11 as a whole, Zechariah's two sign-acts powerfully present his contemporaries with the possibilities and dangers the future holds for them. The shout that goes up in chapter 9, 'Rejoice greatly … Jerusalem! See, your king comes to you!' means, at the very least, that the disaster that overtook their forefathers has not brought to a complete end God's commitment to them as his people. The Israel of the past may have been fractured beyond repair. The old covenant God made with them at Sinai may have had its final outworking in curse and judgment. But the undertakings God gave to Abraham and to David still stand. The 'Branch' of 3:8 and 6:12 will come as promised. There will be a new beginning, a new covenant, so to speak, and the restoration and rebuilding that were already under way in Zechariah's time were the advance instalments of it. The question was, when their God came to them again in this new way – in the person of his representative, the Messiah – would they repeat the mistake of the forefathers? Would the flock again 'detest' its true Shepherd, or rejoice at his coming and be willing to be ruled by him? If our understanding of 10:1 – 11:3 is correct, Zechariah did not see the path ahead as a smooth one. Israel had not yet seen the last of bad shepherds, and therefore the Messiah, when he came, would hardly be met with universal acclaim. It would in fact bring the relationship between God and Israel to a new, and terrifying point of crisis. That is how the two signs of 11:4–17 lead into what follows. They set the stage for the final showdown in God's relationship with his people, and ultimately with the world at large. It is in this context, too, that we can see the appropriateness of the way Matthew's Gospel quotes the passage about the thirty pieces of silver with reference to the betrayal of Jesus.[153] In the time of fulfilment Zechariah's teaching

---

[153] Matt. 27:9–10. On the surprising reference to Jeremiah here, see the note on this passage in the introduction, p. 48 (note 101). Cf. the discussion in Morris, pp. 696–697.

about the clash between God and the false shepherds gets transposed into a higher key, and played out in the person of Jesus the Messiah.

5. Oracle 2: Day of destiny in Jerusalem (chs. 12 – 14)

With the opening of chapter 12 the pace begins to quicken. The goal in view is kept steadily before us by the frequent repetition of the expression 'on that day' – no fewer than sixteen times in the three chapters. Some of the themes we have met previously recur here, but with added intensity as the book moves towards its climax. On view are the events that will usher in the end of history.[154] The place where they will be enacted is Jerusalem. Chapter 12 begins with 'all nations' gathered against Jerusalem to make war on her. Chapter 14 ends with the 'survivors from all the nations' going up to Jerusalem to worship God there, and to acknowledge his universal kingship. So the two poles the oracle revolves around are war and worship, and the overall movement is from the one to the other. But it is not a simple, straight-line progression. Chapter 14 starts by returning us to the point from which we set out (vv. 1–2), before moving us to our final goal. So while the overall trajectory is clear, it is traversed in two complementary ways. In chapters 12 and 13 it is God's troubled relationship with his own people, Israel, that is brought to its final resolution, and then in chapter 14 his relationship with the world at large. Again, the kingdom (rule) of God is the general theme that ties all the material together. Worship by a vast multitude from all the nations is the ultimate expression of his kingdom having come. But since not all will acknowledge him willingly, battles must be fought. The world (and Israel) being as it is, war is the necessary prelude to worship.

The short heading *An Oracle* introduces the whole of chapters 12 – 14. The first major movement, as we have just noted, spans chapters 12 and 13. It begins with the introductory statement *This is the word of the LORD concerning Israel* in 12:1, and concludes with statements that confirm God's special covenant relationship with Israel in 13:9:

> They will call on my name
> and I will answer them;
> I will say, 'They are my people,'
> and they will say, 'The LORD is our God.'[155]

---

[154] I.e. the day on which history will reach its divinely determined goal.
[155] Cf. the *call* and *answer* here with the 'ask' and 'answer' of 10:1 and 6.

So chapters 12 and 13 as a whole are about the restoration of God's covenant relationship with Israel, and it will be accomplished from God's side. He himself will do it, and the way he introduces himself indicates that it will be no mean feat. In fact, it will be a work comparable to the creation of the world! The declaration of intention is made by *The LORD, who stretches out the heavens, who lays the foundation of the earth, and who forms the spirit of man within him* (1).[156]

It will be a work of new creation, ultimately involving the whole world, but beginning with Israel. For Zechariah (14:8, 16–21), as for Isaiah, the new creation will have a new Jerusalem at the centre of it.[157] That is where the final battles that will usher in the kingdom of God will be fought and won.

The expression *On that day* runs right through the passage, as we have seen, and serves to establish and maintain its focus on the end to which everything is finally moving. But it is too frequent to serve as a marker of significant sections. It is more like a refrain, or a pulse, that permeates and energizes it all. On the basis of content and movements of thought, however, several parts may be distinguished, as follows:

1. A promise to defend Jerusalem against the final assault the nations will make against her (12:2–9).
2. A promise to pour out on the people of Jerusalem (both royalty and commoners) a spirit of contrition for a 'pierced one' (12:10–14).
3. A promise of cleansing from sin and impurity (13:1–6).
4. A promise that the suffering to come will produce a purified remnant who will truly be God's covenant people (13:7–9).

A great deal in these two chapters is taken up, directly or indirectly, in the New Testament and can therefore be fully understood only when looking back from the fulfilment that comes in Jesus. However, if I keep detouring to trace out all those connections and developments it will be difficult to appreciate the development of thought within the material itself. So apart from the occasional hint here and there, I shall save up reflections on what it all means in the light of the further revelation given to us in the New Testament until we reach the end of chapter 13.

---

[156] Cf. Is 42:5; 44:24.
[157] Is. 65:17–19; 66:18–24; cf. Ezek. 40:1–4; 47:1–12; Mic. 4:1–2.

a. Jerusalem's enemies to be destroyed (12:1–9)

The message concerning *Israel* (1) in these two chapters is focused on *Judah* and *Jerusalem* in particular. There is an obvious reason for this, of course. By Zechariah's day, what had once been the nation of Israel, made up of all the twelve tribes descended from Abraham, Isaac and Jacob, had been reduced to a small Persian province centred on Jerusalem. *Judah* was no longer the kingdom or tribe of that name from earlier times, but the people of this province (Yehud). In a sense it was all that was left of Israel,[158] and it existed precariously in a pagan world – always under virtual siege from hostile forces, and threatened with extinction. Furthermore, this opening part of chapter 12 is hardly reassuring, at least in one very important aspect of its message. It shows that as the final day approaches, hostility against Judah and Jerusalem will intensify rather than diminish. Jerusalem is where the nations of the world will assemble for their conflict with God and his people. The good news is that God will triumph in that last battle, and that his people will share his victory – a good example of a theme we have met before in Zechariah being repeated and intensified.[159]

The figure of Jerusalem as a *cup* that causes people to 'reel' or stagger (as though drunk, 2) draws on traditional prophetic language about 'the cup of judgment' that God will cause his enemies to drink. Like a host serving his guests, God is pictured as giving people various drinks he has specifically prepared for them. The 'cup' can be very pleasant.[160] More often, however, especially in the preaching of the prophets, the cup was a symbol of God's wrath; a cup he would make his enemies drink to the very dregs.[161] The suffering of Jerusalem and its people during the exile was likened by Isaiah to the drinking of just such a cup.[162] But here it is Jerusalem herself that is the *cup*. The nations will be drawn to it like drinkers to fine wine, but it will be a deadly draught for them. In drinking this cup they will meet the doom God has prepared for them. In verse 3 the image shifts from cup to *rock*, and from reeling to injury caused by collision with an immovable object. But the message is the same: the nations that gather to attack Jerusalem will encounter God's wrath there, overwhelmingly and finally.

There are echoes here of earlier battles: every *horse* struck with *panic*, and every *rider* with *madness* (4a). That is the kind of thing

---

[158] The rest of 'Israel' was still scattered among the nations, most of it (i.e. them) with little prospect of ever returning.
[159] Cf. 9:12–16.
[160] As in the 'cup of salvation' of Ps. 116:13, or the 'overflowing' cup of Ps. 23:5.
[161] E.g. Jer. 25:15–16, 27–28. Cf. Baldwin 1972, p. 188.
[162] Is. 51:17.

that happened when the Lord overthrew the army of Pharaoh at the Red Sea,[163] when Joshua led the Israelites into battle against the Canaanites,[164] and when Sisera's forces were swept away at the river Kishon.[165] The 'blinding' of the enemy (4b) recalls the blindness suffered by Syrian invaders in the time of Elisha.[166] And above all, the sudden reversal here when Jerusalem's situation seems hopeless is like the miraculous deliverance of the same city from Sennacherib's forces in the time of Isaiah.[167] God has fought for his people before. But this is not just 'another' battle; it is the last one – the battle of *that day* which will usher in the kingdom of God.

The emphasis throughout falls on the initiative of God, and his total sovereignty over everything that happens. He has summoned the nations to this final battle; they *are gathered* by his determination, not their own.[168] He 'makes' Jerusalem a cup that sets them reeling and a rock they cannot move. He 'strikes', 'keeps watch', 'blinds', 'saves', 'shields' and 'destroys'. It is his battle, first and foremost. But it is also the battle of his people. The expression *the house of Judah*, in verse 4, may be a general term for the people as a whole or (like *house of David* in v. 7) for their leaders. The latter is more likely in view of what follows in verse 5: *Then the leaders of Judah will say* ... In fact, the leaders (under God) are shown as playing a key role in the victory. God makes them *like a brazier in a woodpile, like a flaming torch among sheaves*, so that they *consume right and left all the surrounding peoples* (6). Here at last are leaders worth the name! How different they are from the false shepherds of chapter 11 who exploit and devour the very people they are supposed to care for (11:4–5, 16)! And, as promised in 10:4, it is 'from Judah' that this leadership comes. This passage looks to the day when false shepherds will be no more, and Israel will no longer suffer at their hands. And the people themselves will be strong, *because the LORD Almighty is their God* (5).[169] They will be strong, fundamentally, because their relationship with God will at last be fully restored, and he will be in their midst as their mighty protector and deliverer.[170] Much of what follows (to the end of ch. 13) will be concerned with just how this complete healing of the relationship between God and his people will be achieved.

[163] Exod. 15, especially vv. 1, 4.
[164] Josh. 2:8–9.
[165] Judg. 5:21–22.
[166] 2 Kgs. 6:18.
[167] 2 Kgs. 18:17 – 19:37.
[168] The verb is passive (a Niphal). Cf. 14:1, where the active verb (with the Lord as subject) expresses the same reality.
[169] Anticipating the climax reached in 13:9.
[170] LORD Almighty is a military title: literally 'Yahweh of hosts [i.e. armies]'.

But first, in verses 7–8, there are hints of other relationships that will at last be healed. No community is without its tensions, even a community united at the most fundamental level by a common faith in God. In the community Zechariah ministered to, as we saw, there were tensions between returning exiles and permanent residents, and between 'southerners' and 'northerners'.[171] Other kinds of tensions emerged with time: tensions between leaders and people, and between the people of Jerusalem itself (where power and wealth became concentrated) and the less affluent rural areas. There is great sensitivity to such matters in the description here of how the LORD will deal with the different segments of the population on the final day. He *will save the dwellings of Judah first, so that the honour of the house of David* [the leading families] *and of Jerusalem's inhabitants may not be greater than that of Judah* [the people of the province as a whole] (7). And as for the people of Jerusalem itself, *the feeblest among them will be like David, and the house of David* [the leaders] *will be like the Angel of the LORD going before them* (8). So there will be leadership, but it will be a leadership that truly cares for the weak, and draws people together rather than scattering them; in other words, leadership like that of God himself.[172] The leaders *on that day* (8) will be true undershepherds of God, the great leader and true shepherd of his people.[173]

So ends this first part of this prophetic message, with verse 9 acting as a summary. God will destroy those who try to destroy Jerusalem. Chapter 14 shows why: it is from there that he will manifest himself as King to the whole world. But as these verses have shown, he will not do that alone, but in and through his people. The oracle as a whole, we recall, is about *Israel* and *Jerusalem* (1, 2). But it's far more about people than places. It is through the *people* of Jerusalem (5), not just the city itself, that he will manifest his glory to the world. So now deeper issues begin to be probed – issues that go right to the heart of what has troubled God's relationship with his people in the past and what must happen if a complete mending of that relationship is to happen.

b. Mourning for the One they pierced (12:10–14)

Now indeed we are on holy ground, for we are approaching the most mysterious and profound part of Zechariah's message, and it has to do with the necessary place of suffering and weeping in the coming of the kingdom of God.

[171] See the introduction, p. 25.
[172] Cf. Is. 40:11.
[173] Cf. Zech. 10:3; 1 Pet. 5:2–4.

The reference to the 'pouring out' of *a spirit of grace and supplication* in verse 10 seems to mark a sudden change of subject. But this is not so. The people on view are still *the house of David* and *the inhabitants of Jerusalem* (as in v. 7), and the reference to someone who has been 'pierced' (10) suggests that the general context is still a battle, or at least the aftermath of one. If there is a sudden change, its nature and meaning must be sought by reading these verses in close connection with what has gone before, not as an entirely new and unrelated piece. In general the picture that unfolds here is of a victorious army suddenly plunged into grief by the realization that its supreme commander has been slain in the battle and (worst of all) that his own followers have been responsible for his death. Which brings us to the key issue of this passage, and arguably of the message of the whole book. Who is the 'pierced one' of verse 10? The answer cannot be given wholly from this passage alone as there are things still to come (in the next chapter) that are relevant to it. But for now we shall stay with the verses directly before us and see what we can glean from them.

The 'pierced one' is none other than God himself, for it is he who expressly says so: *they will look on me, the one they have pierced.*[174] There is the essence of the matter. The victory that will usher in the kingdom of God will not be won without suffering, and none will suffer more keenly than the King himself. The word translated *pierced* here is the same word used for the 'stab' that kills the false prophet in 13:3, and the 'sword thrust' with which Abimelech is killed in Judges 9.[175] It is not a mere wounding, but a death blow; a piercing to the heart. But even that is not the worst of it. The deepest pain is caused by the knowledge of who has done it. It is not the enemy that pierces God in this battle, but his own people, just as the son of 13:3 is stabbed by his own parents. This act must surely spell the end of Israel's covenant relationship with God! What else could possibly follow?

Of course, there is mystery here. We are dealing with things inexpressible. How could God be pierced? And even granting the possibility, how could his own people do such a violent act unwittingly, and how and when will they *look on* the One they have

---

[174] NIV; cf. AV. The speaker is clearly God in v. 10, as in v. 9. Many scholars emend the Hebrew text (MT) to read, 'they will look on him (*'lyw*)' to agree with the expression 'they will mourn for *him*', which immediately follows (cf. RSV). The proposed emendation is a minor one, and reasonable in that sense, but it is unsupported by the ancient versions, and is unnecessary in order to make sense of the text (as my exposition of this passage and what follows it, esp. 13:7, will show). For a recent discussion see Meyers and Meyers 1993, pp. 336–337. The authors conclude, 'we find no reason to depart from the MT'.

[175] Judg. 9:54 (Heb. *dqr*); cf. 1 Sam. 31:4.

pierced? No answers are given here, but this is not the whole story. Zechariah has not yet said all he has to say about this matter; we have not reached the end of his book yet! And some things presently obscure will become clear only in the light of a dawn that will break much later.[176] What we can say is that the 'piercing' is not the only mystery in this passage. There is also the mystery of God's grace to those who have done it. He pours out on them *a spirit of grace and supplication* (10), so that they are able to weep for what they have done, and seek his forgiveness for it. As the NIV translates this verse, what is poured out is a certain disposition, or state of mind. It is much more likely, however, that the primary reference here is to *God's* Spirit (capital 's').[177] Isaiah, Joel and Ezekiel had all spoken of a day when God would pour out his Spirit on his people, and had associated this with the dawning of the new age when everything that had been promised would at last be fulfilled.[178] In the same way, the pouring out of the Spirit here in Zechariah is linked to the dawning of *that* (final) *day* (11). *Grace* and *supplication* are terms that describe the effects the Spirit will produce. He will impart divine (unmerited) favour,[179] and turn the hearts of the recipients towards God in prayer. The prayer on view is plainly one of contrition, as indicated by the references to 'mourning', 'grieving bitterly' and 'weeping' (10–11). And the reason: *they will look on me, the one they have pierced* (10). The Spirit will produce insight; they will see God in a new way, and realize at last how grievously they have sinned against him.

The depth and intensity of the grief they will feel is emphasized by comparing it to mourning over the death of *an only child* and *a firstborn son* (10). There are echoes here of the night before the exodus, when 'a great cry' went up throughout the whole land of Egypt because of the death of the firstborn sons,[180] and of Abraham's anguish when he lifted the knife to slay Isaac.[181] The scope of the grief (involving the whole nation) is emphasized in verse 11 by likening it to the weeping for king Josiah, who was killed on the *plain of Megiddo*.[182] We know from the books of Chronicles that mourning Josiah's tragic death became an annual event in later times,

---

[176] See Matt. 4:16–17; John 1:1–9; and especially Rev. 1:7.
[177] As in the NIV footnote.
[178] Is. 32:15; Joel 2:28–32; Ezek. 39:29.
[179] Hebrew *ḥēn*.
[180] Exod. 11:6; 12:30 (AV).
[181] Called, in Gen. 22:2, 'your son, your only son ... whom you love'.
[182] 2 Chr. 35:22–25; 2 Kgs. 23:29. *Hadad Rimmon* is probably to be understood here as a place name, although there may be a secondary allusion to an ancient ritual associated with a pagan god of that name (cf. the 'mourning for Tammuz' in Ezek. 8:14). The place was probably named after this god. See Baldwin 1972, pp. 192–193.

including (probably) Zechariah's day.[183] The apparent allusion to it here is especially apt because Josiah died as a result of being pierced – with an arrow.[184] The weeping that will follow the pouring out of the Spirit will likewise be a grief shared by the entire community, the whole *land* (12). But in verses 12–14 the community is broken down into its various components, and each is shown mourning *by itself*, and within each group men and women mourn together, the men *with their wives*. In other words, there is no pointing the finger at others; each individual and group accepts its own responsibility for what has been done, and owns the sin. The 'houses' of *David* and *Nathan* (one of David's sons) are presumably people of royal blood, from which the civil leadership would mainly have been drawn. Those of *Levi* and *Shimei* are presumably those of priestly lineage, from whom the religious establishment was drawn.[185] Historically (as we have seen) it was the leaders who were most to blame for the sins of the nation. But here, when the Spirit is poured out, people do not blame the leaders nor the leaders the people. All mourn for their own part in what has happened, not just the groups that are named, but also *all the rest of the clans* (14). The grace to say 'the sin is mine (or ours)' and to grieve over it and seek God's forgiveness for it is the essence of true repentance, and that, in a word, is what this passage says the Spirit will produce in the people of Jerusalem when he is poured out on them on the last day.[186]

But of course repentance is of no value at all unless it is met with some action on God's part to deal with the sin that has been committed. The fact that the Spirit who is poured out here is described as a Spirit of *grace* strongly suggests that further grace will follow; that the resulting *supplication* will not go unheeded. And indeed it is so. The form that further grace will take is spelled out in what comes next.

c. Cleansing from sin (13:1–6)

From a flood of tears we come, at the beginning of chapter 13, to a fountain of cleansing; from one kind of 'fountain', we might say, to

[183] 2 Chr. 35:25.
[184] 2 Chr. 35:23.
[185] Alternatively, the houses of David, Nathan and Levi may represent the royal, prophetic and priestly components of the community. But the prophetic office was not normally inherited in the way the other two were, and this approach leaves Shimei unaccounted for. It seems better to take the four names in two pairs as above. For Shimei as a levitical, priestly name see Num. 3:21; 2 Chr. 29:14; 31:12–13; Ezra 10:23. See the excellent discussion in Meyers and Meyers 1993, pp. 346–349, and 359–360.
[186] Cf. Acts 2, especially v. 37.

another.[187] And there are other points of connection too. In 12:10 a 'Spirit (*rûaḥ*) of grace and supplication' is poured out; here *the spirit (rûaḥ) of impurity* is removed (2). In 12:12 the 'land' (*'ereṣ*) mourns; here the *land* (*'ereṣ*) is cleansed (2). Most striking of all, perhaps, the 'piercing' (*dqr*) of God in 12:10 finds its negative counterpart here (as we have seen) in the 'stabbing' (*dqr*) of a false prophet (3). There is a lot going on here, and at first sight it can be very confusing. But at the very least we can see at once that it is no accident that this passage occurs where it does. The connections with chapter 12 run deep, and exploring them is one of the ways to unlock the message of this part of the book as it continues to unfold.

What better news could there be for people weeping for their sin than the opening of a *fountain* to cleanse them from it (1)? Here, as elsewhere in the Old Testament, the *fountain* is a metaphor for overflowing, never-failing, inexhaustible supply. It is the image David used to describe the abundant life he had found in God: 'with you [God] is the fountain of life'.[188] For Jeremiah, God was the 'spring [fountain] of living waters' that his people had foolishly forsaken for their own 'broken cisterns'.[189] For Solomon, the fear of the LORD was a 'fountain of life', and the wisdom based on it was itself a 'fountain' and a 'bubbling brook'.[190] For Zechariah the *fountain* represents total cleansing, the complete answer, at last, to the *sin* and *impurity* that has marred Israel's relationship with God over the long course of its history, and in particular (given the strong connections with the previous passage) the sin of 'piercing' him. It is the fulfilment of the promise given to Joshua the high priest in 3:9: 'See ... I will remove the sin of this land in a single day.' The 'day' in question is now specified as *that day*, the day that has been on constant view since the beginning of chapter 12. No sin will be too heinous, and no stain too stubborn for this fountain to deal with. The only requirement is repentance, a repentance that, in any case, God himself will bring about by the pouring out of his Spirit. No specifics are given at this point about the precise nature of the fountain. If we are curious (as well we might be) we shall have to wait for more light to be shed on the matter. We simply note here that it will be on the same 'day' that the people of Jerusalem look on the one they have pierced (12:10–11), that they will find that the cleansing fountain has been opened for them (13:1).

But there is more to the cleansing on view here than this. From

[187] Cf. Jer. 9:1 (MT 8:23): 'Oh, that my head were a spring of water / and my eyes a fountain of tears!' The word for 'fountain' (*māqôr*) is the same as in Zech. 13:1.
[188] Ps. 36:9.
[189] Jer. 2:13. The same Hebrew word as in Zech. 13:1.
[190] Prov. 14:27; 18:4.

the cleansing of the people in verse 1 we move to the cleansing of their *land* in verses 2–6.[191] This is typical of the healthy 'material-ism' of the Bible. Biblical religion, from the Genesis account of creation onwards, affirms the material world – not as something to be worshipped as divine, nor exploited, nor escaped from into some purely 'spiritual' realm, but as something good to be ruled by human beings in obedience to God.[192] The image of man as gardener in Genesis 2 captures nicely the duty of care involved in his relationship to his environment as God intended it to be. So the Bible recognizes that human beings and their environment are inextricably linked, for good or for ill. When the first human pair rebelled against God in Genesis 3, it was not just they who suffered, but the 'ground' as well.[193] According to the apostle Paul, the whole creation is now in bondage to decay, and will be liberated from it only when our own redemption is brought to completion on the last day.[194] What we have here in the present passage is a microcosm of this. Given the focus on Israel in chapters 12 and 13, the *land* on view here is not the entire earth but the land of Israel. But the same theological principle is at work – which is why a passage about the cleansing God will bring about *on that day* (1, 2, 4) cannot stop with only people, or with cleansing that is only inward and 'spiritual'. It must deal also with what is outward and material. Verse 1 must lead to verses 2–6!

God promises to rid the land of three things: *idols, prophets* and *the spirit of impurity* (2). But only one of them (prophets) is taken up and spoken of at length in the following verses, so our basic task is to understand what is meant by the removal of prophets. At first sight the whole notion that prophets will be 'removed' by God is startling, since to this point in the book prophets have been viewed positively. Zechariah himself was a prophet (1:1, 7), and there is pointed reference in chapters 1 and 7 to the 'earlier prophets' through whom God had warned a former generation of the judgment he would send if they did not repent. They were God's 'servants'; through them God spoke 'by his Spirit' (1:6; 7:12). So what are we to make of the apparently very negative view of prophecy in the present passage?

---

[191] The two are closely connected, so that in 3:9 *the sin of this land* is metaphorical for 'the sin of the people of this land' (the entire community). Here in ch. 13 the *land* is cleansed by the removal of offending people from it. The essential point in both places is the intimate connection between the two: a truly clean people can exist only in a truly clean land.
[192] Gen. 1:28, 31.
[193] Gen. 3:17–19.
[194] Rom. 8:22–25.

First, these prophets can hardly be the same kind of people as those whose ministry is so strongly endorsed earlier in the book. It would be possible, as the apostle Paul does in the New Testament, to speak of true, God-given prophecy coming to an end on the last day (because it will no longer be needed),[195] but one could hardly speak of it being removed by God (along with idols) in order to rid a land of impurity! We must conclude therefore, that what is on view here is not prophecy as such, but false prophecy – the very antithesis of what is spoken of so approvingly earlier in the book – and the details of the passage clearly bear this out. The 'spirit' associated with these prophets is not the Spirit of God, but *the spirit of impurity* (2). They speak *lies* rather than the truth (3). They wear a prophet's garment *in order to deceive* (4),[196] and (very probably) the *wounds* on their bodies are self-inflicted, like those of the prophets of Baal on Mount Carmel (6).[197] Finally, and most telling of all, their removal here goes hand in hand with the 'banishing' of idols (2). We have seen this connection between idolatry and false leadership before, back in 10:2:

> The idols speak deceit,
>> diviners see visions that lie;
> they tell dreams that are false,
>> they give comfort in vain.
> Therefore the people wander like sheep
>> oppressed for lack of a shepherd.

There is the nub of the matter: idolatry and false prophecy always go hand in hand. Where idols are worshipped, the preaching of the Word of God is extinguished, and people wander from the truth and fall under oppression. Worst of all, their whole environment becomes defiled – filled with things abhorrent to God and degrading to themselves.[198] Idolatry breeds false prophecy and false prophecy breeds more idolatry. It is a vicious circle that only God

---

[195] 1 Cor. 13:8–12.

[196] Cf. Gen. 27:11, 16, where Jacob wears hairy goatskins in order to deceive his blind father. Cf. Gen. 25:25.

[197] 1 Kgs. 18:28. *Ashamed of his prophetic vision* (4) does not portray the false prophets as repentant, but as trying to deny that they are prophets in order to avoid detection and punishment (cf. Is. 2:19–21, where men, terrified of God's judgment, throw away their idols and take refuge in caves). The explanation that the wounds were received in a drunken brawl (*at the house of my friends*, 6) is 'an unlikely story' (Baldwin 1972, p. 197). Baldwin comments that 'the friends could be "lovers"; that is, associates in idolatrous worship, which is a usual connotation of the [Hebrew] word (e.g. Hos. 2:7, 10ff; Ezek. 23:5, 9)'.

[198] Rom. 1:18–32.

can break. The good news of this passage is that he will do so, finally and forever, *on that day* (2, 4). And his people, themselves cleansed, will utterly repudiate and condemn everything that defiles, just as God himself does. It will no longer be possible for any false prophet to deceive and corrupt them.

We may be shocked by the awful picture of a son being 'stabbed' by his own parents in verse 3. But before we simply dismiss it as primitive, barbaric and so on, and turn away in disgust, we need to ponder two things. First, it reflects the following commandment given to Israel through Moses:

> If your very own brother, or your son or daughter, or the wife you love, or your closest friend secretly entices you, saying, 'Let us go and worship other gods' (gods that neither you nor your fathers have known, gods of the peoples around you, whether near or far, from one end of the land to the other), do not yield to him or listen to him. Show him no pity. Do not spare him or shield him. You must certainly put him to death. Your hand must be the first in putting him to death, and then the hands of all the people. Stone him to death, because he tried to turn you away from the LORD your God, who brought you out of Egypt, out of the land of slavery. Then all Israel will hear and be afraid, and no-one among you will do such an evil thing again.[199]

This was indeed a 'hard' word from God to his people, but it was intended to protect them from being trapped in the downward spiral of false prophecy and idolatry to which we have just referred. It was also intended to impress on them the extreme seriousness with which God himself viewed the sin of misleading people by speaking falsely in his name. It is 'such an evil thing' that even the most precious ties of human love and family solidarity must not be allowed to become excuses for making light of it.

There is no record in the Old Testament of this commandment ever being implemented; perhaps because it was never enforced by the judicial authorities, or because no father or mother could ever bring themselves to do it. Certainly the occasion for it must have been there often enough. But enforced or not, the very existence of the commandment served as a constant reminder of the extreme evil of false prophecy and the danger of tolerating it. It was a 'shocking' commandment, and it was intended to be.

But there is one significant difference between the commandment itself and the way Zechariah alludes to it. The commandment itself

[199] Deut. 13:6–11.

spoke of 'stoning' the false prophet, but Zechariah speaks of 'stabbing' him (3). This can hardly be accidental, given the reference to the 'piercing' of God in the previous chapter (12:10). As we have already seen, the same Hebrew word (*dqr*) is used in both passages.[200] This surely gives Zechariah's words a special edge. It means that we must all finally choose either to stand with those who 'pierce' God, or with those who 'pierce' those who speak falsely in his name. There is no middle ground. Nor is this simply an Old Testament issue. It is put just as starkly at the end of the New Testament, in the message of the risen Christ to the church of Thyatira:

> I have this against you: You tolerate that woman Jezebel, who calls herself a prophetess. By her teaching she misleads my servants into sexual immorality and the eating of food sacrificed to idols. I have given her time to repent of her immorality, but she is unwilling. So I will cast her on a bed of suffering, and I will make those who commit adultery with her suffer intensely, unless they repent of her ways. I will strike her children dead. Then all the churches will know that I am he who searches hearts and minds, and I will repay each of you according to your deeds.[201]

Truth matters to God, and speaking falsely in his name promotes idolatry and defiles God's people. It is a lesson we need to take to heart today when there is so much pressure on us, even within the church, to tolerate false teaching in the name of 'Christian' charity and humility. We simply cannot do it; our Lord forbids it, and none was more charitable or humble than he was. The love he commands is never divorced from truth in the way that tolerance is often urged on us today. There is false tolerance, just as there is false prophecy.

What, then, are we to make of Zechariah's words about the 'stabbing' of a false prophet in our passage? They are probably not intended as a literal description of something that will happen in the future, but (like the commandment of Deut. 13) are meant to give us a salutary shock, and to assure us that on the last day all lying in God's name and all compromising with the truth on the part of his people will be over. The people of God, purified at last from their own sin, will share totally in God's own condemnation of evil, and be free from all the defilement it brings. They will be a clean people in a clean land.

---

[200] The RSV translates it as 'pierce' in both 12:10 and 13:3.
[201] Rev. 2:20–23; cf. Rev. 2:14–16.

d. The shepherd struck, the sheep scattered (13:7–9)

These three verses are a short poem that at first sight seems quite self-contained and unrelated to what has gone before. But in fact it is the masterstroke that brings the whole message of chapters 12 and 13 to a conclusion and ties all its threads together. In this respect it is like the short poem (also about a shepherd; 11:17) that concludes chapters 9 – 11.

It begins with God calling for a sword to strike someone whom he calls *my shepherd* and *the man who is close to me* (7a). The rest of the poem is about what will follow from this. When the shepherd is struck the *sheep* will be scattered, and God's hand will be turned against the *little ones* (7b). As 'shepherd' and 'man' are parallel to one another (both referring to the same person), so are 'sheep' and 'little ones'. The sheep are *little ones* in the sense that they are weak and vulnerable. So this verse is very surprising; it shows God 'striking' and 'turning his hand against' people whom we would normally expect him to protect: a shepherd (man) he describes as his 'own', and sheep (people) he describes as weak and vulnerable. If the picture of a parent stabbing his own child in the previous section was shocking, this is even more so. At least there the victim was clearly guilty! What are we to make of this extraordinary action of God? It is a question that demands an answer, and we shall have to return to it. But first, let us read on to see what ensues.

The striking of the shepherd is the trigger that sets the whole poem in motion. From there on, however, the focus is on the sheep. In verses 8–9 they are divided into thirds. Two-thirds are *struck down and perish*, and only one-third is *left* (8). The terminology used (people being 'struck down') and the huge scale of the slaughter involved seems to imply a battle, a battle fought, not in some mythical realm, but in a particular *land* (8a). Given the context of the poem, this can only be one land, the land of Israel (12:1), and more particularly the territory of Judah and Jerusalem (12:2). So the poem brings us back to the battle with which this oracle opened in chapter 12, the battle that will usher in the kingdom of God on the last day (12:2–9). We have already seen that that battle will not be won without great cost, especially to God himself (12:10). As we return to it here we see that it will also not be without cost to God's shepherd, and that shepherd's weak and vulnerable flock (8).[202]

---

[202] The precise significance of the *two-thirds* and *one-third* of v. 8 is not clear. At the very least it speaks of severe suffering and dispersal. In view of the quotation of v. 7 by Jesus in Matt. 26:31 and Mark 14:27, v. 8 should probably be seen as having its fulfilment in the persecution and scattering of the early church (Acts 8:1; 11:19).

But the poem is not finished yet. The last verse focuses particularly on the one-third who survive the battle itself. They will undergo even more suffering, but (and here is the good news!) their suffering will have a glorious outcome. They will pass through it like *silver* and *gold* being refined in a furnace,[203] and afterwards they will *call* on God and he will *answer* them; God will own them as his people, and they will gladly own him as their God (9). The closing words of the poem echo the classical way in which the covenant relationship between God and Israel was expressed in the law of Moses: 'I will walk among you and be your God, and you will be my people.'[204] Historically that relationship turned out to be a very troubled one, constantly marred – especially by idolatry and false prophecy on Israel's part. But this poem ends on a note of tremendous confidence. Out of the suffering that will usher in the kingdom of God will emerge a new, cleansed, people of God, who will truly know him. Out of the last battle will come a renewal, the restoration at last of God's covenant with Israel. So looking back we can now see how fittingly this poem concludes the whole of chapters 12 and 13. It picks up the themes of battle (12:2–9) and cleansing (13:1–6), and weaves them together under the heading of covenant renewal.

But two final things remain for us to consider if we are to appreciate the great richness of this poem. The first has to do with the identity of the 'stricken' shepherd (7). We have already seen God portrayed as the true shepherd of Israel in 11:4–14, and God himself as the 'pierced one' in 12:10. But the stricken shepherd here cannot be God, because he is expressly distinguished from him. God refers to him as the *man who is close to me* (7).[205] He is clearly a 'good' shepherd, approved by God, and is someone intimately connected with God – but he cannot simply be equated with God. The book of Zechariah has provided us with only one person who fits this description, namely the ideal king of 9:9, whose coming was anticipated in the promises concerning 'the Branch' in 3:8 and 6:12. In other words, the stricken shepherd is the Messiah. Here is perhaps the profoundest and most precious aspect of the theology of this book: like the great prophet Isaiah before him, Zechariah understood that the Messiah would have to suffer if sin were to be atoned for and Israel's relationship with God were to be restored. Furthermore, this suffering would be expressly brought about by God. In Isaiah 53:10 it is God who 'crushes' his Servant, and 'causes

---

[203] Cf. Is. 1:25.
[204] Lev. 26:12.
[205] The Hebrew word *'āmît*, used of the shepherd here, is used elsewhere only in Lev. 6:2, and 18:20, where the NIV translates it as 'neighbour'.

him to suffer'; here in Zechariah it is God who *strikes* the shepherd. He does not strike him because he deserves it, but because he has assumed responsibility for the wrongdoing of others.

Furthermore, in the light of the New Testament we see that the shepherd was not only someone close to God, but his Son. In smiting the shepherd, God himself acts with the severity he required of his people when he gave them the 'shocking' law of Deuteronomy 13.[206] However that law may have fared in the life of Israel, this poem speaks of a time when God will fully implement it in the person of his shepherd. The good shepherd will die the death of the most heinous offender against God's law, and God himself will be his executioner. It might be tempting, in view of this, to regard God as some kind of unfeeling monster, far removed from the pain that would be suffered by a 'normal' person in these circumstances. If so, however, all we need to do is recall 12:10, and the 'piercing' of God himself. In Zechariah's inspired prophecy the suffering of God and the suffering of his shepherd go hand in hand. In chapter 9 we saw a similar close connection between the coming of God and the coming of the king. But here the connection goes even deeper. We can (indeed *must*) say that in the striking of the shepherd God himself is struck.[207] Or to put it in the timeless words of the apostle Paul, 'God was in Christ, reconciling the world unto himself.'[208]

Finally, we should note carefully the way this poem adds a new, vitally important dimension to the theme of cleansing we met earlier in chapter 13. There is a cleansing that comes from the *fountain* (1); but there is also a cleansing (refining) that comes via the *fire* (furnace, 9). As far as those who experience them are concerned, the only requirement for the first kind of cleansing is repentance. The second, however, comes only via the hard discipline of suffering. Both have their foundation in God, who is both holy himself and the sanctifier of his people. Holiness, in biblical terms, is not just about being forgiven; it is also about transformation.[209] We need the furnace as well as the fountain if we are to be as God wants us to be. That is why suffering should not cause us to lose heart, or to feel (when it comes) that God has somehow abandoned us. It is a

---

[206] So Jones, p. 151; cf. Baldwin 1972, p. 197.

[207] Cf. Simeon's prophecy concerning Mary: 'a sword will pierce your own soul too' (Luke 2:35).

[208] 2 Cor. 5:19 (AV).

[209] For an excellent treatment of the general subject of biblical sanctification, see D. G. Peterson, *Possessed by God: A New Testament Theology of Sanctification and Holiness*, New Studies in Biblical Theology (Apollos, 1995).

vital and precious part of his way with us: he 'disciplines us for our good, that we may share in his holiness'.[210]

e. Let there be light! Zechariah 12 – 13 and the New Testament

We have already begun to see how the message of these chapters finds its ultimate meaning in the fuller revelation about the coming of the kingdom of God in the New Testament. That should hardly surprise us, given the fact we are constantly directed to *that day* – a time in the future – when the things spoken about here will come to pass.[211] We have also noted the crucial significance of the fact that when Jesus arrives in Jerusalem to set in train the events which will lead to his crucifixion, Matthew and John both draw our attention very pointedly to Zechariah 9:9: 'See, your king comes to you ... having salvation' (Matt. 21:4–5; John 12:14–15). In effect we are told that if we truly want to understand the significance of that critical moment in the history of God's dealings with Israel (and ultimately with the world), we need to recall what had already been said about the coming of God's kingdom in the book of Zechariah, especially in chapter 9 – *but not only there!* Other significant quotations from or allusions to Zechariah follow, particularly to the material in chapters 11, 12 and 13. These may be summarized as follows:

- The estimation by Israel's leaders that Jesus was 'worth' thirty pieces of silver: Matthew 27:9; cf. Zechariah 11:12.[212]
- The return of the money to the temple authorities, who give it to a potter: Matthew 27:3, 10; cf. Zechariah 11:13.[213]
- The 'piercing' of Jesus on the cross, and the 'looking' on him by those responsible for his death: John 19:37; cf. Zechariah 12:10.

---

[210] Heb. 12:4–11, especially v. 10.

[211] See Zech. 12:3, and the many similar references to *that day* thereafter.

[212] The *actual* estimation of his worth is zero, since they crucify him. They pay the money only to secure his betrayal. Although Jeremiah is named as the prophet whose words were fulfilled in all that followed, the mention of the thirty pieces of silver is clearly an allusion to Zechariah. See further below, and cf. Morris, pp. 696–697.

[213] It could be that the naming of Jeremiah as the prophet whose words were fulfilled has reference primarily to the involvement of a potter and the purchase of the field (see Jer. 18:1–12; 19:1–15; 32:6–9). The words (and acts) of Jeremiah associated with the potter and the field are about the coming judgment on Israel for its rejection of God, and it could be that this is the larger significance of the betrayal and death of Jesus to which Matthew wishes to draw our attention. But allusions to Zechariah are also clearly present. See the previous note.

- The 'sudden flow' of blood and water from Jesus' side: John 12:34–35; cf. Zechariah 13:1.[214]
- The 'mourning' and 'wailing' for him by 'a large number of people': Luke 23:27, 48; cf. Zechariah 12:10–13.
- The 'smiting' of the shepherd (Jesus) and the 'scattering' of the sheep (his followers): Mark 14:27; Matthew 26:31; cf. Zechariah 13:7.

What are we to make of all this? We could, perhaps, take a fairly minimalist approach to the whole thing and say that the events which unfolded after Jesus entered Jerusalem fulfilled some *parts* of Zechariah 9 – 13 (the bits quoted or alluded to by the Gospel writers). But given the way our attention is drawn to Zechariah 9:9 at the beginning of it all, it is much more likely that we are meant to understand that what Zechariah said about the coming of the kingdom was being fulfilled in *all* of what followed. The subsequent quotations and allusions are there to keep reminding us of this.

In order to appreciate how the New Testament writers refer to Zechariah we need to understand two things. First, *all* the Old Testament promises about the coming kingdom of God find their fulfilment (ultimate meaning) in Jesus Christ.[215] Furthermore, they are not fulfilled in some very general way (i.e. the fulfilment is 'somehow' related to Jesus Christ), but in the very specific *events* of his birth, life, death, resurrection, ascension and coming again. This means (among other things) that the fulfilment does not come all at once, but in two major phases. As Jesus both has come and will come, so the kingdom of God has come and will come. As we saw in the introduction, the same Jesus who told his disciples that the kingdom was already present, told them to pray for its coming.[216] The key to understanding this apparent contradiction is to grasp the basic truth at the heart of it, namely the kingdom of God comes *in Jesus Christ*. In the New Testament the time of fulfilment that Zechariah spoke about as *that day* opens out into *the last days* – the whole period beginning with the first coming of Christ to make atonement for sin, and his second coming in glory to judge the world.[217] This is the age we now live in![218]

[214] The very pointed way in which our attention is drawn to this by John suggests that it is highly significant for him. It may be that it is just proof that Jesus really did die, but the association of blood and water with purification rites in the Old Testament strongly suggests a larger significance, namely the efficacy of Jesus' death to provide cleansing from sin.
[215] 2 Cor. 1:20.
[216] Luke 11:2, 20.
[217] Heb. 1:2; Acts 2:17; 2 Pet. 3:3.
[218] 2 Cor 6:2: '*now* is the day of salvation' (my italics).

The second major thing we must grasp is the landmark significance of the birth of Jesus Christ. In that momentous event God became incarnate; he entered our world *in the person of his Son,* Jesus Christ.[219] In Zechariah God himself and the Messiah (the Branch, the king) are closely connected, but always distinguished from one another. In the New Testament, however, the two become one in the God-man, Jesus Christ. It is no longer merely a matter of intimate, close relationship; God *really is present* in Jesus Christ.[220] This is why the New Testament writers can refer to passages in Zechariah that refer specifically to God and point to Jesus as the one in whom they are fulfilled. So in Zechariah it is God whom Israel values at 'thirty pieces of silver'; in the New Testament it is Jesus. The same is true of the identity of the 'pierced one'. In Zechariah it is God who pours out his Spirit to bring about true repentance; in the New Testament it is the risen and ascended Christ.[221] This (at first sight) puzzling use of Zechariah in the New Testament makes perfect sense in the light of the incarnation of God in Christ.

Armed with these important insights we can now appreciate some other ways in which Zechariah is taken up in the New Testament, especially in the book of Revelation. This is the climax of the whole Bible, and has mainly to do with the very end of history, when God will judge the world and reign in glory over the whole (renewed) creation. It has hardly started, however, before there is a very pointed reference to the book of Zechariah. The apostle is speaking about the return of Christ, which will usher in the last things:

> Look, he is coming with the clouds,
>   and every eye will see him,
> even those who pierced him;
>   and all the peoples of the earth will mourn because of him.[222]

At his return, Jesus Christ will *again* be seen by 'those who pierced him', and they will 'mourn because of him'. But this time it is not just Israel, but 'all peoples of the earth' who are in view. The rejection of Jesus, God's Messiah was not the sin of Israel alone, but of the whole human race, and all will face judgment for it on the last

---

[219] John 1:1–18.
[220] 2 Cor. 5:19.
[221] Acts 2:33–38. While the primary reference is to the fulfilment of Joel 2, the strong repentance theme suggests an allusion to Zechariah as well. Both Joel and Zechariah speak of the 'pouring out' of the Spirit.
[222] Rev. 1:7; cf. Zech. 12:10.

day unless they repent. And again, as in the passion narratives of the Gospels, many allusions to Zechariah follow. The opening vision of the risen Christ standing among the 'seven golden lampstands' (which represent seven churches) recalls Zechariah's fifth vision, in which God's presence among his people in Jerusalem is symbolized by a 'gold lampstand' with 'seven lights' (4:2, 10b). The two witnesses who are (like) two 'olive trees', standing 'before the Lord of the earth' in Revelation 11, recall the way the two leaders (Joshua and Zerubbabel) are represented in that same vision.[223] The four coloured horses of chapter 6, which are sent out by the LORD to judge the earth, are the New Testament counterpart to the coloured horses of Zechariah's first and eighth visions.[224] These allusions to Zechariah are obvious, and there are more to come. When we look, shortly, at chapter 14 we shall see that there are many echoes of that in the book of Revelation as well.

So in many ways the New Testament tells us that Zechariah's message about the coming of the kingdom of God finds its fulfilment in Jesus Christ. The first stage of the climactic battle to usher in the kingdom of God has already been fought in Jerusalem, in the death, resurrection and ascension of Jesus Christ. The final stage will be fought there also, when he returns. In the meantime it continues to be fought everywhere we go as Jesus' followers, preaching the kingdom of God in the power of the Holy Spirit whom he has poured out upon us. The battle is not easy; Jesus never said it would be![225] But we are well equipped for it,[226] and our cause is just: to set captives free and bring people of all nations under the lordship of Jesus Christ, so that God may be given the glory due to his holy name. His kingdom come, and his will be done!

But we are already beginning to anticipate chapter 14, which brings us to one final thing we must consider before moving on. We noted when we began our study of chapters 12 and 13 that they are focused throughout on Israel, and conclude with the renewal of God's covenant with Israel.[227] So in the light of all we have now seen, how should we think of this being fulfilled? The answer must surely be *in Jesus Christ*. It is important to remember that Jesus was *from* Israel (as far as his humanity was concerned) and that his ministry was primarily directed *to* Israel. His presentation of himself to Israel as the king (Messiah) promised by God (which he

---

[223] Rev. 11:4; Zech. 4:14.

[224] Rev. 6:1–8; Zech. 1:8; 6:1–8.

[225] John 15:18–25; John 16:33; Matt. 10:17.

[226] 2 Cor. 10:4; Eph. 6:10–18.

[227] See Zech. 12:1 (*the word of the LORD concerning Israel*); and 13:9 (the covenant renewal language echoing Lev. 26:12).

did conspicuously by entering Jerusalem the way he did at the beginning of his passion week) brought the covenant relationship between God and Israel to crisis point. Israel could not go on any longer as it was: a choice had to be made. There was the possibility of a fully restored relationship with God, of covenant renewal – but only under the headship of Jesus Christ. In the time of David there was no being in the kingdom of God without being in the kingdom of David. In the same way the kingdom of God and the kingship of Jesus (the great Son of David) were now indivisibly linked, since the kingdom of God had come *in Jesus*. It is a matter of record that Israel in general chose to reject Jesus and fell under God's judgment. But it is also a matter of record that Jesus had prepared the way for the emergence of a new (renewed) Israel, by preaching the kingdom of God, calling for repentance, and preparing the twelve apostles to lead the new community he was calling together. And before he went to the cross he spoke with his disciples about a new covenant in his blood.[228]

It would be wrong, however, to see a complete break with the past, as though the past were simply discarded. On the contrary, the New Testament sees the relationship between the past and what happened in Jesus in terms of *fulfilment*: 'What God promised our fathers he has fulfilled for us, their children, by raising up Jesus.'[229] In other words, Israel's special relationship with God was brought to completion (fulfilment) in Jesus Christ, *but participation in that fulfilment* depended on acceptance of him as God's Messiah. That is the essence of the powerful gospel message Peter preached to the great gathering of Israelites in Jerusalem on the day of Pentecost. He was offering them participation in the fulfilment of God's covenant with Israel by accepting Jesus Christ as their Messiah. They would become members of the new 'reborn' Israel that had emerged out of the old.

The Israel of the Old Testament had failed to live up to its calling as the covenant people of God. But what Israel had failed to do, Jesus himself did *for* Israel. He loved God perfectly, with all his heart, mind, soul and strength, as Israel should have done, and then he took total responsibility for Israel's failure and gave his own perfect life as a sacrifice to atone for their sin. The prophet Isaiah had seen clearly that Israel's covenant relationship with God, and her God-given mission, could be fulfilled only in the person of God's perfect, suffering Servant. In the second of Isaiah's so-called Servant Songs God effectively takes the name 'Israel' from the

---

[228] Luke 22:20; cf. 1 Cor. 11:25.
[229] Acts 13:32–33.

faithless nation and gives it to the Suffering Servant as the one to whom it will henceforth properly belong: 'You [singular] are *my servant*, / *Israel*, in whom I will display my splendour.'[230] The next two Songs speak of the Servant's suffering, atoning death, and exaltation,[231] which is precisely the path Jesus trod. God's covenant with Israel was fulfilled in him, God's perfect Servant or, in Zechariah's terms, God's Shepherd-King.

The high point we have reached here in Zechariah's message is so magnificent that it is difficult to conceive of anything that could possibly lie beyond it. But there is something – an even higher summit – and we have already caught glimpses of it. The goal of the whole biblical revelation is the glory of God. In the New Testament we are told that when everything has been brought into subjection to Christ, then he himself will be subject to the One who put all things under him, 'so that God may be all in all'.[232] This means that the end of the story of the coming of the kingdom of God must involve much more than the renewal of his covenant with Israel. It must culminate with the whole creation worshipping him as king, including (and especially) his human creation – people of all nations. This is the point we move to in chapter 14 as this magnificent book comes to its climax. The movement from the renewal of God's covenant with Israel (chs. 12 – 13) to the inclusion of people of all nations in the blessings of that covenant (ch. 14) is a natural one. Israel was never called into a special relationship with God merely for its own sake, but for the glory of God and the ultimate blessing of 'all peoples on earth'.[233]

f. The LORD comes and reigns (14:1–21)

This chapter completes the oracle that began in chapter 12, and also completes the whole book. If we think of the book of Zechariah as a long-distance race, the beginning of chapter 14 is the turn into the final straight. The coming of the future *day of the LORD* (1) is not a new theme, but this chapter brings us to the final development of it. Chapters 9 – 13 have been largely taken up with events associated with the coming of the shepherd king (Messiah) to atone for sin. Chapter 14 is concerned with the final coming of God himself, to judge the world and reign in glory. As we have already seen, in view of the incarnation of God in Christ in the New Testament, the coming of the Messiah and the coming of God cannot ultimately be

---

[230] Is. 49:3; my italics.
[231] Is. 50:4–9; 52:13 – 53:12.
[232] 1 Cor. 15:28.
[233] Gen. 12:3.

separated from one another. Nevertheless, there are two main phases to the coming of the kingdom of God, and this final chapter of Zechariah has to do with the second of them. We were already at the beginning of the end in chapter 9, but now we have come to the end of the end, the awesome finale.

While chapter 14 is the continuation and completion of what has gone before, it is also a unit in its own right. The sixfold repetition of *on that day* throughout the chapter divides it into seven parts, and nests all its content under the heading given at the beginning: *A day of the* LORD *is coming* (1).[234]

The 'day of the LORD' is an ominous theme in the Old Testament prophets. Take, for example, the way Isaiah spoke of it:

> Wail, for the day of the LORD is near;
> It will come like destruction from the Almighty!
> ...
> See, the day of the LORD is coming –
> a cruel day, with wrath and fierce anger –
> to make the land desolate
> and destroy the sinners within it.[235]

The day of the LORD is the final day of reckoning for those who have refused to acknowledge God. In Old Testament times many Israelites looked forward eagerly to this day, assuming God would judge everyone but themselves. But Amos warned that this was dangerous presumption. The nations that had resisted God's rule would be judged – true; but so would Israelites who had refused to repent of their own wrongdoing. It would be a day of final reckoning for sinners everywhere, within Israel as well as outside it. Only a remnant would be saved.[236] The same double-edged nature of the coming day is clear here in Zechariah 14, as we shall see. The chapter oscillates between the negative and positive aspects of the day of God's final intervention, but comes to rest on the positive. Like chapters 9 – 14, as a whole, it moves from one kind of gathering (for war) to another kind (for worship), with verse 16 serving as a neat summary. War (judgment) is not an end in itself, but the divinely ordained means of purging the world. The *survivors* will be worshippers (16), beyond the reach of sin and its corrosive

---

[234] The variation to '*And* on that day' (NIV; my italics) in the last verse does not introduce an eighth unit, but closes the seventh. In the underlying Hebrew text it is just 'on that day' (the same as the other six occurrences) but closes the entire chapter by coming at the very end of the verse.
[235] Is. 13:6, 9; cf. Ezek. 13:5; Joel 1:15; 2:11, 31; Obad. 15; Zeph. 1:7, 14; Mal. 4:5.
[236] Amos 5:18; 9:9–10.

effects forever (21b). This chapter has a lot in common with chapter 9, but the focus on the emergence of a saved remnant is one of the things that gives chapter 14 its special character. Enough of overview, however; it is time to try to trace the development of thought through each of its seven parts.

If *your plunder* (1) is taken in its natural sense as 'the plunder you have acquired', then the opening verse suggests that the coming day will be a day of victory – a day for the sharing out of plunder (an activity of conquerors).[237] But verse 2 at once introduces the sober note of suffering. The nations God will bring against Jerusalem will do much damage to both the city itself and its people, and half its population will be taken into exile. But the other half will remain, and it is presumably these who will divide the plunder. This leaves us with a puzzle, however: how can such a battered remnant be viewed as, or become, victors? The answer is given in verse 3: the LORD will fight for them. When it seems that the enemy has won, God will intervene and turn the tables.

This theme is developed in the second unit, which begins in verse 4. The LORD's 'going out to fight' (3) is now particularized in terms of his taking a stand on the Mount of Olives, to the east of the city. It is not entirely clear here whether he has 'gone out' from Jerusalem, or from his dwelling place in heaven, but the latter is altogether more likely in view of the earlier references in Zechariah to the final battle between God and his enemies. For example, in chapter 6 his war chariots emerge from between two mountains of bronze, representing the entrance to his heavenly temple, and in chapter 9 the LORD appears 'over' his people to give them victory (6:1; 9:14). Here he descends from heaven to *stand* upon the earth as its rightful ruler and judge.[238] And, as in similar passages elsewhere in the Old Testament, God's coming causes the earth to convulse.[239] The Mount of Olives splits in two, opening a way for the survivors in the besieged city to escape,[240] as their fathers had fled from an earthquake in the days of King Uzziah (5).[241] It is clearly, at one level

[237] Sweeney (p. 698) apparently takes v. 1 in a negative sense: 'the spoil *of the city* will be divided in its midst' (my italics).
[238] As in Deut. 11:24 and Josh. 1:3, 'standing' is symbolic for 'taking possession'. Cf. Job 19:25: 'I know that my Redeemer lives, / and that in the end he will stand upon the earth.'
[239] Cf. Exod. 20:18; Is. 2:19; Hag. 2:6.
[240] The location of *Azel* is unknown; presumably it was somewhere to the east of the Mount of Olives. The 'mountain highway' is reminiscent of the highway through the desert of Is. 40:4, created by the levelling of the mountains and the raising up of the valleys.
[241] I.e. in the eight century BC (2 Kgs. 14:18–21; Amos 1:1). This earthquake had clearly left a deep impression on the people of Jerusalem.

at least, a moment of terror, as mere human beings are confronted with the world-shaking power of God.[242] But for the survivors (and this is where the accent falls) it is a moment of liberation: their great and awesome God has stepped in to save them. The splitting of the Mount of Olives recalls the dividing of the Red Sea at the exodus from Egypt – the experience of deliverance par excellence in the Old Testament.[243] The 'coming' of God in verse 5 is the counterpart of his 'going out' in verse 3. It brings his act of intervention to an end, presumably in Jerusalem itself. The *holy ones* of the same verse may be his angelic servants, the armies of heaven, who come with him.[244] But there is another possibility, namely that they are his holy people, the survivors, who have fled from the city to meet him, and come with him as he enters the city as conqueror and liberator.[245] This second alternative better fits the logic of the whole unit, but need not exclude the first. Most likely, the survivors join with the hosts of heaven at this supreme moment of victory.[246]

The first two parts of the chapter have described the 'coming' of the day of the LORD – the dramatic intervention of God that will usher it in. The next three focus on the nature of the 'day' itself. The third unit (6–7) describes it as a *unique day* of unending light. As the six days of creation in Genesis climax in the unique seventh day of rest, so here the 'day' of the dawning of God's kingdom, which has been in steady view since the beginning of chapter 12, at last opens out into eternity. The paradox of *no light* (6) and *there will be light* (7) beautifully expresses the truth that the old creation will give way to the new, in which there will no longer be *cold* or *frost*, or the darkness caused by the setting of the sun. The light of the new creation will be the never-failing, unchanging glory of God, enveloping all in its purity and brilliance. The fourth unit (8) opens with *living water* flowing out from Jerusalem, as the life-giving rivers once flowed out of the garden of Eden.[247] This river will not ebb and flow with the changing seasons, as rivers presently do, but flow all year round, in *summer* as well as *winter*. This can only mean that the 'seasons' will be transformed, just as the light is. All things will become new in ways that our present limited minds can only dimly grasp.[248]

[242] Cf. Is. 2:10–21.

[243] Exod. 14:21–22.

[244] As in Deut. 33:2; Is. 13:31.

[245] Cf. Is. 40:10–11, where, when the LORD returns to Zion, he brings his 'flock' (people) with him.

[246] Notice how, in Deut. 33, the expression 'holy ones' refers both to angelic beings (v. 2) and the people of God (v. 3).

[247] Gen. 2:10–14; cf. Ezek. 47:1–12. The *eastern* sea is the Dead Sea, and the *western* the Mediterranean (see NIV footnotes).

[248] Rev. 21:5 (AV).

The cause of all this light and life and newness is the presence of God. Verse 9a lifts our eyes from the creation to the Creator with a statement of his universal kingship, which is amplified in the fifth unit (which follows immediately) in terms of the 'Shema' of Deuteronomy 6:4.[249] What Israel had been taught to confess as the essence of its own faith, will finally be recognized by all: the LORD God of Israel is the creator and ruler of the whole earth, the One and only God. At *his name* every knee will bow; at last there will be no more idolatry. In the next two verses (10–11) this is given geographical expression in the picture of the lifting up of Jerusalem – the city of this one and only God, and the centre of his universal reign – above all the surrounding terrain.[250] The comparison with Isaiah 2:1–4 is obvious and striking, and the climactic statement that Jerusalem will be *secure* (11) echoes the imagery of the so-called Zion psalms, where the security of the city of God is guaranteed by the presence of God within her.[251] It is as though the entire Old Testament Scriptures as Zechariah knew them are being ransacked for images and language to express the wonder of what is happening at this climactic moment. Everything that has been confessed, prophesied, sung about and hoped for has at last come to fulfilment. This unit closes, in verse 12, with the negative counterpart of Jerusalem's security – the utter destruction of her enemies. The horrific depiction of the enemy ravaged by plague is a reminder of the fate that befell the Egyptians at the time of the exodus, and of Sennacherib's besieging army in the time of Isaiah.[252] These terrible events within history are seen here in their true light as shadows of a far more dreadful judgment to come. The fourth and fifth units together make up the largest and most complex passage in the entire chapter, and end here on a particularly sobering note.

The sixth unit, beginning in verse 13, develops the idea of the plague further, and at last provides the full explanation for the opening image of the victors dividing the spoil. Struck down by plague, the hostile armies around Jerusalem will become a rich source of plunder, which will be collected and (by implication) brought into the city (14).[253] The message is clear – even those who

---

[249] The word 'Shema' (Heb. *šᵉmaʿ*) means 'hear' – the first word of Deut. 6:4.

[250] The naming of the borders of the land and the gates of the city recall the detailed description of the ideal land and city of God in Ezek. 40 – 48.

[251] Ps. 46:5; cf. Pss. 47 – 48.

[252] Exod. 7 – 12; 2 Kgs. 19:35.

[253] The statement *Judah too will fight at Jerusalem* (14) is puzzling in this context, since the battle seems to be over at this point. It seems best to take it as an allusion to 12:1–9 (esp. v. 7), and a reminder that the people of Judah, as participants in the battle, will also participate in the spoils.

continue to resist God's rule will end up by surrendering their wealth, *great quantities of gold and silver and clothing*, to enrich his city and those who will live in it.[254] In other words, the 'survivors' of verses 1–5 will not just survive – they will inherit all things![255] In verse 16 the notion of *survivors* is expanded. So far the focus has been on the survivors of Israel, with the nations seen purely as enemies. But now we see that there will be other survivors as well, *from all the nations*. These too will share in the worship of the new Jerusalem: they *will go up year after year to worship the King, the LORD Almighty, and to celebrate the Feast of Tabernacles* (16). This is where we pass beyond war to worship. But why this particular festival?

The Feast of Tabernacles (or Booths) stood in the mainstream of Israel's religious life, along with the other two great festivals, Passover and the Feast of Weeks,[256] and by the Persian period, in which Zechariah lived, it had become the highlight of the religious year.[257] It was a joyful autumn festival, lasting seven days, and marked the end of the agricultural year, when the produce of the wheat and grape harvests had been gathered in.[258] At the same time it recalled the very different circumstances of Israel's ancestors, who had lived in temporary shelters (booths) in the desert, on their way to the land God had promised to give them.[259] It was particularly the occasion when Israelites gathered to worship God and celebrate his goodness to them as a nation. For all these reasons it is the perfect climax to the book of Zechariah, combining the twin themes of journey's end and harvest home. And what a harvest this is! It is *people* – formerly enemies, but now worshippers – gathered in from *all the nations*, to *worship*, at last, their rightful LORD and King (16).[260] The festival is celebrated by both the 'survivors' of Israel and the 'survivors' of the nations, at last worshipping as one people. What worship! What celebration! What joy!

But the joy of salvation, in the Bible, never descends into sentimentality; it is always grounded in reality and truth. And so it is here, for the term *survivor* is a two-edged sword. Not everyone will survive; some will be overthrown by God's judgment. And the reason is simple: not everyone will *go up* to Jerusalem to worship

[254] See v. 11.
[255] Rev. 21:7.
[256] Deut. 16:16.
[257] See Ezra 3:4; Neh. 8:14–17; and cf. Hanson (p. 386), who traces the rise to prominence of this particular festival to the period of the monarchy.
[258] Deut. 16:13–15.
[259] Lev. 23:43.
[260] Cf. v. 14, where it was the *wealth* of the nations that flowed into Jerusalem.

the King (17). They will maintain their defiance to the end; and for them there will be no victory, and no joy, but want (*no rain*), *plague* and *punishment* (17–19). Zechariah's vision of the coming kingdom of God is wonderfully inclusive: it embraces people of all nations. But it is not *universalist* in a sentimental, truth-evading way. Belonging to the people of God is not merely a matter of survival, as though all that is required is to be alive; it is also, more fundamentally, a matter of personal decision. One must choose to come to the feast, and join the worshippers. And Zechariah is quite clear that not everyone – nor even the majority – will choose to do so. There is hell as well as heaven. But arching over both is the truth that God reigns, and he will be glorified as much by saving those who willingly bow the knee to him as by judging those who don't. The kingdom of God *will* come, and that means there are decisions to be made.

The keynote of the seventh and last unit (20–21) is holiness, which is another name for God's supremacy and perfection. These closing verses of the book show us the whole of *Jerusalem and Judah* as one vast sanctuary, in which everything is holy, from the explicitly religious vessels of the temple to the most common cooking pots (20). Everything is sanctified by God's presence, and partakes of his perfection. What was once written only on the high priest's turban ('Holy to the LORD')[261] will be written over everything, even *the bells of the horses* (20).

At first sight the reference to the *Canaanite* in the last verse introduces a discordant note by apparently excluding some on purely racial grounds. But 'Canaanite' is almost certainly metaphorical for 'idolater' here. The idolatrous religion of the Canaanites was a constant source of temptation and defilement for the Israelites, especially in the centuries leading up to the exile. Chapter 13 spoke of a time when God will 'banish the names of the idols [and therefore idolaters] from the land' (13:2). But the word *Canaanite* is well chosen, because it also has another meaning, and this too would have been well known to Zechariah's original audience. Its literal meaning is 'trader',[262] and, as we saw in chapter 5, trading was another area in which 'wickedness' had invaded and defiled the covenant community. Joyce Baldwin has nicely captured this aspect of the statement about 'no Canaanite' here at the end of the book: 'Once the King comes, money-making will no longer mar the Temple courts, nor merchants' greed take the joy out of sacrificial giving.'[263] It was a truth that Jesus reinforced with a whip of small

[261] Exod. 28:36.
[262] See the NIV footnote.
[263] Baldwin 1972, p. 208.

cords![264] So the presence of holiness and the absence of the 'Canaanite' are two sides of the same reality – perfect purity. Here at last is the complete fulfilment of the promise of chapter 3 that the sin of the land will be removed 'in a single day' (3:9).[265] The double reference to the LORD's *house* (20, 21) completes the picture of the elevated Jerusalem of verses 11–12. Free at last of all impurity, and filled with the redeemed of all nations, Jerusalem has at last become 'the mountain of the LORD's house', in perfect agreement with the vision of Isaiah, whose powerful words had inspired so much of Zechariah's preaching.[266] Zerubbabel's temple has given way to the reality it symbolized: God the King in the midst of his saved people – forever.[267]

Just two comments to conclude. First the apparent absence of the Messiah from this final chapter. In one sense that is as it should be, for the theme of the whole book has been the coming of the kingdom of God; so it is entirely fitting that it should conclude with God all in all. But at the same time it is somewhat strange, given the way the coming of the kingdom is so closely connected in the preceding chapters with the coming of the Messiah. The reality, of course, is that he is not absent here at all, but only the fuller revelation given in the New Testament allows us to recognize his presence. As we noted earlier, the key that unlocks so much of how the New Testament refers to Zechariah is the incarnation. When Jesus was born in Bethlehem it was not just God's Messiah who had come to us, but God himself. And when Jesus Christ comes again it will be the coming of God. The One who ascended bodily from the Mount of Olives will one day stand there again.[268] He will come again in glory to judge the world and restore all things:

---

[264] John 2:15 (AV); Cf. Matt. 21:12, 13 and parallels.

[265] In NT terms Zech. 3 and Zech. 14 represent the two complementary aspects of salvation: freedom from condemnation involved in being a sinner, and freedom from the very presence of sin itself.

[266] Is. 2:1–2.

[267] Cf. Ezek. 40 – 48, and especially 48:35: 'THE LORD IS THERE.'

[268] In view of the largely symbolic nature of apocalyptic writing (cf. the book of Revelation), it would be unwise, generally speaking, to take the description of the last things in this chapter too literally. It is language stretched to breaking point to describe the indescribable. However, we do have warrant for believing in the literal, bodily return of Christ. The words spoken by the angelic messengers at Jesus' ascension make it clear that his return will be just as literal and observable as his departure was: 'After he said this, he was taken up before their very eyes, and a cloud hid him from their sight. They were looking intently up into the sky as he was going, when suddenly two men dressed in white stood beside them. "Men of Galilee," they said, "why do you stand here looking into the sky? This same Jesus, who has been taken from you into heaven, will come back in the same way you have seen him go into heaven"' (Acts 1:9–11).

When the Son of Man comes in his glory, and all the angels with him, he will sit on his throne in heavenly glory. All the nations will be gathered before him, and he will separate the people one from another as a shepherd separates the sheep from the goats.[269]

For he must reign until he has put all his enemies under his feet. The last enemy to be destroyed is death. For he 'has put everything under his feet'. Now when it says that 'everything' has been put under him, it is clear that this does not include God himself, who put everything under Christ. When he has done this, then the Son himself will be made subject to him who put everything under him, so that God may be all in all.[270]

The coming of the kingdom of God is inseparable from the coming of Christ, and we who pray, as Jesus himself taught us, 'Our Father … your kingdom come', also cry out every day, in the agony and joy of our waiting, 'Amen. Come, Lord Jesus.'[271]

The final comment concerns the great harvest *from all the nations* (16) and how it comes about. The short answer this last chapter of Zechariah gives us is, through battle (1–5, 12–15) – a battle in which many people finally come to realize that their rebellion against God is futile, and decide to join those who worship him as their King (16). So far so good, but there is more to be said, and it is the important reference to the pouring out of the Spirit in 12:10 that holds the key to it. As we saw in chapter 12, the pouring out of the Spirit leads to heartfelt repentance among the people of Israel gathered in Jerusalem, and their restoration to true covenant relationship with God (12:10 – 13:9). How wonderfully that was fulfilled on the day of Pentecost, when the Spirit came in power and the apostle Peter stood up to confront his fellow Israelites with their sin in crucifying the Lord Jesus! They were cut to the heart, and turned to God for forgiveness,[272] and out of that momentous event a mighty missionary movement was born – exactly as God intended it should![273] For the Spirit was not given simply to grant forgiveness to repentant Israel, but to send Israel on mission to the world. Jesus himself authorized that mission and set its agenda: 'you will receive power when the Holy Spirit comes on you; and you will be my

---

[269] Matt. 25:31–32.
[270] 1 Cor. 15:25–28.
[271] Rev. 22:20.
[272] Acts 2:37.
[273] This missionary aspect of the kingdom of God, which is only implicit in Zechariah, is explicit in Isaiah. See especially Is. 66:19–21.

witnesses in Jerusalem, and in all Judea and Samaria, and to the ends of the earth'.[274]

The rest of the book of Acts describes the progress of that mission out of Palestine into Asia Minor, into Europe, and finally to Rome, the capital of the Gentile world. At the end of the book of Acts we find Paul there, preaching essentially the same message Peter had preached on the day of Pentecost: 'For two whole years Paul stayed there in his own rented house and welcomed all who came to see him. Boldly and without hindrance he preached the kingdom of God and taught about the Lord Jesus Christ.'[275]

It is a movement that continues to the present day, and will not end until a vast multitude from every nation, tribe, people and language stands before God's throne, worshipping him and saying:

> Praise and glory
> and wisdom and thanks and honour
> and power and strength
> be to our God for ever and ever.
> Amen![276]

This great harvest will be gathered by the preaching of the kingdom of God in the power of the Holy Spirit.

The distinct contribution of the closing chapter of Zechariah is to remind us that this mission involves a battle. The decisive, opening campaign of that battle was fought when Jew and Gentile conspired together to nail the Son of God to the cross, only to have the futility of their rebellion exposed three days later by his resurrection from the dead. The battle continued in the months and years that followed as the Jewish and Gentile authorities combined again to try to destroy the church and silence its gospel witness. It continues today whenever a hostile world is confronted with the truth that God reigns, and it will be ended only when Jesus returns in glory. It is a titanic battle, and there is a cost to being involved in it. But it is no futile struggle; indeed, it is a battle that has already been won. Continued resistance is futile, for God is King, and his kingdom will come. There will be a great harvest! That is the note on which Zechariah's message concludes.

So if that is the vision that fires us, how should we live? What does it mean to live now in that light of the coming kingdom of God? If we are sensitive to the many facets of Zechariah's message it means to be committed to honesty, justice and compassion (5:1–11;

[274] Acts 1:8.
[275] Acts 28:30–31.
[276] Rev. 7:12.

7:8–10). It means being identified with a worshipping, serving community (2:7; 6:15). It means being prepared to stand up and be counted, and to suffer if necessary for our allegiance to God and his purposes (9:12–17; 12:1–9; 14:1–5). But above all it means giving ourselves to the preaching of the kingdom of God to all nations in the power of his Spirit. May his kingdom come, and his will be done!

Other titles in The Bible Speaks Today series

New Testament

The Message of the Sermon on the Mount (Matthew 5 – 7)
Christian counter-culture
John Stott

The Message of Matthew
The kingdom of heaven
Michael Green

The Message of Mark
The mystery of faith
Donald English

The Message of Luke
The Saviour of the world
Michael Wilcock

The Message of John
Here is your King
Bruce Milne

The Message of Acts
To the ends of the earth
John Stott

The Message of Romans
God's good news for the world
John Stott

The Message of 1 Corinthians
Life in the local church
David Prior

The Message of 2 Corinthians
Power in weakness
Paul Barnett

The Message of Galatians
Only one way
John Stott

The Message of Ephesians
God's new society
John Stott

The Message of Philippians
Jesus our Joy
Alec Motyer

The Message of Colossians and Philemon
Fullness and freedom
Dick Lucas

The Message of Thessalonians
Preparing for the coming King
John Stott

The Message of 1 Timothy and Titus
The life of the local church
John Stott

The Message of 2 Timothy
Guard the gospel
John Stott

The Message of Hebrews
Christ above all
Raymond Brown

The Message of James
The tests of faith
Alec Motyer

The Message of 1 Peter
The way of the cross
Edmund Clowney

The Message of 2 Peter and Jude
The promise of his coming
Dick Lucas and Christopher Green

The Message of John's Letters
Living in the love of God
David Jackman

The Message of Revelation
I saw heaven opened
Michael Wilcock

Bible Themes

The Message of the Living God
His glory, his people, his world
Peter Lewis

The Message of the Resurrection
Christ is risen!
Paul Beasley-Murray

The Message of the Cross
Wisdom unsearchable, love indestructible
Derek Tidball

The Message of Creation
Encountering the Lord of the universe
David Wilkinson

The Message of Salvation
By God's grace, for God's glory
Philip Graham Ryken

The Message of Heaven and Hell
Grace and destiny
Bruce Milne

The Message of Mission
The glory of Christ in all time and space
Howard Peskett and Vinoth Ramachandra

The Message of Prayer
Approaching the throne of grace
Tim Chester